J. Boon
Anthropology
Cornell Univ.

Muslim Puritans

Muslim Puritans

Reformist Psychology in Southeast Asian Islam

James L. Peacock

UNIVERSITY OF CALIFORNIA PRESS
BERKELEY · LOS ANGELES · LONDON

University of California Press
Berkeley and Los Angeles, California

University of California Press, Ltd.
London, England

Copyright © 1978 by
The Regents of the University of California
ISBN 0-520-03403-1
Library of Congress Catalog Card Number: 76-55571
Printed in the United States of America

1 2 3 4 5 6 7 8 9

Contents

Acknowledgments

THIS study derives from library, field and survey research that was begun in 1969 and has been pursued intermittently since. Many individuals and agencies have been helpful, and space permits only listing, without bestowing on each the appreciation that is deserved.

The National Science Foundation and the American Council of Learned Societies supported a year of research in Singapore, Malaysia, and Indonesia during 1969-70, and NSF provided essential funds for analysis in two subsequent years. The Wenner-Gren Foundation supported library research in the Netherlands during the summer of 1972, and the Faculty Research Council of the University of North Carolina funded supplementary data analysis.

David Johnson and Larry Wood provided indispensable help in quantitative analysis, while Angell Beza, Dorothy Clement, and Kenneth Hardy contributed valuable advice in this sphere. Barbara Brick, Adji Ruslan Hurjowidojo, Hind Khattab, Edy Salendeho, and Reinhart Tampobolom helped enormously with the coding of data; Frank Manning, Brett Sutton, and Isabel Terry helped in other ways; and the Institute for Research in Social Science, University of North Carolina, provided computer facilities as well as help in typing. Michael Trinkley drew the map. Aid in administering the survey in Singapore and Malaya was given by the Far Eastern Research Organization, and in Jogjakarta by the University of Gadjah Mada; Dr. Joseph Tamney, then of the University of Singapore, was helpful in pre-testing the Singapore schedule. James Boon, Dorothy Clement, Thomas Kirsch, Niels Mulder, and Steven Piker kindly read and criticized the entire manuscript, which was edited by Marjorie Hughes. To Djarnawi Hadikusma, head of the Muslim Party of Indonesia, is due the deepest gratitude for meticulously checking a draft of the manuscript on behalf of the Muhammadijah.

Dean Harsja Bachtiar and Ms. Sjamsiah Achmat of the Lembaga Ilmu Pengetahuan Indonesia were kind enough to sponsor my field research in that country in 1970, while the Institute for Southeast Asian Studies sponsored it in Singapore in 1969 through the help of the Directors at that time, John Legge and the late Harry Benda.

I am grateful to the following libraries for permitting me to examine their resources: Wassom Collection, Cornell University; Library of Congress, Southeast Asia Collection; School of Oriental and African Studies and Institute of Commonwealth Studies, University of London; Colonial Office Library, London; Koninklijk Instituut voor Taal-, land- En Volkenkunde (Royal Institute of Linguistic, Folklore, and Anthropological Studies), University of Leiden; Department van Kolonien, Ministerie van Binenlandse Zaken (Colonial Department, Ministry of Interior), the Hague; Singapore-Malaya Collection, University of Singapore; Pustaka, Pimpinan Pusat Muhammadijah (Library, Central Office of Muhammadijah), Jogjakarta. Among the individuals whose cooperation was helpful in obtaining the use of library resources, I should mention Abdul Kohor and Professor Patrick de Josselin de Jong.

Deepest appreciation must go to the Muslim bodies which permitted an alien researcher to query their members and investigate their affairs. In Singapore, this body was the Majlis Ugama Islam; in Indonesia, which was the focus of this monograph, it was the Muhammadijah. I shall not forget the kindness and courtesy of those Muhammadijah leaders who permitted me to study their movement during 1970, especially Messrs. Malik

Ahmat, Djarnawi, Hamka, Sanusi, and Singadimedjo of Djakarta, and, in Jogjakarta, the President and Secretary-Treasurer of Muhammadijah, Pak H. A. R. Fachruddin and Pak Djindhar Tamimy. To the Muhammadijah, in recognition of remarkable achievement under difficult circumstances, I dedicate this study.

J.L.P.

A Note on Orthography

ALTHOUGH Indonesian orthography has recently been modified slightly to correspond with the Malay, the present monograph retains the standard orthography for each language which was extant at the time of fieldwork (1969–70) and is utilized by the majority of written sources cited. However, several terms which have identical meaning and pronunciation in the Indonesian and Malay languages, but vary slightly in spelling, are given a single spelling, the Indonesian, throughout this text.

This rationalization of conduct within the world, but for the sake of the world beyond, was the consequence of the concept or calling of ascetic Protestantism.

Max Weber [1]

If adequacy with respect to meaning is lacking, then no matter how high the degree of uniformity of process (whether overt or subjective) and how precisely its probability can be numerically determined, it remains an incomprehensible statistical probability. On the other hand, even the most perfect adequacy on the level of meaning has causal significance from a sociological point of view only insofar as there is some kind of proof for the existence of a probability that action in fact normally takes the course which has been held to be meaningful.

Max Weber [2]

1. Weber (1958, p. 154).
2. Weber (1947, p. 99; 1966, p. 11). This quotation differs in one particular from Parsons' 1947 translation, which reads: "No matter how high the degree of uniformity and how precisely its probability can be numerically determined, it is still an incomprehensible statistical probability, whether dealing with overt or subjective process." Weber's original is more literally translated as above: ". . . uniformity of process (whether overt or subjective) . . . ," which makes clearer the relation between "uniformity," "its," "overt or subjective," and "process."

1

Introduction

THIS book's central question is: To what extent and in what sense does cultural change imply psychological rationalization? Religious reformism is the type of cultural change considered, and its psychological rationalization covers spheres ranging from autobiography to family life and work. Theoretical guidance in understanding this relationship derives from Max Weber, and data through which to explore the relation come from the major Islamic countries of Southeast Asia: Malaysia, Singapore, and Indonesia. The methods are statistical, ethnographic, and historical, and one byproduct of the study is to suggest both possibilities and difficulties in the integration of these several approaches.

WEBERIAN RATIONALIZATION AND REFORMATION

A CENTRAL thesis in the writings of Max Weber[3] is that history moves toward rationalization. One type of rationalization is of action: the organization of means so that they thrust

3. Weber (1947, 1958, 1964, 1966); Gerth and Mills (1958); Winckelmann (1973). See Weber (1947, p. 115) for Weber's definition and Parson's discussion of the concept of *Zweckrationalität*. In some usages by Weber, the concept is related to the simple notion of efficiency or rationalization of means discussed here, although originally Weber defined it as rational choice of ends.

1

ever more efficiently and methodically toward whatever ends are deemed significant by the actor. Examples of this type of rationalization include capitalism and bureaucratization; the objective of capitalism is to harness economic means efficiently to economic ends, while bureaucracy is at least ideally oriented toward efficient administration. Capitalism and bureaucracy are two examples of a world-historical trend toward rationalization of action.

Rationalization of action cannot, Weber believed, proceed without spiritual changes capable of rendering the process meaningful and legitimate to the actors involved. Such change of spirit is embodied in myriad forms, but the most dramatic, rapid, rationalizing spiritual force that Weber could discern in modern history was the reformation movement exemplified by Protestantism, culminating in the Calvinism of the sixteenth- and seventeenth-century Puritans. The Puritan, as analyzed by Weber, was driven by his doctrinally induced terror of damnation to rationalize his actions into an ever more methodical and single-minded movement toward glorifying God and demonstrating that he, the Puritan, was of the elect predestined for salvation. As Weber puts it in the quotation heading this chapter: "rationalization of conduct within the world, but for the sake of the world beyond."

Rationalizing his life, the Puritan amputated his traditions. He was the purist, the ascetic—the purifier of action by stripping it of nonrational ritual, aesthetic, cosmological, and social structures. The results, as Weber was morbidly aware, were demonic as well as productive. Consequences ranged from the creativity of technology to alienation within the industrial state, from the efficiency of bookkeeping to wild mass movements.

Weber's theoretical framework bore, of course, on the question of the economics of rationalization and reformation, exemplified by the common interpretation of his most famous work, *The Protestant Ethic and the Spirit of Capitalism.* But it illuminates also the broader question of the psychology of these processes. What does rationalization of action imply for the personality development, the mental health, the patterning of consciousness and character[4] of the individual? It is this question which inspired the present study. Exploring the psychology of a particular type of reformist movement, I hope also to lay bare aspects of the psychology of rationalization—that immense process which Weber saw dramatically embodied in a particular time and place by the Protestant Ethic.

The data for the present study derive from a geographic region and a religious tradition outside the realm of Protestantism and the West. Indeed, they are outside even the Asian canvas on which Weber sketched his comparative study of religion in China and India. They are Southeast Asia and Islam —the major Asian region and the major salvation religion to which Weber did not extend his comparative study.[5] But the objective in utilizing these data is not to add a new case to the Weberian *Religionssoziologie*. It is to deploy new data in exploring a level of analysis that has not been plumbed by Weber and the Weberians: the psychological.

Cultural Analysis

A central tenet in Weberian methodology is the so-called "interpretive understanding" *(Verstehen)*, the formulation of the meaning *(Sinn)* of action to the actor. Social action *(soziales Handeln)* is not simply behavior, but behavior capable of being understood in terms of subjective categories—behavior which is meaningful. Understanding is accomplished by "placing the act

4. Honigmann (1967, p. 69) defines character as a pattern abstracted from the overt data of behavior and constituting "the personality's nuclear region comprising broad, organizing value orientations, enduring dispositions, and policy-setting premises that guide an individual in a variety of situations. . . . This nuclear region I call character-structure." Honigmann (1967, pp. 136-37) also refers specifically to a "Protestant Ethic character structure," the elements of which resemble Weber's Calvinist-capitalist configuration and, in some respects, the reformist psychology elucidated in this study.

5. Weber's planned work on Islam was not completed owing to his early death (Bendix, 1962, p. 258). For a consideration of Weber's work with respect to Southeast Asia, see S. H. Al-Attas (1963b).

in an intelligible and more inclusive context of meaning, a *Sinn-zusammenhang.*"[6] While empathy with the actor may facilitate such interpretative understanding, Weber makes clear that Verstehen depends ultimately not on empathy but on the analytical construction of the actor's subjective categories.[7] Insofar as these categories are shared by a plurality of actors, such analysis is what Weberian anthropologists term "cultural";[8] the "more inclusive context of meaning" is, in a word, culture.

As the second quotation at the head of this chapter makes plain, interpretation of meaning is not assured by analysis of statistics. No matter how exhaustive and successful the analysis of statistical regularities of behavior, that behavior remains incomprehensible unless its meaning to the actor is discerned. Following this trend of argument, cultural analyses give relatively little attention to measurement of uniformity and covariation among events; they are preoccupied instead with constructing the framework of meaning in terms of which the actor understands any event. Clifford Geertz' analysis of the Balinese cockfight is an elegant example, and he provides a seminal program for cultural analysis in his concept of "thick description,"[9] the construction of layers of subjective meaning which illuminate the event.

When the question is raised of generalizing from a particular interpretation in order to construct theory, Geertz—the most relevant spokesman for cultural analysis applied to Southeast Asia—remains very much within the Weberian viewpoint. He states:

> Believing, with Max Weber, that man is an animal suspended in webs of significance he himself has spun, I take

6. Weber (1966, p. 5; 1947, p. 89).
7. "One does not need to be Caesar in order to understand him" (Weber, 1947, p. 90).
8. C. Geertz (1973). By "culture" is meant a system of shared categories such as beliefs, values, and symbols. "Cultural analysis" is the elucidation of these patterns of consciousness—that is, as deployed by such cultural analysts as Geertz, it resembles Weber's *Verstehen.*
9. C. Geertz (1973).

culture to be those webs, and the analysis of it to be therefore not an experimental science in search of a law but an
interpretative one in search of meaning.[10]

Again, Geertz favors the interpretive method, which constructs
frameworks of meaning, rather than the statistical or experimental one, which measures uniformity and covariation among
events. Tackling the question of generalization, Geertz rejects
the notion of the "law," which posits such uniformities and
covariations. In place of "law," he proposes an "interpretative
science." What type of generalization does such "science" offer
to replace the "law" of analytical science? Geertz offers no ready
answer, but he writes that "what generality it contrives to
achieve grows out of the delicacy of its distinctions, not the
sweep of its abstractions."[11] He states further that these interpretations will achieve generality not in verification through fit
with events but as they illuminate new phenomena that swim
into view.

What Geertz proposes sounds much like Weber's "ideal" or
"pure" (rein)[12] type, though with more delicate distinction (or
thicker description) and less "sweeping abstraction." The ideal
type is exemplified by the Protestant Ethic, the Spirit of Capitalism, and rationalization. The type is ideal in that no empirical
behavior perfectly fits it; no society perfectly exemplifies the
Protestant Ethic or the Spirit of Capitalism, and no behavior is
perfectly rational. Like the literary caricature of a Babbitt or a
Becky Sharp, the ideal type is based not on a count of traits that
permits computation of an average or correlations, but on
exaggerated and purified description of individual cases.
Through the clarity that such idealized portrayal permits, the
patterning of life is highlighted. As in Geertz' notion, the ideal
type was designed to substitute for the probabilistic law. Derived through interpretative analysis of individual phenomena
rather than statistical analysis of regularities, its aim was neither

10. C. Geertz (1973, p. 5).
11. C. Geertz (1973, p. 25).
12. Weber (1947, p. 89; 1966, p. 6).

refutation nor verification, but the illumination of events by placing them in a conceptual frame.

Why the antipathy between Verstehen and statistics? The obvious problem with statistics is their thinness and indelicacy. Statistics reveal too little, too grossly, about many events; Verstehen delicately discloses much about few—through reconstruction of the meanings that underlie them. The problem with statistical analysis is exemplified by the concept underlying the present study: reformism. Even superficial encounter reveals that the configuration of meanings denoted by "reformism" is complex for any single Southeast Asian, and varies among them. For some persons, the classical tenets of Muslim reformism—i.e., personal analysis of the Qur'an *(idjtihad)* and the purge from Islam of tradition *(adat)* —are its central features; for others, these features are marginal; for all, the subjective configuration within which such features are positioned is complex. Yet statistical analysis requires simplification. To compare numerous responses, some standardized measure of the variable in question, some construct, such as "reformism," is required, and this construct necessarily fails to take full account of the rich particularities of the subjective worlds from which it remotely derives.

Psychological Analysis

Weber sharply distinguished the Verstehen analysis from the psychological, at least in certain senses of the word. He excluded from the concerns of Verstehen "those aspects of psychopathology which are devoid of subjective meaning" and other "psychic or psychophysical phenomena such as fatigue, habituation, memory, etc."[13] Recognizing that these types of psychological states and processes may have causal significance for action, he nevertheless considered them irrelevant for Verstehen except insofar as they become part of the subjective world under analysis. On the same ground, while recognizing that some facets of psychology overlap with interpretive sociology, he stated bluntly that psychology "using methods of the natural

13. Weber (1947, pp. 101 and 97).

sciences" has no more relevance to the analysis of action "than do the natural sciences."[14] (Here he would seem to refer to those measurements and assessments of psychology which are objective rather than introspective—e.g., such psychophysical and physiological measures as galvanic skin response—and of course he has in mind the pre-clinical psychology of his time.) The boundary that Weber draws is between the subjective and objective worlds, as well as between methods that penetrate subjectivity versus those that do not. The boundary is not sharp, however, since that which is unconscious can be included in the analysis of consciousness; Weber states that the interpreter of action must understand the full motivation of the actor, whether or not such motives are completely conscious *(Bewusstzein)*.[15]

Despite the vague boundary, the Weberian distinction between cultural *(Verstehen)* and psychological analysis is useful in distinguishing between (1) those frames of meaning that are formulated in the shared consciousness of individuals and (2)

14. Weber (1947, p. 101).

15. Weber (1966, p. 14; 1947, pp. 115 ff.). The distinction between cultural and psychological analysis employed in this study would seem to catch the spirit of Weber's distinction between Verstehen and psychology; cultural analysis and Verstehen treat understandings that the actors hold consciously and articulate explicitly, while psychological analysis delves into patterns not articulated nor part of the actor's conscious awareness—e.g. relations between cultural orientations and various behavioral patterns. The extent of awareness and explicitness of articulation varies from person to person and even from moment to moment depending on external cues. For example, in the course of a few minutes' conversation with a leader of the reformist Muslim women's movement, the leader's answers to questions regarding the reformist view of child-rearing varied according to the stage of the interview and the level of question asked. At the beginning she was asked generally about the movement's view of proper child-rearing, and she gave a general answer: "that which upholds Islam." Later she was asked about specific practices, such as weaning or cuddling, and she gave specific opinions revealing a more detailed awareness of relationships than was elicited by the general question. The point of the cultural/psychological distinction is not subtle phenomenological interpretation of details but to roughly demarcate areas of analysis as an aid to organization and presentation of bulky data.

those linkages of behavior patterns to these frames of meaning that are hypothesized by the analyst but not explicitly recognized by the subjects. Thus Southeast Asian reformists spontaneously, explicitly, and lengthily expound the meanings of *Tauhid* (the unity of God), but they do not normally spontaneously expound linkages between belief in Tauhid and such behavioral patterns as early weaning and depressive psychosis. In Weber's terms, Tauhid is more open to Verstehen, whereas the connection—if any—between Tauhid and the weaning or the psychosis is impervious to Verstehen if that connection is not in the actor's ken.

Given that the actor himself does not readily expound a connection between Tauhid and weaning, what is one to do? In terms of strict Verstehen methodology, one should concentrate on elucidating the subjective world and ignore the weaning and the psychosis. Essentially, this has been the tack of Weber and the Weberians, with the result that Weberian analysis of rationalization has included relatively little of so-called "depth" psychology. Weberian methdology does, however, provide for this type of analysis.

Weber has stated that interpretive social science should strive both for "interpretive understanding" *(Verstehen)* and "causal explanation" *(ursächlich erklaren)*. Guided by this dictum, should one search for a causal linkage between weaning and Tauhid? Precisely such a link has been a major concern of psychologies ranging from the psychoanalytical to the experimental, and has been dominant in the so-called psychological anthropology. In these frameworks, early events in the life cycle are seen as causing later ones, or at least as bearing a functional relationship to them. Human existence is conceptualized after the model that Clifford Geertz (following Sorokin) terms "causal-functional," as compared to the "logico-meaningful" model of Verstehen analysis.[16] While recent paradigms of psychological anthropology[17] are certainly more sophisticated and complex than the early ones, they remain "causal-functional" in a broad

16. C. Geertz (1959).
17. LeVine (1973).

sense: one is more concerned to elucidate a condition–consequence relationship between events than a logical fit among
categories.

At this point, Weber recognized a use of statistics. In the
second sentence of the second quotation at the head of this
chapter, he states that statistics are necessary (though not sufficient) to demonstrate causality—for in order to establish that X
has affected Y, one must show what course Y would take
"normally," i.e., if without X. Establishing such a regularity
requires counting and the calculation of probability.

By this logic, "psychological analysis" would seem to call
for statistical analysis. If the actors themselves do not recognize
a connection between, e.g., weaning and Tauhid, then one
strategy is to show that the two are nevertheless statistically
correlated—that those who believe in Tauhid most strongly
wean their children earliest, for example. The correlation is not
at the level of causal or functional analysis; the next step is to
show that the correlation reveals a link between events and
experiences that works in an ongoing system. If the system in
question is the personality, within the context of society and
culture, then the analysis is properly deemed psychological.

*Cultural Analysis, Psychological
Analysis, and Statistics*

Following the logic of the Weberian distinctions, we seem to
have arrived at a conclusion that statistical analysis is appropriate for psychological but not for cultural or Verstehen analysis.
This distinction is too simple. On the one hand, causal-functional analysis of a psychological system cannot be achieved by
statistical correlation alone; on the other, statistics can serve
Verstehen.

Geertz suggests that the cultural analyst is like the clinical
diagnostician in his concern with particularities of the individual case. Yet it should be recalled that even the clinician is
guided by knowledge of regularities. In the medical profession,
many of these have been established by statistical analysis of
experimental data, though impressionistic generalization drawn

from experience also plays its part; similarly, the cultural analyst brings his systematic and impressionistic knowledge of a shared pattern to the service of interpreting a particular event or utterance. Not only must he interpret the event, the cultural analyst must also generalize about the culture: To what extent is a given pattern shared? Because of their grossness, statistics are not an entirely satisfactory way of answering this question, but they are one way.

As the premier practitioner of the Verstehen methodology within the Southeast Asian context, Clifford Geertz provides an excellent example. He has developed, for Java, the widely known typology distinguishing *abangan* (syncretist Muslims) and *santri* (purist Muslims), differentiating the latter into *santri modèren* (reformist Muslims), and *santri kolot* (traditionalist Muslims).[18] The labels and their associated attributes are formulated not only by Geertz, but are also used by the Javanese themselves. However, a statistical analysis to be explained later suggests that empirically the types differentiate into subtypes; thus, the *santri modèren* who gained his ideology in youth and is largely reformist in that he rejects traditional ritual is distinct from the *santri modèren* who gained his ideology in adulthood and manifests his reformism through affirmation of an Islamic ethic. Thus a statistical and psychological analysis (which links an experience to an ideology in a way the actors themselves do not normally do) suggests refinement in a cultural classification derived through Verstehen. Here ethnography generates insight into cultural categories; statistics suggest ways in which these categories are distributed in relation to diverse experiences of the population; and further ethnography is required to explore the phenomenological reality of these statistical relationships. Ethnography and statistics dialectically contribute to cultural analysis.

Psychological Implications of Weberian Theory

A broad spectrum of Weber's thought is relevant to the present study. This includes the so-called "Weber thesis" which explicates the relationship between Calvinism and capitalism;

18. C. Geertz (1960b).

comparative analyses of India, China, and Judea which suggest essential themes in traditionalism that contrast with the reformist thrust; Weber's synthesis of sociology of religion which develops the notion of rationalization; that aspect of his political sociology concerning sects and movements; and central tenets of his methodology.[19] All of these materials have been thoroughly discussed elsewhere,[20] as have the controversies surrounding them,[21] most of which are irrelevant here.

Weberian scholarship is vast; put simply, it divides into two broad phases. The first phase, reaching its peak before the Second World War, was primarily critical and was concerned with the connection between Calvinism and capitalism.[22] The second phase, emerging after the war, expends less energy on economics, criticism, and the West and is primarily interested in utilizing Weber's ideas for understanding society, culture, and history outside the West.[23] While the present study derives from the second phase, it attempts to add a psychological aspect.

Despite the lack of psychological emphasis among the Weberians, the kernels of such an orientation are apparent in the work of Weber himself. Consider his characterization of the Calvinist-capitalist in *The Protestant Ethic and the Spirit of Capitalism*. The Calvinist-capitalist's rationalization of meaning is exemplified by his increasing concern for doctrine, law, and sanction, and his correlated rationalization of action is exemplified by a number of tendencies: emphasis on saving time, a purge of ornamentation, ceremony, art, and other sensuous forms which distract from ultimate objectives; treating others as instruments rather than kinsmen or friends; personal asceticism, as in taboos on strong drink, promiscuity, and ecstasies that tempt from the straight and narrow; capitalistic and other work that is oriented toward efficiency and asceticism.

19. Weber (1947, 1951, 1964, 1966, 1967a, 1967b).
20. See Aaron (1964), Bendix (1962), Parsons (1968).
21. See Eisenstadt (1968), Peacock (1975b), and Winckelman (1972).
22. Eisenstadt (1968), Green (1959), Parsons (1968), Samuelson (1961), Winckelmann (1972).
23. Bellah (1957, 1963, 1965), Ames (1964), Eisenstadt (1968), Kirsch (1967), C. Geertz (1960b), Piker (n.d. and 1973), Spiro (1970).

In describing these tendencies, Weber characterizes not only an ethic, in the sense of a set of normative prescriptions, but what some anthropologists would term an ethos[24]—a configuration of character, a pattern of emotion, a set of dispositions. Indeed, in the original German text, Weber himself frequently uses the term *Ethos* to capture the psychology of the *Ethik*; he also uses other terms referring to psychological dispositions— for example, *Charakterzüge, psychologisches Antriebe, Angst,* and *psychologischer Entwicklungsreiz.*[25]

In short, Weber was genuinely concerned with reformist psychology, a topic that has received less attention in Weberian commentary than have the economic, political, social, and cultural aspects of his perspective. Without question, Weber possessed great psychological insight; his forte was what Bendix has termed "existential psychologizing":[26] inferring an actor's logically plausible subjective dispositions by analyzing the objective conditions of his existence. Note that this framework goes beyond strict "Verstehen" in that circumstances external to the actor's ken are related to the meanings that the actor himself reveals; the analysis is psychological in the sense defined earlier. Yet Weber's genius in constructing psychological ideal types was limited by a refusal, perhaps based on moral and personal as well as methodological grounds,[27] to invade the privacy of the person by empirically exploring in depth his consciousness, and especially his unconscious. This tenet is reflected in Weber's rejection of Freud.

Though the years have, in part, vindicated Weber's anti-Freudianism, basic premises of the psychoanalytical framework continue to be fundamental in the field of psychological anthropology, and these suggest important questions for understanding the psychology of reformism and rationalization. A first major question concerns the life cycle. If, as Weber argues,

24. Bateson (1936, pp. 2, 32); cf. Bateson's notion of "ethos" to "character" as elucidated by Honigmann (1967, p. 69).
25. Winckelmann (1972, pp. 34, 43, 117, 124-5).
26. Bendix (1962, pp. 269 ff.).
27. Gerth and Mills (1958, p. 20).

reformist doctrine restructures the life of the believer, harnessing it relentlessly toward search for proof of his salvation, what, exactly, is the effect on the life cycle (in Leighton's more appropriate term, "life arc")?[28] How does the life cycle of the believer differ from that of the nonbeliever? While psychoanalysis would emphasize the childhood phase, the Weberian framework obviously calls for study of the rationalization of the total life arc as it unfolds from birth to death.

A second major question suggested by psychoanalysis concerns the psychopathology of rationalization: What are the repressions, frustrations, stresses, and resulting pathologies that flow from reformist rationalization of life? One can speculatively discern in the classical neurotic and psychotic syndromes an exaggerated analogy to the rationalization exhorted by the Protestant Ethic: the obsessive-compulsive's precision of scheduling, his ascetic purification and stifling of impulse; the paranoid's insistence on systematizing reality into order; the neurotic's repression of sexuality. All of these symptoms seemed to flower especially in the aftermath of an historical epoch marked by a modernizing rationalization. Psychosis and neurosis lie within the realm of a psychology that Weber saw as off-limits to Verstehen, presumably because of the unconscious and involuntary origins of the symptoms. Yet precisely for this reason, psychopathology is a challenge to cultural analysis. The challenge is to show that cultural rationalization penetrates even the nonrational, the involuntary and unconscious layers of the personality—that culture is not confined to articulated ideology.

For similar reasons, a third major question suggested by depth psychology is the relationship of culturally defined rationalization and reform to expressive behavior, as in the arts, in recreation and release, in manners and other realms that are not explicitly included within the consciously demarcated doctrine or viewpoint elucidated by Verstehen, but can be hypothesized to bear a relation to such cultural frameworks. It may be remarked again that when the actors themselves do not articulate

28. Leighton (1959, p. 24).

the relationship, a likely method for exploring it is to check statistical correlation.

These questions have of course not been entirely ignored by Weberian-derived analysis. The most comprehensive psychological elaboration of Weberian theory remains David C. McClelland's *The Achieving Society*.[29] McClelland not only investigates the motivational dispositions implied by the Protestant Ethic (which he translates into his "Need to Achieve" or *n-ach*) but also certain of the life-cycle and expressive features associated with these motivational tendencies. A second comprehensive study is Hagen's,[30] which is especially useful in addressing the question: What childhood experiences and family configurations regularly give rise to the rationalizing impulse, and what historical forces give rise to these patterns of child-rearing and family life?

The present study is not on the comprehensively cross-cultural scale of McClelland's and Hagen's. In one respect, however, it can help to fill a gap in these researches. Neither McClelland nor Hagen give sufficient account of what was central in the Weberian approach: the cultural definitions of the actors, as discerned through Verstehen. By cultural definition is meant not only explicit doctrines and philosophies of life, but also the actor's essential structure of meaning, including values, symbols, and world-view. McClelland, as a psychologist, is more interested in measuring the behavioral and motivational implications of the "need to achieve" than with formulating the cultural premises that underlie it; and Hagen, too, tends to focus on motivational dynamics rather than the cultural premises that define achievement.[31] The present study endeavors to perform a cultural analysis as a necessary step in interpreting psychology.

29. McClelland (1967).
30. Hagen (1962).
31. One instance of McClelland's analysis failing to incorporate adequately Weber's definition of the cultural basis of the Protestant Ethic is given in Peacock (1973b). A more extended example of Hagen's seminal study is appropriate, inasmuch as he deals specifically with the Javanese materials. Hagen (1962, pp. 166-71) gives a psychoanalytic interpretation of the Javanese father's becoming very distant from his

INDONESIA, SINGAPORE, AND MALAYSIA[32]

Islamic groups are found in both Buddhist Thailand and the Christian Philippines, but the predominantly Islamic nations of Southeast Asia are Indonesia, Malaysia, and Singapore. The three countries are closely bound by geography, migration, language, and culture such that their Islamic sphere has long formed a unity.

Geographically some portion of each of these nations either touches or is visible from the others; note on the map the proximity of Singapore to the peninsula of Malaya (in Malaysia) and the island of Sumatra (in Indonesia). This proximity has encouraged a variety of intermigrations. In Malaya, for example, the state of Negeri Sembilan is dominated by Minangkabau migrants (from Indonesian Sumatra); and Buginese migrants

---

son when the child reaches 5 (see Chapter 3 of the present study). Hagen stresses that this distancing occurs during the oedipal period, and he believes that the father's formality toward the son leaves the son feeling not only submissive but also sexually inadequate. As a result, Hagen suggests, the son has difficulty relating to women and therefore takes refuge in a marriage based on hierarchy and respect.

In a society where bourgeois equality between the sexes is a norm and ideal, hierarchical relations may indeed reveal fears of sexual inadequacy. But in Java, as will be seen, this hierarchical relationship accords with the entire sociocosmic structure derived from centuries of history; it is not simply the result of an oedipal fear. Furthermore, it is necessary to understand the cultural structure in order to interpret the oedipal experience itself. Hagen writes as though the rivalry of father and son were direct, such that the father is out to defeat (indeed, castrate) the son in order to take control of the mother. In actuality, the father's behavior accords with Javanese notions of power and hierarchy dominant throughout the culture (see Chapter 4 of the present study). The father withdraws to a higher plane, there to concentrate his spiritual energies. The son's reaction to this withdrawal is a poignant sense of loss, rather than any blatant fear. Obviously this situation warrants further analysis, but any interpretation should take account of the Javanese cultural framework.

32. Facts on Indonesia cited here are elaborated in McVey (1963), Wertheim (1959), and other standard works listed in Peacock (1973a); on Singapore Malays, see Djamour (1965, 1966); on peninsula Malays, see Roff (1967, 1974).

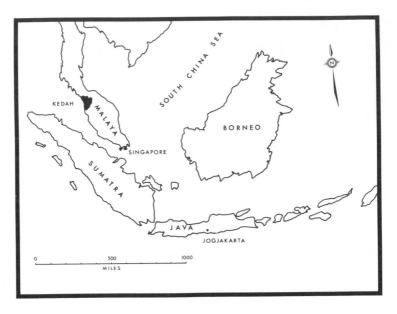

(from Indonesian Sulawesi) comprise ruling families in other states. In Singapore, a large minority of the so-called "Malays" are first-generation migrants from Indonesia's Java, Sumatra, and Bawean. And in Indonesia, the so-called "coastal Malays" are found throughout the network of ports. Within the Islamic sphere specifically, the three countries have enjoyed a continuous exchange of religious teachers and students, and the writings of such famous authors as Hamka are published and read in all three. It is the Malay language, mutually comprehensible (though varying greatly in dialect), which eases intercourse, and subtle cultural and phenotypic similarities help too; sharing syncretic (animistic, Buddhist, and Hindu) undercurrents, a tradition of courteous harmony, and an agrarian background, the Malayo-Muslims of Indonesia, Singapore, and Malaysia even tend broadly to "look alike."

The three nations differ, however, in ethnic composition. In Malaya (here I refer to the Malay Peninsula, which is our primary concern, rather than the entire nation of Malaysia), the Muslims, who are largely Malays though also Arab, Indian, and

Pakistani, comprise approximately half the population, while the largely Chinese non-Muslims comprise the other half. In Singapore, the estimated 350,000 Muslims are in a minority by comparison to the Chinese. And in Indonesia, the Muslims (at least nominal ones) are in the majority.

Differences are apparent, too, in the relation between economics and ethnicity. In Malaya, Chinese dominate the economy while Malays dominate government. In Singapore, Chinese dominate both and the Malays are relegated on the whole to low positions, although a handful of Arab, Pakistani, and Indian Muslims possess great wealth. In Indonesia, Chinese dominate business and the "Indonesians" (peoples of "Malay" stock) dominate government, but pious Muslims go into business to a greater extent than in either Malaya or Singapore.

Finally, Islam itself is differently associated with ethnicity. In Malaya, "Malayness" is synonymous with being Muslim in a way not true of Indonesia; to *masuk Melayu* (become a Malay) means to *masuk Islam* (become a Muslim), and virtually no Malay is anything else. The same is true in Singapore. In Indonesia, however, persons of Malay or "indigenous Indonesian" race and ethnicity (as they put it, *bangsa*) are Christians, Buddhists, and Hindus as well as Muslims.

And these differences are linked to broad contrasts in the organization of each place as an Islamic society. In Indonesia, where "Indonesianness" is not "Muslimness," the nation is not Islamic after the fashion of Malaya, where each sultan is the religious as well as political head of his state and maintains a religious bureaucracy to enforce the faith. Yet while Indonesia is no Muslim state, it does have a Ministry of Religion which is predominantly Islamic and a system of Islamic courts which exists beside the civil one. Singapore's Muslim minority must content itself with a small Muslim court and Muslim council to serve Muslim interests within a pluralistic city-state embracing a variety of faiths.

What is Islamic reformism, and what has been its fate in these varied societies? The Islamic faith penetrated Southeast Asia as early as the eleventh century A.D. and spread widely during the fifteenth, sixteenth, and seventeenth centuries. This Islam was not pure; it was syncretic, mixed with local custom *(adat)*, mystical and magical practices, and the Hinduist, Buddhist, and animist beliefs that preceded it. During these years there existed a few purist believers, but the most decisive move toward purification came when the nineteenth-century introduction of the steamship enabled great numbers of Indonesians and Malays to travel to Mecca for pilgrimage and study. Some of the more devout and astute of these students came under the influence of reformism emanating from Muhammad Abduh of Cairo's Al-Azhar University. When they returned to their homeland, these reformists founded schools, published tracts, and organized movements to spread the doctrine of reform. Flourishing in early twentieth-century Singapore, spreading widely in Indonesia, resisted strongly by the Malay sultanates, this movement became known as the Kaum Muda (New Faction) of Malayo-Indonesian Islam.

The tenets of the Kaum Muda were essentially two: *idjtihad* and purification. Idjtihad—rational interpretation by the individual of the Qur'anic scripture and Muslim traditions *(hadith)* —is opposed to the method of relying on the word of the teacher; the reformists were contemptuous of the *taklid buta* (blind obedience) of disciples to teachers, who represented not the pristine and pure original word of Allah but the particular schools of canonical law that had been elaborated by Qur'anic scholars during the medieval age of Islam. Purification of religious practice was necessary because of all the non-Islamic mysticism, magic, animism, Hinduism, and Buddhism that had been incorporated into the Malayo-Muslim syncretic "Islam," yet were not decreed by the holy text.

Purifying through fundamentalism, the reformist sought to rediscover the original, the pure, the true Islam. Both ancient and contemporary, the faith was eternal, and with it the believer could rationalize much of the modern world. Thus the reformist embraced much that was new, yet he retained a hard core of his Islamic identity.

During the three-quarters of a century since the flowering of reformism in Southeast Asia, the movement has developed differently in Singapore, Malaya, and Indonesia. Only in Indonesia has a reformist organization remained a major force. Represented in the early twentieth century by numerous movements, the Indonesian Kaum Muda has resolved into a few large regional organizations, such as Persis centered in West Java, and a single national organization, the Muhammadijah. Boasting hundreds of branches distributed throughout the islands, Muhammadijah is certainly the most powerful Islamic reformist movement ever to exist in Southeast Asia, perhaps in the world. Essentially a missionary movement that teaches pure Islam, Muhammadijah has made impressive social and educational contributions as well. Its clinics, orphanages, poorhouses, and hospitals, together with several thousand schools, render it easily the most important private non-Christian social, educational, and religious organization in Indonesia. Its women's branch, 'Aisjijah, is probably the most dynamic of any in the Muslim world. Its former political affiliate, Masjumi, was for a time the most powerful in Indonesia. In short, Muhammadijah is an organization of importance and influence.

Singapore boasts no such organization; there is a branch of Muhammadijah, but with only some 200 members, and otherwise reformism is not represented by any cohesive body. Yet at the turn of the century the bustling port city of Singapore was the seat of the Southeast Asian Islamic reformation, the gathering place for teachers and students, the wellspring of associations, the distribution center for tracts sent throughout the tropics. Reformism exists still in Singapore, but as an ideology without organization. Singapore Islamic reformism is an attitude, vaguely associated with a lively past, heralded by a few dedicated teachers. The fascinating question to be asked in Singapore is whether reformism reduced to attitude, dissociated from organizations and institutions, still breeds the expected psychological rationalization.

The Kaum Muda never had the influence in Malaya that it had in Indonesia and, for a time, in Singapore. Blocked by the religious bureaucracies of the sultanates and the religious teachers in the villages, Kaum Muda did manage to stir conflict in some communities; and though the label itself became highly suspect, the reformist ideas do seem to have made inroads, as is suggested by a survey to be described later. Yet these ideas are apparently dissociated from any organization officially bearing the banner Kaum Muda.

Consonant with the relatively weaker role of organized reformism in Malaya and Singapore, few major English-language works on the subject are available,[33] whereas numerous important English-language studies concern reformism in Indonesia. There have been major surveys of Indonesian Islam, including reformism, during the pre-World-War-II period, the World War II period, and the postwar period.[34] Detailed monographs and theses cover such reformist organizations as Persatuan Islam,[35] Muhammadijah,[36] Masjumi,[37] and the Kaum Muda movement in Sumatra.[38] There exist general assessments of the Indonesian movement[39] and analyses of its social and cultural aspects,[40] its ethnographic context in such regions as Java and Atjeh,[41] its political aspects nationally,[42] and its relationship to the Weber thesis with reference to economic development.[43] Thus the reader has access to material on the sociology, history, economics, politics, and organizational aspects of Indonesian reformism. The present study focuses on the psychological component.

THE PRESENT STUDY

Having surveyed aspects of theory, method, and case, it is now possible to state the objective and design of the present

33. Roff (1967) and Zaki (1965).
34. Noer (1973); Benda (1958); Boland (1971).
35. Federspiel (1970).
36. Alfian (1970), Ali (1957), Salam (1965).
37. Noer (1960).
38. Abdullah (1971).
39. Berg (1932), Drewes (1955), Palmier (1954), Reid (1967).
40. C. Geertz (1960b and 1968), van Nieuwenhuijze (1958), Wertheim (1959).
41. C. Geertz (1960b); Siegel (1969).
42. Samson (1968):
43. S. H. Al-Attas (1963b), Castles (1967), Alfian (1971), Kuntowidjojo (1971), C. Geertz (1960b, 1963), Wertheim (1959, 1965).

study. The objective is not to "test" Weberian theory, but to explore in an exotic milieu certain of its psychological implications. In order to achieve this, two types of analysis must be accomplished. The first is cultural analysis; Muslim reformism as a cultural category in the lives of Southeast Asians must be defined. The second is psychological analysis; behavioral correlates of reformism that are not necessarily recognized by the reformists themselves must be detected. The guiding assumption, derived from Weber, is that cultural rationalization—i.e., reformism—will be reflected in psychological rationalization— i.e., the rationalization of a range of behaviors that is not doctrinally part of reformism itself.

The method to be utilized in exploring this assumption is basically statistical; given that the reformists themselves do not normally define a given behavioral pattern as part of reformism, then an obvious technique is to check whether, nevertheless, that pattern is statistically correlated with reformism. Aside from this reason to utilize statistics, there is the objective of comparing several groups (reformists versus others) within several nations; the survey method facilitates some degree of uniformity of procedure so as to permit comparison of results.

Although the core data of the present monograph are statistical, the questions asked and the interpretations suggested derive largely from a type of research that is both ethnographic and documentary. Documentary sources concerning the relevant themes and in the several relevant languages (English, Dutch, German, Indonesian, and Malay) have been combed, and relevant ethnographic exposure was provided in two of the three countries analyzed: Singapore from July to December 1969, and Indonesia from January to July 1970. The third region, Malaya, was inaccessible to me save for brief trips, owing to the disruption beginning on May 13, 1969, which apparently accounted for my inability to obtain a visa. The ethnographic work differed between Singapore and Indonesia. In Singapore, I concentrated on gaining a general picture of the little-reported life of the Malayo-Muslim community and on collecting life histories of Muslim leaders. In Indonesia, I took advantage of some knowledge of the wider context acquired through earlier fieldwork[44] and concentrated on participant observation of a single movement, the Muhammadijah.[45] Only after the ethnographic work in Singapore did I design the Malay-language survey schedule concerning reformism and other attributes, which was administered in Singapore through interviews in some 400 households and in Kedah, Malaya, to 200 households, during the spring of 1970. The parallel schedule for Indonesia was also designed toward the end of my ethnographic work, and was administered by interviews in some 400 households in Jogjakarta, Java (the home-base of Muhammadijah), in early summer 1970. Additional surveys were administered to Muslim students and leaders in Singapore and Jogjakarta. The map shows sites of the surveys: Singapore, Jogjakarta, and Kedah.

Because Jogjakarta is one of the dominant heartlands of the reformist movement today in Southeast Asia, while Singapore and Malaya are on the periphery of this movement, the present analysis will focus on Jogjakarta, and Singapore and Malaya materials will be presented briefly. For each country, the plan of presentation is as follows: The first step is to clarify the cultural dimensions of reformism, and the second step is to explore psychological correlates of this cultural category (in contrast to psychological correlates of the traditional syncretic orientation). Issues raised through the analysis are considered in the conclusion.

44. Peacock (1968).

45. In Peacock (forthcoming) I present some of this material, including analysis of the autobiography of the founder of Muhammadijah, K. H. A. Dahlan, and of the Muhammadijah training camp, Darol Arqom, in which I was a participant-observer.

2

Reformism in Jogjakarta: Cultural Analysis

THE "SPECIAL *(Istimewah)* Region of Jogjakarta" on the island of Java, Indonesia, covers over 1000 square miles, inhabited by more than 2 million people, some 200,000 of whom live in the city of Jogjakarta. Divided into four districts, each with subdistricts which in turn are divided into villages and hamlets *(desa* and *dukuh),* the rural area is administered separately from the city. The city is divided into wards or *kampung,* such as the famed Kauman in which Muhammadijah originated.[1]

A "special" region in cultural as well as administrative terms, Jogjakarta is for the Javanese a major center of that syncretic (Hindu-Buddhist, Javanist, Muslim) civilization sometimes known as *abangan.* Jogjakarta (often called simply 'Jogja') shares with Surakarta the honor of being a living sultanate of the old empire of Mataram, but in Jogja the sultanate is more viable. This is partly because the Jogja Sultan, Hamengku Buwono, threw the weight of his traditional charisma behind the national revolution of Indonesia; Jogjakarta became the revolutionary capital of Indonesia, and the sultan became influential in national affairs (he was at the time of this research Minister of Finance for the Republic). Though his palace has been converted in part

1. See Selosoemardjan (1962) for general description of Jogjakarta (pronounced "Jog-ya-kar'ta").

23

into lecture halls for the University of Gadjah Mada, Indonesia's oldest university, it remains a locus for civic ritual. Thousands flock to the syncretic Sekaten fair on the palace green, and the Garabeg ceremonies annually link the Sultan to Islam through a ritual parade of *gamelan* orchestras from the palace to the Great Mosque. Expressive of a lively syncretic Javanism, mystical cults abound in Jogjakarta, as do puppet theaters, dance performances, and refined manners.

In Jogjakarta one finds the full spectrum of Javanese Islam, ranging from a perfected syncretic, abangan culture to the militant reformist Islam known as *santri modèren*. The national headquarters of the most powerful anti-Javanist santri modèren reformist movement (Muhammadijah), Jogja is also the place of origin of the most powerful pro-Javanist abangan movements (Budi Utomo and Taman Siswa). Only the middle type, the traditionalist Islamic *santri kolot*, has failed to flourish in Jogjakarta; whereas numerous kampungs in Jogjakarta are known as strongly Muhammadijah, the only one famed for its santri kolot sympathies is Krapjak, the site of a traditionalist Islamic school on the edge of town.

Muhammadijah in Jogjakarta

Founded in Jogjakarta in 1912 by K.H.A. Dahlan, Muhammadijah boasted some 4000 members by the time of his death in 1923, most of whom resided in Jogjakarta. By 1970, Muhammadijah claimed around 6 million members with more than 2000 branches distributed throughout the islands. The organizational format has remained essentially the same since 1930, when the movement was differentiated into various committees such as social welfare and health care, Islamic law, education, youth, economics, politics, material resources, evangelism, and the women's division, 'Aisjijah. Although the more worldly committees (education, economics, politics, material resources, and social welfare) have recently moved to the capital of Indonesia, Djakarta, in order to be at the hub of the bureaucracy, the national headquarters continue to be in Jogjakarta.

The center of Muhammadijah in Jogjakarta is a two-story white building on 99 K.H.A. Dahlan street. The building contains a library, a distribution center for literature (a commercial Muhammadijah bookstore is nearby), files of membership that go back to the time of the Japanese occupation, workrooms for the Muhammadijah magazine and bulletin, headquarters for the women's and student organizations, a prayer room, an auditorium, and a small office for Pak Djindhar Tamimy, the administrator who oversees much of the local and national operation. Here, too, are the President of Muhammadijah, Pak H.A.R. Fachruddin, and the President of Aisjijah, Professor Siti Baroroh. Those who drop by range from aged figures of the movement's early history to youth leaders, and at one time or another most of the active organizers throughout the city and region appear.

Also in Jogjakarta are located a Muhammadijah hospital, headed by the physician-husband of the head of 'Aisjijah, orphanages, schools, kindergartens, the Great Mosque, small mosques, women's mosques, and the theological faculty. Certain neighborhoods, such as Kauman and Karang Kadjen, are full of Muhammadijah members and properties, such as prayer-houses, kindergartens, and cottage industries. Throughout the Jogjakarta Muhammadijah community, life is organized around the five daily prayers, the Friday sermon, the Fast, and most distinctively, study sessions (pengadjian). Pengadjian are held by neighborhoods, youth groups, women's organizations, and other divisions within the Muslim community. The format is not rigidly set, but consists essentially of lecture and discussion on some topic concerning Islam, and the topics vary widely; indeed, the subject of several 1970 pengadjian was my findings concerning Muhammadijah.

The other major Muhammadijah institution in Jogjakarta is the school. In Jogjakarta there are both government and private schools—primarily Christian, Muslim, and syncretist—at the elementary (Sekolah Rakjat or SR), junior high (Sekolah Menengah Pertama or SMP), and high school (Sekolah Menengah Atas

or SMA) levels. These can lead to university study. Muhammadijah also has religious schools *(madrasah)* which can lead to
theological study at government seminaries or Muslim univer-
sities abroad, as well as kindergartens, normal schools, missionary schools, and other specialties. The total number of Muhammadijah schools in Jogjakarta is 42, manned by 610 teachers and
instructing 15,000 pupils.

In sum, the required rituals of Islam, the study groups, and
the schools provide the major source of reformist participation
and eduation for the generality of the Muhammadijah membership in Jogjakarta. A select group takes part also in such gatherings as council meetings, committee meetings, and training
camps. The wider Jogjakarta public is exposed to the Muhammadijah orientation throughout such media as mass prayers,
posters displayed at the Sekaten fair, and a street named after
K.H.A. Dahlan.

Types of Religious Orientation

Even a cursory sketch of Muhammadijah in Jogjakarta
reminds us that involvement in reformism varies in kind and
degree. One may "be" a reformist by formal membership in the
Muhammadijah, by the type of schooling one has experienced,
by participation in other activities, or simply by attitude. Each
of these modes of being a reformist can be subdivided according
to intensity of involvement or commitment. And the same
individual may wax and wane in dedication or completely shift
viewpoint as he passes through the life cycle. Who, then, is a
reformist and who is not?

An important answer to this question is given in Clifford
Geertz' *The Religion of Java.*[2] Geertz postulates three ideal
types: *abangan* (syncretist Muslim), *santri* (purist Muslim), and

2. For ethnographic exposition of the abangan/santri constructs, see
C. Geertz (1960b), Jay (1963), Peacock (1967), Snouck-Hurgronje
(1927a). For historical explanation, see Johns (1966), Pigeaud (1938, pp.
471 ff.), Sardjono (1947), Soebardi (1971). Muskens (1970) and Polak
(1973) treat the sharpening of the abangan category with the rise of
Hinduist movements since 1965.

prijaji (aristocratic Muslim). The santri in turn divide into the reformist *(santri modèren)* and traditionalist *(santri kolot)*. Inspired in part by Weber, the Geertzian classification is founded on cultural analysis, a definition of how the Javanese render the world meaningful—whether through a syncretic, reformist, or other type of world-view. Geertz goes beyond the purely cultural analysis in that he also portrays ramified behavioral patterns, as in socioeconomic status, educational systems, and political organizations, that correlate with each distinctive cultural orientation.

Geertz' seminal work was based on qualitative, largely ethnographic research, distilled into an ideal typical formulation of the logic underlying each distinctive orientation and style of life. The value of his work is enhanced by the fact that his ideal types more or less correspond to labels that the Javanese themselves use in making order of reality. Despite the great utility of his scheme, a simple question remains, which can be answered only by statistics: To what degree is each trait, supposedly an attribute of a given type, actually associated with other traits which also supposedly characterize that type? This question was approached through what I shall term the Jogjakarta survey.

THE JOGJAKARTA SURVEY

Following several months of participant observation of the Muhammadijah branches on several islands, I settled in Jogjakarta in March 1970 and continued these observations among the Muhammadijans there. In May 1970 I decided to attempt a survey in Jogjakarta similar to one I had already gotten underway in Singapore and Malaya, and I began by drafting a schedule in the Indonesian language which was modified after consultation with informants. This draft served as the instrument for trial interviews, which I conducted myself, with informants representing the several broad types of interest (santri, syncretist, etc.), and this experience resulted in a final draft which was mimeographed for use in the interviews with a sample of 400. These interviews were carried out by a team of students at Gadjah Mada University who were experienced in survey research. After attending initial interviews with several of the students, I did. not attend the remaining interviews. It should be noted, however, that owing to numerous speeches I had by that time given in Muhammadijah circles, my name, which appeared on the interview schedule (see Appendix A), was known by numerous reformist respondents. (As a foreign visitor to the.Muhammadijah, I had, by the time of the survey, spoken at evening and dawn study groups to audiences ranging from forty or fifty to many hundreds, and my visit had received both local and national coverage in the Muslim media.) This association, together with a letter of introduction from the Muhammadijah authorities, allegedly allayed suspicion and increased receptivity to the interviews among Muhammadijans. A letter of introduction from the municipal authorities of Jogjakarta was also shown to respondents.

Jogjakarta-region is divided into villages, and Jogjakarta-city into neighborhoods, each with an official headman. These neighborhoods and villages were the basic units of the Jogja survey. Ten such units were selected by inquiry and observation to represent a range of social types including rural and urban, reformist and traditionalist, rich and poor. The interviewer would present the headman of a unit with a letter explaining the project and a letter from the authorities legitimizing it, obtain from him a list of households in the unit containing a married couple with a son, and then visit each house on the list until the quota for that unit had been achieved. The interview focused on the male household head; only questions in Part III of the Jogjakarta Household Survey schedule (see Appendix A) were directed to the wife. Accordingly, except in the case of these questions (which mainly deal with child-rearing, discussed in Chapter 3), responses noted come from male household heads.

This procedure resulted in 391 acceptable completed interviews (9 were discarded because the wife did not complete her portion). These completed interviews were distributed as follows among the ten units: Kauman (40 respondents) and Karang Kadjen (39), two neighborhoods known for their high concen-

tration of Muhammadijans; Krapjak (35), a semi-rural neighborhood bordered by rice fields on the edge of town, site of a large
religious school run by a santri kolot figure and reputedly high
in concentration of traditionalists; Dipowinatan (40), reputedly
high in concentration of syncretist members of the nationalist
party (PNI); Kota Baru (42), a suburb reputedly high in concentration of Dutch-educated, white-collar elite; and several mixed
neighborhoods: Godean (80), a rural area to the west of Jogjakarta-city, and Kraton (26), Bulaksumur (12), Njutran (39), and
Kritjak (38). As was hoped, approximately half of the total
sample turned out to be members of Muhammadijah. This proportion is higher than the proportion of Muhammadijans in the
Jogjakarta population, since the objective was to insure that
there was a large enough proportion of reformists in the sample
to permit secure comparison of reformists and others. While the
sample obtained is proper for this purpose, it is a quota sample
and not a random sample that permits generalization to the
Jogjakarta population as a whole.

In addition to the 400 household heads in Jogjakarta, 34 of
the 38 participants in a Muhammadijah training camp for
branch leaders, Darol Arqom, also completed a portion of the
survey schedule (that part which does not require the wife to be
present). This camp was an intensive two-week, seventeen-hour-
per-day routine of physical training, study, and self-criticism
held in a village near the town of Klaten. Its aim was to intensify
the commitment of leaders in local branches, and many of its
lecturers were national leaders from Jogjakarta. I was a participant in this camp but did not interview each branch leader
separately; instead, I distributed the questionnaires at the beginning of the camp and collected them two weeks later, at the end.

A survey was also made of the attitudes of students in
Jogjakarta secondary schools. Again, quota sampling was used
in order that approximately half of the students would be at
Muhammadijah schools and half not. Two types of Muhammadijah schools were surveyed: the most highly regarded Muhammadijah coeducational high school (Muhammadijah SMA)
and the two famous Muhammadijah madrasah, Mualimien for

boys and Mualimaat for girls. The other half of the sample of
somewhat over 1000 students came from two of Jogjakarta's best
and largest government high schools, SMA I and III. Unlike the
household surveys, which were administered by interview, the
school surveys required each student to fill out a questionnaire
(which was a shortened version of the household schedule; see
Appendix B) distributed in classes. In the government high
schools, only those students enrolled in the Islamic religion
classes were sampled, since the desire was to include only
Muslims in the total sample.

For economy of space, I shall refer to the two questionnaires as follows:

H = household survey
S = school survey
Q = question number

By consulting the appendices, the reader can find translations of
all questions discussed in the text.

*Religious Orientation: Operational
Definitions and Associations*

The central goals of this chapter are, first, to delineate the
essential attributes of reformism and each of the other religious
orientations, and second, to ask the question: If a person pos-
sesses one attribute, does he possess all? Three attributes were
selected as defining the extent of religious orientation: educational background, organizational membership, and theological
or doctrinal attitude (see Table 2). These were considered to
reflect the major varieties of reformist or nonreformist experience in the Jogjakarta setting, and they touch on the cultural
(doctrinal), social (organizational), and personal (socialization /
enculturation / educational) patterns.

Household Survey

In terms of educational background, respondents were classified as Western, reformist Muslim, traditionalist Muslim, or
syncretist. A respondent was classified as having a "Western

educatíonal background" if he indicated on HQ I-6 and 21 that his *and* his father's longest period of school within each of the levels (primary, intermediate, and secondary) either had attended was in a Dutch school; "reformist Muslim educational background" if his and his father's longest period of schooling within each level was Muhammadijah (either government or madrasah type, i.e., mualimien); and "traditionalist Muslim educational background" if his and his father's longest period of schooling was at the traditional type of Islamic school known as a *pesantren* (HQ I-6 and 21, part 17). Each of these categories, then, includes only those respondents whose dominant schooling, and that of their fathers, at all levels was of a single type: either Western, reformist, or traditionalist.[3]

3. "Longest period of school" at a given level was determined as follows: HQ I-6, 21, and 35 first ask the type of school attended at each level (elementary, intermediate, secondary), then ask how long the subject (respondent, father, son) was there ("from class _____ to class _____"). If the subject attended more than one school, the one at which most time was spent counted as the type at that level; if time spent was equal, the school checked last was counted. Instances of multiple schooling at the same level were few. While the categorization into elementary, intermediate, and secondary is based on the current Indonesian government system (SR, SMP, and SMA) and oversimplifies the more variegated Dutch government system, pre-testing indicated that respondents with Dutch schooling had little difficulty categorizing their education in terms of the current three levels. (See Table 1.)

Alternative 18 of HQ I-6, 21, and 35 permitted the respondent to list any schooling which he felt did not fit the elementary / intermediate / secondary and other pre-coded categories. These responses were coded into the following types: (1) advanced government Muslim schooling (usually at a government Islamic seminary known as IAIN); (2) advanced government technical schooling; (3) advanced Muhammadijah schooling (at a Muhammadijah college); (4) non-Muslim university or teacher's college; (5) Muslim university or teacher's college; (6) study in Mecca or other private but advanced Islamic study; (7) study of Javanese culture, as gamelan or dance; (8) technical training courses, other than governmental; (9) syncretic combinations, e.g., Christian plus Islamic study. Responses in these categories were so few, however, that they were not taken into account here in defining the basic categories of reformist, syncretist, traditionalist, and Western by schooling.

The fourth category, "syncretist," is not so pure, as befits the phenomenology of syncretism; the impurity also had the methodological advantage of including most of the remainder of the respondents. Into this residual category fell all individuals whose longest period of schooling at *some* level was in a government Indonesian school or a private nationalist-nativist Javanese or Indonesian school, such as Taman Siswa and various later types that sprang up during the Revolution of 1945-50. Some of these "syncretist educated" had also experienced some schooling of the first three types, and the category also includes those whose dominant type of schooling differed from their fathers. (See Table 1 for a summary of the types of schooling just outlined.)

Respondents' doctrinal or theological attitudes were classified as Muslim reformist, Muslim traditionalist, or "syncretist" ("Javanese" or "abangan"), depending on response to two items:

HQ II-2. Which of the following sentences most fits your own belief?:
1. The carrying out of the law of Islam must be cleansed from folk customs that do not fit the teachings of Islam.·
2. Folk customs *(adat istiadat)* that have long been followed by Muslims should not be changed.
3. Not certain.

HQ II-3. Which of the following sentences most fits your own belief?:
1. Better for an individual to draw his own conclusions about the rules of Islam through the teachings of the holy Qur'an and the codified traditions (Sunnah).
2. Most people are better off depending upon the religious authorities to inform them about the law of Islam.
3. Better if each person relies on the voice of his inner spirit.
4. Better if each person relies on the great teachings of the ancestors expressed at the shrines, together with his own inner voice.

TABLE 1.
Types and Levels of Schooling Among Jogjakarta Respondents

Type	Levels
Western Dutch	Elementary (e.g. Volksschool) Junior high (e.g. Meer Uitgebreid Lager Onderwijs) High school (e.g. Hoogere Burger School)
Reformist Muslim Madrasah	Approximately equivalent to late junior high and early high school
Government-type Muhammadijah	Elementary (Sekolah Rakjat) Junior high (Sekolah Menengah Pertama) High school (Sekolah Menengah Atas)
Traditionalist Muslim Pesantren	Not divided into levels
Syncretist Government or nativist- nationalist	Elementary (SR) Junior high (SMP) High school (SMA)
Variety of schooling	

Educational background
  of father different
  from that of son	

Persons who chose alternative 1 on both questions were classified as holding a reformist attitude; those who chose alternative
2 on both questions were classified as traditionalist Muslims.
Those who had mixed answers (1 and 2, or 2 and 1) or who
chose 3 or 4 on HQ II-3 were classified as syncretist.

HQ II-2 is designed to check the extent of belief in reformist
purification as opposed to traditionalism or syncretism (alt. 1
vs. alt. 2). HQ II-3 is designed to divide respondents into those

who believe in the reformist *idjtihad*, or personal analysis (alt. 1), those who believe in the traditionalist *taklid buta*, or reliance on authorities (alt. 2), and those who trust the inner spirit or the sacred shrine more than either of these santri alternatives. The category "syncretist" is again residual and impure, since it is possible for a person classified as "syncretist" to choose *either* alternative 1 or 2 on HQ II-2, as long as he mixes his answers or chooses 3 or 4· on HQ II-3. The objective is to distinguish individuals who are *consistently* reformist; I assume that two out of two reformist responses are less likely due to chance than one of two. A certain validity of the questions is suggested by the fact that in a sample of known reformists, the heavily indoctrinated Darol Arqom training camp participants—branch leaders of Muhammadijah—all chose both reformist items.

Classified as reformist in organizational or party membership were individuals who indicated in response to HQ II-39 that they belonged to one of the reformist groups—Muhammadijah, HMI, Persis, or the PMI—but to no traditionalist Muslim or syncretist Javanese organization. Those who indicated that they belonged to either the traditionalist Muslim party (NU) or its youth wing (Ansor), but to no reformist or syncretist organization, were classified as conservative (traditionalist) in membership. Respondents who indicated that they belonged to the syncretic national party (PNI) or the associated youth organization (Gerakan Pemuda Marhaen) were classified as syncretist Javanese in membership. Again, syncretism is the residual category, so that a person who belonged to PNI as well as NU or Muhammadijah (unlikely but possible) would be classified as syncretist.

As anticipated, differing characteristics of reformism are not evenly distributed. These differing measures of religious orientation slice the sample differently, resulting in differing numbers of respondents overall and within each category. Thus, of the 387 respondents who answered both questions concerning theology, 194 gave reformist answers, 111 traditionalist, and 82 syncretist. Of the 376 respondents who had been to school, 75 were classified as Western schooled, 47 as reformist schooled, 38 as traditionalist schooled, and 216 as "syncretist" schooled. Of the 253 who divulged party or organizational membership classifiable in terms of this trichotomy, 163 were reformist, 16 traditionalist, and 74 syncretist.[4]

Cross-tabulation[5]—To what extent and in what manner are these measures of attitudes intercorrelated? Two major techniques were employed to answer these questions: first, analysis

4. Additional Jogja household survey indications of reformism vs. syncretism or traditionalism were: designation of neighborhood and indication of whether one believed in mazhap (HQ II-44—i.e., the scholastic texts derived from medieval Islam). Analysis shows that these indices predict basically the same cultural and psychological patterns as the indices reported here.

5. Textual statements based on cross-tabulation represent several steps of interpretation of the data generated by the questionnaires reproduced and translated in the appendices. The first step was coding. Many of the survey questions were multiple-choice. If questions were open-ended, coding categories were developed by the investigator after the data were collected. The coded data were stored on computer cards and tapes. The types of religious orientation were then constructed from this coded data and cross-tabulated with the "dependent variables"—i.e., the psychological traits represented by most of the rest of the data. Such cross-tabulations are a simple device to show how frequently a respondent with response A also gave response X; they also allow calculation of tests of significance, i.e., the probability that the association between variables is actually zero in the population from which the sample is drawn. These cross-tabulations have been condensed into tables too bulky for publication here. Footnotes report percentages abstracted from these tables, often lumping similar percentages (e.g., 5–10%) when the percentage obtained varied according to measurement used, but the overall trend is the same regardless of measure used. Notes and text also sometimes simplify, for analytical purposes, categories used in the coding.

These footnotes do not give results of measures of association and tests of significance for the cross-tabulations, largely because such results imply unwarranted assumptions about the sampling procedure. Percentages can be compared by inspection; in order to know roughly the sample size on which each set of percentages is based, the reader should refer to that portion of Chapter 2 which gives the number of responses according to the measure of religious orientation utilized: the number varies from approximately 400 to 200 for Jogja, but remains at approximately 400 for Singapore and 200 for Kedah, since only one

of cross-tabulations, and second, factor analysis. Simply by examining the percentages of persons who respond here in one way and there in another, we begin to answer such questions as how frequently a person who undergoes reformist schooling also adopts reformist attitudes and/or joins reformist organizations. The correlation is evident, but the pattern is not simple. If a person is a member of a reformist organization, to what extent is he also reformist in theology and educational background?

The great majority (83%) of those who belong to the reformist organizations also show reformist theology. By contrast, most of those (90%) who belong to the syncretist organization show syncretist theology, and only 10% show reformist theology. Thus, the sample splits fairly neatly between those who are both organizationally and theologically reformist and those who are both organizationally and theologically syncretist; there are, however, some mixed types. Only a small number of respondents belong to the traditionalist organization.

While reformists by organization tend to be reformist by theology, they represent a mixture in educational background. Virtually all of the Islamic schooled, whether reformist or traditionalist, join the reformist organization. Half of the non-Islamic schooled, whether Western or syncretist, do so as well (compared to only one-third who join syncretist organizations). Thus, in Jogjakarta, education of any kind appears to encourage membership in the reformist organization. This result, based on the household survey, is confirmed by ethnographic work and

---

indication of religious orientation (theology) was used in these two places. As a rule of thumb, many statistical tests would yield an acceptable level of significance (defined as $p \leqslant .05$) with samples of these sizes if the difference in percentages is 10% or greater. In many instances, as can be seen, the differences are much greater than this, indicating that the significance levels obtained are more stringent than the conventionally accepted .05 or .01 levels. However, lesser degrees of difference also obtain, and these are also discussed when they are consistent with general trends and patterns revealed both statistically and qualitatively. Notable inconsistencies are also reported. Citation of statistics in the text itself is kept to a minimum, in order to avoid distraction from the thrust of the analysis.

analysis of Muhammadijah membership lists; for example, the majority of the Darol Arqom training camp participants had experienced government schooling rather than, or as well as, reformist schooling. Islamic schooling of any kind almost certainly results in reformist membership, within this Jogjakarta sample. The reason is probably that Jogjakarta is a stronghold of Muhammadijah and weak in traditionalist Muslim organization, so that the devout Muslim of any persuasion gravitates toward Muhammadijah.

All educational types also gravitate toward reformist theology: 84% of the traditionalist schooled, 68% of the reformist schooled, and the majority of the syncretist and Western schooled as well. Few of the Islamic schooled show syncretist theology, and only about one-third of either the Western or syncretist schooled do so. Not only do the traditionalist schooled have the highest percentage with reformist theology of any group, but they also have the lowest percentage of traditionalist theology (13%). Thus, traditionalist Islamic schools (known as *pesantren*) appear to strongly encourage both reformist theology and membership. This pattern is apparent also from biographical and life-history data. Even though certain specific features of method and doctrine in pesantren schooling oppose reformism, and even though pesantren are organizationally affiliated with the *santri kolot* parties, something about the general psychology of pesantren schooling (perhaps the sheer intensity and asceticism of the experience) appears to encourage the development of reformist orientations. This psychological dynamic will be explored further in the next chapter.

In sum, theological orientation and organizational affiliation are strongly associated; reformists in one aspect tend to be reformists in the other, and syncretists in the one tend to be syncretists in the other. Educational background is not as strongly associated with theological orientation and organizational affiliation as these latter features are with each other. Reformists theologically and organizationally come from a variety of backgrounds; while the majority of the reformist educated become reformists theologically and organizationally, an even larger proportion of the pesantren educated do so, and a fairly large proportion of the syncretist educated do so as well.

Factor Analysis—The question of what goes with what is answered somewhat differently by factor analysis. Three clusters were derived which both parallel and refine the associations discussed above.[6] These three factors, which correlate with stages of the life cycle, are: (1) adult theology and organizational membership, (2) youth schooling and organizational membership, and (3) childhood schooling and family heritage. These three categories distinguish three subsets of "reformist experiences." The first type includes present, adult membership in the Muhammadijah organization and the reformist Indonesian Muslim Party (PMI), as well as reformist theological orientation. The second type of experience involves schooling and membership during youth, i.e., in a Muhammadijah junior and senior high school and in the Muslim Student Association (HMI), the highly active youth reformist movement sympathetic to but not affiliated with Muhammadijah. The third type of experience includes elementary schooling in the Muhammadijah and a father whose dominant schooling was also Muhammadijah.

These three stages of experience summarize as simply as possible the results of a rather complex factor analysis which revealed that the traits or experiences *within* each type (e.g., schooling in a Muhammadijah junior and senior high school and membership in HMI) tend to be strongly intercorrelated. Conversely, computation of intercorrelations *between* factors indicated that they are relatively independent of one another; in other words, the correlation between the types was not great— e.g., the person who in his youth joined HMI *and* attended a Muhammadijah junior and senior high school was not necessarily the same person who had attended a Muhammadijah elementary school and whose father was educated by Muhammadijah.[7]

6. This method and these results are elaborated in detail in Wood (1975).

7. In more detail: Muhammadijah and PMI membership and reformist theology "loaded" (see Wood, p. 10) .50 to .80 on the factor we have

School Survey

Students were classified according to their school and their theological orientation, the latter being defined just as in the household survey (SQ 19, 21 equal HQ II-2, 3). By type of school, the 1190 student respondents were approximately half Muhammadijah and half government, with 252 at the Muhammadijah high school, 318 at the Muhammadijah madrasahs, and 620 at the government high schools. The 790 students classifiable into either group split into 754 reformists and 36 syncretists by theological orientation. The low number of syncretists in our sample is probably due to the fact that only students enrolled in Islamic religion classes were interviewed in the government schools, so that the full-blown, anti-Muslim syncretists in these schools were largely omitted.

The Branch Leaders and the National Leaders

With respect to the ideological and organizational indices of reformist orientation, the 34 Muhammadijah branch leaders in the training camp Darol Arqom were in complete unanimity: 100% favored *idjtihad* on HQ II-2, 100% favored purification on HQ II-3, and, of course, 100% were members of the Muhammadijah. With respect to schooling, however, as was noted above, few were of pure reformist background. The majority were graduates of the government elementary school, while none had attended the premier Muhammadijah madrasah (Mualimien in Jogjakarta) and only a half-dozen had attended other reformist madrasahs. The absence of pure reformism in

---

termed "adult," whereas other indices of reformism had much lower loading on this factor. ("Loading" indicates the extent to which a given element correlates with the dimension or "factor" characterizing a cluster of elements.) Intermediate and secondary Muhammadijah schooling, together with membership in HMI, all loaded on the "youth" factor at levels ranging from .44 to .85, with much less loading by other indices of reformism. Elementary Muhammadijah schooling and having a father with similar schooling loaded .45 to .53 on what we have termed the "childhood" factor, whereas other indices were much less related to this factor.

educational background reflects a general heterogeneity of background revealed as the participants (23 of them) narrated their autobiographies to the training group at large; some came from syncretist families, some from traditionalist (NU) families, and few reported hard-line reformist family backgrounds.

The national leaders of Muhammadijah were not administered the survey questionnaire, but were interviewed concerning their philosophies and backgrounds. Interviews of this type were held with the President and the Secretary-treasurer of Muhammadijah, with the head of the reformist Muslim party (PMI), and with heads of major divisions within the Muhammadijah. Based on these interviews, almost all of these national leaders exemplify the "pure" type of reformist. All favor the tenets of *idjtihad* and purification, all are of course members of the Muhammadijah, and virtually all have gained their dominant education within the reformist Muslim school system of the Muhammadijah, either at the Madrasah Mualimien in Jogjakarta or equivalent madrasahs elsewhere or in the Muhammadijah SR, SMP, SMA system.

Reformist Types

In sum, there appears to be a hierarchy of reformist types. At the level of national leaders, one finds the purest reformist in the sense that almost every leader is reformist according to all three criteria: doctrinal, organizational, and educational. At the level of the branch leaders, one finds the second-purest: these are unanimously reformist in ideology and organizational affiliation, though not in educational background. At the level of the general populace of Jogjakarta, as sampled in the household survey, there exist numerous mixed types: persons who are reformist in one attribute but not in the others. Factor analysis suggests a further refinement—that varied combinations of reformist experience produce subtypes of reformists. Thus, the ideal-type analysis, of which Clifford Geertz' *santri/abangan/ prijaji* trichotomy is a seminal instance, appears to hold best for the leaders and least for the general populace in the Jogjakarta sample. This suggests a certain relation between the conceptual purity of the ideal type and the function of the leader as expressing in pure form the ideals of the culture.

FURTHER CULTURAL ORIENTATIONS

Clearly "reformist" is not a unitary type in the sense that every "santri modèren" in Jogjakarta can be expected to have the same ideological, organizational, and educational attributes. Yet when further cultural orientations are explored, it is apparent that all of the attributes are associated with the same orientation in certain cultural spheres. That is, regardless of whether one is a reformist by virtue of schooling, ideology, or membership, he will tend toward certain beliefs and practices. The object of the remainder of this chapter is to summarize these relationships as confirmed by the Jogja survey. Unless otherwise noted, the relationships summarized here hold true for all types of reformists.

On two items of the Jogjakarta household survey, respondents of all types, reformist or other, were in agreement. Virtually all (96%) claim to believe that God will reward and punish in the afterlife (HQ I-65), and virtually all customarily ask forgiveness of parents on the Lebaran day, which celebrates the end of the fast month (HQ II-11). The first response indicates consensus concerning a belief basic to Islam. The second response indicates conformity to a ritual basic to Malayo-Indonesian society.[8]

Aside from these basic areas of agreement, respondents varied according to type, largely in the direction predicted by the santri-abangan typologies and prescribed by ideologies of such organizations as the Muhammadijah. Among the household heads, it was reformists who *least* often professed belief in sacred relics, the coming of a charismatic messiah-like prince,

8. See C. Geertz (1960b, p. 319) on the central significance of this rite in Javanese society; the Singapore and Malaya surveys suggest that the rite has fully as much significance there, i.e., is pan-Malayo-Muslim rather than uniquely Javanese.

and the various spooks and spirits, except for the *djin* or "genie," which are recognized by santri as affirmed by the Qur'anic scripture (HQ II-38). Syncretists (including the Western schooled) *most* frequently believed in these elements.[9] In frequencies of belief, traditionalist Muslims fell between the syncretists and reformists, sometimes resembling the one and sometimes the other, depending on which spirit or sacred element was considered. The majority of students from all types of schools claimed disbelief in these elements (SQ 23), and the theologically reformist students were the most frequent disbelievers, except in the messianic prince and the genie.[10] The branch leaders were almost unanimous in disbelief, except in djin.

Factor analysis of the household data confirmed that belief or disbelief in these sacred elements (excluding djin) is a unitary trait; a person who professes disbelief (or belief) in any one item on the list of HQ II-38 very likely professes the same for the other items. But he who disbelieves in all other items believes in the djin.[11]

In interpreting these results, we should recall the general

9. The difference was greatest when comparing the groups in terms of party and theology, where reformist disbelief in the elements listed varied from two to three times that of other groups except in the case of djin; e.g., 50–75% of syncretists (percentages varying according to type of spirit) believed in all but *ratu adil*—the messiah or "Just Prince" who, in Javanese mythology, will right all wrongs—compared to only 4–24% of reformists in all but djin. By schooling the differences were less, but in the same direction. C. Geertz (1960b, esp. p. 29) gives useful interpretation of these spirits.

10. No more than 20% of any group of students professed belief in any entity except djin and sacred relics *(pusaka);* 31% of government SMA students, 15% of Muhammadijah SMA students, and only 6% of madrasah students believed in pusaka. But 80% of the Muhammadijah (SMA and madrasah) students, compared to 60% of the government SMA students, believed in djin.

11. Wood (1975, pp. 19-20) reports that spiritual elements *tujul, memedi, wewe, lelembut, peri, gendruwo,* and *wedon,* all loaded 0.74 or more on the factor "rejection of spirit belief," whereas djin had a *negative* loading of 0.48 on this factor.

consensus of ethnographic studies[12] that the Javanese traditionally view the world as composed of spiritual energies contained
in forms and images, such as magically potent swords, sacred
shrines, spirits, deities, teachers, and rulers; the Javanese syncretist world is what Weber termed a "garden of magic"—indeed, an animistic jungle.

Islam, on the other hand, holds as its central tenet the belief
in God's uniqueness and His unity *(Tauhid)*. The one God
monopolizes and concentrates all spiritual energy; hence it is
forbidden to believe in the spiritual power of other entities
(except those, like djin, which are in the service of Allah). Since
the reformists profess the purest Islam, the syncretists the least
pure, it is logical that the reformists show the strongest belief in
Tauhid.

Reformists more frequently than syncretists reject belief in
petungan (HQ II-36),[13] a mode of calculating when ritual or
other events should occur in order to mesh with the animistically
conceived cosmos. This suggests that the reformists are rejecting
a Javanist notion of time which has aptly been termed "pulsa-
tive."[14] Time does not accumulate, but instead pulsates between

12. Ranging, for example, from the overviews by Snouck-Hurgronje
(1927a) to C. Geertz (1960b, sect. I).

13. Seven times as many reformists by party, theology, and schooling disbelieve in petungan as do syncretists: 4–8% belief by reformists
(percentage varying by definition of reformism) vs. 27–53% syncretists.
Exemplifying the Muhammadijan attitude toward petungan-thinking,
the President of Muhammadijah, Pak H.A.R. Fachruddin, once remarked
in a speech, "I just came from X town, they are talking about Muhammad's birth on the 12th day. Why? Because the year has 12 months. If
the professor [referring to me] hears talk like this, can he believe Islam is
rational? If I hear it, I feel sick at heart—though not if I smile!" (He
smiles.) Another example: A Darol Arqom participant apologized to the
group for knowing the day but not the year of his birth—a syncretic
trait. The day is important for the syncretists, for it represents the
convergence of cycles, and it will be repeated. The year is important for
Muslims, for it is a phase in a sequence, and it will not be repeated.
Petungan represents a repetitive sense of time, Islam a progressive sense.

14. C. Geertz (1960b, pp. 30-1, 35).

empty periods and auspicious points at which various cycles of days and weeks converge; it is at these points that certain ceremonies should be held, that actions should or should not be taken. One may conceptualize that the reformists are replacing the pulsative-cyclical notion of time with a cumulative-linear conception expressed in an Islam which conceives of a true history passing from Adam to Jesus and climaxing with Muhammad and salvation.

Reformists overwhelmingly reject the communal feasts (slametan) that have traditionally preserved social and spiritual equanimity and thus kept everyone safe, or "slamet." Syncretists overwhelmingly reported practice of the majority of these slametans. Traditionalists were again in-between syncretists and reformists in their reported practice of slametan, and they favored most those slametans with Islamic content yet animistic form, such as celebrations of the birth of Muhammad.[15]

Rejecting slametans, reformists affirm the Islamic prayers (salat). When asked to rank the various ideals of religious action (HQ I-66), santri place first priority on the five daily prayers, with reformists leading the other groups in this emphasis.[16] The ideology is confirmed in reported practice, in that the reformists

15. Some 60–80% of the reformists by school, party or theology report *not* practicing the life-cycle (birth and death) slametans, compared to 70–90% of the syncretists by party or membership, and 50–80% of Western and syncretist schooled, who *do*. Traditionalists fall in between, approximately half practicing and half not. The difference between syncretists and reformists with respect to the calendrical slametans is less than to the life-cycle slametans, since syncretists less often practice the calendrical and Islamic-related *muludan* and *maleman* (celebrating Muhammad's birth and the end of the fast) than they do the life-cycle slametans; 80–90% of the reformists by schooling vs. 60% of the Javanese and Western schooled report not practicing these two Islamic-related slametans; by party and theology the same differences hold. Traditionalists frequently celebrate muludan and maleman.

16. Whether by schooling, theology, or party, 85–100% of reformists ranked the five prayers of first importance, compared to 64% of the Western and syncretic schooled, 67% of the traditionalists by theology, and 23% of the syncretists by theology and 38% by party.

rank highest among the Jogjakartan household heads in reported regularity of the five prayers (HQ I-70).[17]

Further responses reinforce the notion that for these santri, as generally in the Islamic world, the daily prayers reflect a relationship with God that is ritualistic and communal rather than spontaneous and personal, as in Protestantism. Few reformists seek God's counsel in time of sadness (HQ I-34),[18] and fewer of them than of the Western schooled and the syncretists (by organization and doctrine) rank "meditative communion with God" as of first importance as a type of religious action (HQ I-66).[19] More than any other type, the reformist opts for "regular prayers" instead of "praying to God when one feels the

17. By schooling, 90% of the Islamic schooled (whether reformist or traditionalist) vs. 50% of the Western or syncretist schooled claimed to do the five prayers daily. By theology, 94% of the reformists vs. 67% of the traditionalists and 10% of the syncretists, and by party, 98% of reformists vs. 31% of syncretists, made this claim.

18. Only 1–6% of any group claimed to seek God for counsel.

19. Meditative communion was considered most important by 17% of the Western (Dutch) schooled, compared to 9% or less for any other group; the tendency of Western schooling to correlate with this attitude was also revealed by the survey in Singapore (see Chapter 5), with Western schooling there being English. Thus a "Protestant-like" attitude toward God, a desire to communicate with Him, appears to arise in Western education. Yet a mystical relation to God is also well established in Indonesian Islam; see Archer (1937) and Drewes (1960) on Sufism in Indonesia; Johns (1965) on the Tuhfa of Java; van Nieuwenhuijze (1945) on Islam in Sumatra; Shamsudin (1957) on Atjeh; S.M.N. Al-Attas (1963) on Sufism in Malaya and (1967) concerning Hamzah Fansuri of Atjeh; and Hadiwijono (1967) and Mulder (1970, 1975) on syncretic mysticism in Java and Jogjakarta. Western schooling and syncretic mysticism *(kebatinan)*, pesantren schooling and Islamic mysticism *(Sufi)*, have long been wedded in Java. Only a dozen or so respondents of the entire Jogjakarta sample reported membership in a Sufi (HQ II-36, alt. 16) or kebatinan group (HQ II-39, alt. 29)—which is odd, since my own impressions and studies by Mulder (1975) and others indicate a large kebatinan membership in Jogja; perhaps respondents feared to admit kebatinan or Sufi membership, as the cults carry a taint of Communism.

need to communicate with Him"[20]—confirming the priority of ritualistic prayer, at set times, in set form, in a fixed place.

Factor Analysis—Aside from the general, strong, expected correlations between reformist, syncretist, and traditionalist types and further religious patterns, factor analysis detected three intriguing clusters:

Rejection of petungan was shown to be strongly correlated with claiming not to celebrate slametan associated with the syncretic calendar: the *tingkeban* slametan, held at seven months of pregnancy, the birthday feast *(weton)*, the child's setting of feet on the ground *(tedak siten)*, the birth and death day of the prophet *(muludan)*, and the ceremony *(maleman)* celebrating the end of the fast.[21]

Factor analysis also indicates that it was a somewhat different set of reformists who rejected the life-cycle slametans than those who rejected the calendrical slametans. This "life-cycle slametan" factor showed a strong correlation between rejecting slametans held just before and right after birth *(tingkeban* and *selapanan)* and those held after death (at 3, 7, and 100 days, and 1000 days and one year).[22] These slametans ritualize the life cycle at its extremes, either beginning or end.

Factor analysis also points to a third type, a strong clustering of responses within the realm of Islamic ritualism, legalism, activism, and moralism. An individual who gave any of the

20. Only 10–20% of the Islamic schooled, compared to 30–40% of the Western and syncretist schooled, favored prayer when communication with the deity is desired (as opposed to a set time for prayers), which reflects a general union of Westernism and mysticism vs. Islam and legalism. On the historical shift of Muhammadijah from mysticism to moralism, see Archer (1937, p. 112). On this item, Singapore reformists differ from those of Jogja; largely Western schooled, they show the general Western-schooled tendency to favor the communicative prayer with God when need compels.

21. Rejection of the calendrical slametans loaded this factor at around .50 to .70 (Wood, 1975).

22. Rejection of the five death slametans loaded the "life-cycle factor" at around .90, whereas two birth-related slametans *(tingkeban* and *selapanan)* loaded at around .60 (Wood, 1975).

following responses was likely to give the others as well: ranking the daily five prayers as the most important moral action; considering regular prayer more important than praying to God when the need arises; actually praying five times daily (HQ I-70); giving a high rank to the struggle to build a good society as a moral action (HQ I-66); feeling that one's life is a mission to carry out God's commandment (HQ II-30); and a stress on salvation over interpersonal relations, in that one would prefer to "die alone in the desert but close to God rather than with friends but away from God" (HQ II-30b). Also correlated (but less strongly) was the conviction that drinking liquor is absolutely and invariably sinful (HQ II-27c).[23]

Reformist Subtypes—In sum, reformists in general, whether defined by ideological, organizational, or educational features, predictably and overwhelmingly reject the abangan or syncretic complex, its spiritual world, its rituals, and concepts which integrate the two, such as petungan. However, within this broad patterning, factor analysis suggests some subtypes. The three just mentioned are: those who reject the calendrical complex; those who reject the life-cycle slametans; and those who do not necessarily reject either of these, but whose reformism is expressed by affirmation, i.e., the affirmation of an Islamic ethic one could almost say an Islamic Protestant Ethic. According to the factor analysis, consistency is strong within each type—i.e., a positive response to any one item strongly implies a positive response to the others, whereas the correlation between the types is weak, i.e., they are independent.

It will be recalled that factor analysis also detected three types of reformists on other grounds. These were: the reformist on the basis of ascription and childhood experience (having a reformist father and reformist elementary schooling); the reformist on the basis of youthful experience in a reformist school and movement; and the reformist so defined because of his

23. These items loaded the Islamic Ethic factor at levels ranging from .43 to .75, whereas the disbelief in spirits and nonpractice of slametans did not load this factor strongly (Wood, 1975).

current, adult organizational affiliation and ideological commitment.

An obvious question is whether the first set of types (cultural orientation) correlates with the second (reformist experience). Indeed, this is the case.[24] The reformist via youth experience is the cultural negativist; it is he who is reformist by his rejection of slametans, most strongly those of the life cycle. The reformist by virtue of his adult affiliation and ideology is positive; it is he whose reformism affirms the Islamic Ethic. Finally, the reformist on the basis of heritage and childhood education does not exhibit strongly either the negative or the positive reformist attitudes; it is as though his ascribed (rather than achieved) reformist status is not sufficiently strong to orient him consistently toward any distinctive reformist slant. In a kind of Weberian "existential psychologizing," one may further speculate that it is "natural" that the reformist molded most strongly by the radical and rebellious experience of youth would signal his reformism through a negativism, especially directed at the life-cycle ritualization which honors his enemy categories of childhood and maturity (in the extreme, death). Similarly, it is plausible that the adult-based reformist would affirm rather than negate, especially when what he is affirming is the Islamic sphere most likely to be the concern of the aging: an ethic prescribed to guarantee salvation from death.

24. Correlation (r^2) between the two elements of the youth factor (membership in HMI and Muhammadijah SMP and SMA education) and the life-cycle slametan rejection factor was .65 and .75, respectively. The r^2 for the relation of these two youth categories to rejection of calendrical slametans was .34 and .38. An r^2 of .39 was found between the adult factor (organizational and ideological reformism) and the Islamic ethic (Wood, 1975). Differentiation of "reformism" into these life-cycle stages increases the predictive power of the variable in certain areas. Despite this refinement, the gross indications of reformism (education, theology, and membership) instead of the factors are used throughout the ensuing discussion, because the gross indices deal with the entire Jogja sample, whereas the factor analysis treats only the reformists.

Reformist Orientation

Beginning with an ethnographically derived typology of reformists, syncretists, and traditionalists, we proceeded to explore the distribution of attributes of each type within the Jogjakarta sample. The statistics confirm the basic typology, but suggest refinements—for example, differentiation between organizational-ideological reformists versus reformists by educational background, and between culturally negative reformists via youthful experience versus culturally positive reformists via adult commitment.

These statistically derived types cry out for further ethnographic work; the result of tabulating responses by a sample of anonymous persons, they raise the question: What is the phenomenology behind the response? Even intensive investigation of the situation and psychology of every respondent would of course fail to reveal this phenomenological reality in any absolute sense, but any data that approximates this ideal will be helpful; thus the experience of participant observation in the Darol Arqom training camp provided some degree of personal knowledge of survey respondents, and hence at least some ethnographic data against which to compare survey responses. At this point, however, one must entertain the possibility that the statistical results are artifactual, the product of problems of definition, sampling, or measuring. They could also be revelatory of behavioral patterns not represented either in Javanese folk typologies or ethnographic ideal types, and best discernible through computerized analysis.

However tentative the results, they are worth summary (see Table 2). The statistics confirm the general viability of the santri/abangan cultural types but suggest that these are not unitary. In the general populace, reformists by organization and theology are fairly likely to be *non*-reformist by educational background; they may have received a syncretic or Western education, but they are particularly likely to have been educated in a traditionalist Islamic school, the *pesantren*. (At the national

TABLE 2.
Characteristics of Javanese Muslim Reformists

DEFINING FEATURES

Theological: Belief in *idjtihad* (rational personal interpretation of scripture) and purification of tradition

Organizational: Member of Muhammadijah or other reformist organization

Educational: Schooling by Muhammadijah, either "government" style or madrasah

ASSOCIATED FEATURES (in contrast to syncretists)

Less belief in sacred relics, messianic princes, and spooks or spirits, with exception of *djin*

Negation of *petungan* conception of time and space

Less practice of *slametan* ritual

Low priority on meditative communion with God

High priority on the five daily prayers

SUBTYPES

Childhood: reformist family background and early education, lacks reformist orientation in adulthood

Youth: reformist experience in secondary school and youth movements, shows reformist orientation in adulthood by rejecting life-cycle slametans

Adult: holds reformist theology and membership,   affirms Islamic Ethic

level of leadership, life histories suggest that the pure *santri moderèn* type is found: the reformist by education as well as theology and membership.) Reformists are also differentiated by type of experience. Some are reformist by virtue of youthful experience in reformist schools and movements, others by adult commitment to reformist theology and organization, and a third type by virtue of early reformist schooling and a reformist family background. Type of experience is associated with type of reformist orientation: The reformist only by virtue of his childhood and family background is not strong in any of the reformist cultural orientations. The reformist by youthful experience is strong in rejecting ritual complexes, but weak in affirming a positive Islamic ethic, while the reverse is true of the reformist by adult commitment.

Finally, considered as a whole, regardless of the particular attribute under consideration, the reformists exceed the syncretists in what Weber would term a "rationalized" cultural orientation—rationalized at least from the vantage point of a Protestant Ethic type of world-view. Thus, the reformists reject a ritualized, cyclical pattern of activity and conception of time, they weed out the "garden of magic," and they affirm an ethic which systematizes life toward achievement of salvation and fulfillment of the prescriptions of a scripturally defined theology.

3

Psychological Analysis:
The Reformist Life Cycle

PSYCHOLOGICAL analysis explores the relationship between a cultural framework—in this instance Islamic reformism —and patterns of behavior which are not normally explicitly linked to the cultural framework by the culture bearers—in this instance, reformists—themselves. An example given earlier was the linkage between Tauhid and weaning. Here we are interested in exploring the relationship between reformism as a cultural type, or set of subtypes, and such patterns of behavior as child-rearing, the organization of the life cycle, social interaction, artistic expression, and mental illness. Whereas the reformist (Muhammadijan) doctrine explicitly considers such matters as belief in spirits, observance of *slametans*, and commitment to the Islamic ethic, most of the areas of concern here are not explicitly included within the doctrinal formulations of the Muhammadijah or the normal discourse of the Muhammadijan.

The analysis is simple, if lengthy. The first step is to portray the traditional Javanese pattern; the second is to indicate the areas in which the reformists deviate from this pattern more than do other cultural types. Thus an association is explored between reformism as cultural type and deviation from tradition (i.e., a kind of "reformism") in behavioral pattern.

Where all subtypes of reformism are associated with the same behavioral tendency, the text simply states "reformists do this or that," though statistics in footnotes permit the reader to check on different degrees of the tendency among the different subtypes. Where the tendency is not seen in all subtypes, the text states which one(s) display it.

Where relevant biographical data is available, some effort is made to interpret the statistical relations in terms of it, in order to suggest dynamics in the unfolding of the life cycle; but the main focus here is on the aggregate rather than individual patterns.

INFANCY AND EARLY CHILDHOOD

A child is much desired among Javanese, who highly value procreation and maintain a high birthrate.[1] In the neonatal period—before and during birth, and in infancy—the child is considered vulnerable to shock, which opens it to penetration by the ever-present syncretic spirits, throws it out of mesh with the cosmos, and can cause sickness or death. To insure security (slamet) and to place the natural cycle of birth and maturation in harmony with the cosmic cycle, slametans are held in mesh with the cyclical calendar: these include the telonan (at 3 months of pregnancy), tingkeban (at 7 months of pregnancy), brokohan or barbaran (at birth), pasaran (5 days after birth), selapanan (35 days after), pitonan (7 months after), and taunan (one year after birth).[2]

In addition to securing and harmonizing the life cycle, the slametan is also in some sense believed to determine it. During the tingkeban, for example, a needle is presented to insure that the child will be sharp or mind, and at the pitonan, the child's choices of certain objects from a tray are believed to influence his later choice of a job. And the slametan-like puppet play (wajang kulit) is believed to transfer attributes of certain mythic characters to children watching it during a celebration of passage.

1. H. Geertz (1961, pp. 104-5); Nitsastro (1970). Except where noted otherwise, description of child-rearing derives from H. Geertz or personal observation.

2. C. Geertz (1960b, sect. 1) describes these rites; also note statistics in Chapter 2.

According to the Jogja survey, reformists deviate more from these traditional patterns than do other groups. The reformist's first son is more frequently born in the hospital than are first sons of syncretists (HQ III-46).[3] And the allegedly traditional birth of the child at the home of its maternal grandmother is slightly more frequent for children of the Western and pesantren schooled, the theologically syncretist, and traditionalist Muslim party members.[4] As already noted, the slametan cycle surrounding pregnancy, birth, and early childhood is held rarely by reformists, frequently by syncretists. Nor is the puppet play held often by reformists. In sum, reformism loses a framework for ushering the child into the world: birth in the home, surrounded by maternal and other kinfolk, and the cycle of slametans which serve to protect the child from surrounding spirits and harmonize its maturation with the cycles of the cosmos.

For the first 5 days and optionally the next 30, the Javanese child is traditionally massaged so that its body becomes soft and pliable, and it is handled in a "relaxed, completely supportive, gentle, unemotional way."[5] It may be loosely swaddled, and it is carried *(gendong)* in a *slendang*, a long narrow shawl looped over one shoulder and down over the opposite hip to provide a firm place for the baby to sit conveniently near the breast.

The child is suckled on demand and frequently, in public if necessary. It is weaned normally around 14–18 months, but often not until age 2 and sometimes not fully until age 6–7, since

3. By schooling, wives of 77% of the reformist schooled vs. 54% of syncretist and 32% traditionalist gave birth in hospitals; by theology, 49% vs. 59% and 34%; and by party, 56% vs. 50% and 38%. It will be noted that, for brevity, wives were questioned only about the eldest son.

4. By schooling, 13% of the wives of pesantren schooled, 10% syncretist, and 4% reformist gave birth matrilocally; by party membership, 19% traditionalists and 9% syncretists and reformists; by theology, 15% syncretists and 9% traditionalists and reformists. Note that despite reports that the matrilocal birth is traditional, it is rarely reported by any group in the Jogjakarta sample.

5. H. Geertz (1961, p. 92). Cf. Peacock (1968, p. 185), and Bateson and Mead (1942, pp. 13–14).

mothers are reluctant to wean. The child then begins to eat solid food when it desires rather than at scheduled meals. Such snacking, known as *djadjanan*, continues into adulthood and is reflected by the many Javanese snack stands.

The family sleeps together, at least in lower-class households, on mats. At first, the child is put to sleep by being rocked in a slendang, perhaps to a lullaby, and later it is cuddled *(kuloni)* by the mother, who lies on the mat with her arms around the child.

Like eating, excreting is permissively organized as to time and place, and even at age 5 or 6 the child is free to excrete almost anywhere and anytime, indoors or out.

As in the case of ritualized entry into the world, these traditions of early child-rearing are violated by reformists more often than by the other groups. The Jogja survey reveals that the son is *kuloni* and *gendong* by all groups (see HQ III-47),[6] but also that reformists tend to stop these practices earlier in the life cycle. By theology, school, or party, reformists are slightly less likely than other groups to *gendong* beyond age 4,[7] and less likely than syncretists to *kuloni* beyond age 4.[8] Age of weaning (HQ III-54) was about the same for all groups.[9] "Frequent nibbling of snacks" was permitted by somewhat fewer reformists

6. H. Geertz (1961, p. 151); cf. Bateson and Mead (1942, pp. 16, 88). Most mothers in all groups indicated the son is kuloni (80–90%) and gendong (87–97%).

7. By schooling, 7% syncretists, 3% traditionalists, and no reformists gendong to age 5; by theology, 3% syncretists, 7% traditionalists, and no reformists; by party, 10% syncretists and 4% reformists. Cf. Danziger (1960), who found similar differences in gendong and kuloni by class: 9–11 months average age for middle class vs. 13–18 months for lower class.

8. By schooling, 8% syncretists, 3% traditionalists, and 6% reformists kuloni beyond age 4; by theology, 13% syncretists and 5% traditionalists and reformists; by party, 15% syncretists, no traditionalists, and 6% reformists.

9. Reformists wean earlier if the categories are defined in certain ways; thus by schooling, only 17% of sons of reformist fathers, compared to 26% of syncretists and 32% of traditionalists, are weaned later than age 18 months. But divided by party, reformists had the highest percentage (32%) weaned later than that.

than by others (HQ III-60).[10] Greater reformist concern with
toilet-training is suggested by the fact that sons of reformists
were most likely of all groups to be trained by age 2 (HQ
III-53).[11]

Because of the child's presumed vulnerability to spirits and
other dangers, and also to distinguish children from four-legged
animals, they are not permitted to crawl. Children are kept off
floor or ground until after the seven-month *slametan*, which
celebrates their coming to the ground. It has been suggested that
to walk without first crawling strains the child's equilibrium,
and that this strain is compensated by the adult's exquisite sense
of balance and "deep cultural emphasis on psychic equilibrium."[12] One might also note the sharp distinction between
nature and culture signified by the refusal to let the child be as an
animal—a refusal that expresses the strong Javanese pride in the
etherealized refinement of their culture.

Refinement is taught early by etiquette. This is accomplished by pushing and pulling the child through the proper
pattern of postures and gestures. Such training proceeds not so
much through encouraging trials and then discriminating success
and failure by reward and punishment as through a continuous
stream of kinesic molding and verbal instruction (sometimes
known as *tuturi*) that provides the child with little initiative to
explore on its own.

10. Djadjanan are permitted "often" by 49–51% of reformists, compared to 55–68% syncretists and around 60% traditionalists.

11. Sons of 30–41% of reformists, 23–26% of syncretists, and 26–
36% of traditionalists were trained by age 2. More than 50% of sons of
reformist party members, vs. less than 30% of sons of syncretist party
members, were trained by age 3. Cf. Danziger (1960), who found a
similar difference by class, ranging from an average age for training of 2
years (lower class) vs. 15 months (middle), and for weaning of 18
months (low) vs. 11 months (middle). Exemplifying the research tradition from which these queries stem, Whiting and Child's (1953) cross-
cultural survey found greatest "superego strength" when weaning is
between 1 and 3 years, toilet-training between 1 and 2.4 years, and
"independence training" between 2 and 4. Obviously this overall
relationship need not hold *within* a culture.

12. H. Geertz (1961, p. 100).

Prior to age 5 or 6, the child is considered immature; he is *during Djawa* or "not yet Javanese," and he is *during ngerti* or "not yet capable of understanding." After that he is suddenly a cultured Javanese, and he has also changed his relationship to his father. Between ages 2 and 5, the father is close to the child, cuddling him and cradling him in the shawl, taking him with him on visits. At age 5, the child should begin to speak high Javanese *(krama)* to the father, and use formal manners toward him. At this point the child learns hierarchy; he now shifts from the *wedi* (fear) of childhood to the *isin* (embarrassment, as in the presence of superiors) of adulthood, and then to the *sungkan* (neutralization of isin by proper manners) which marks the refined Javanese.[13]

The results are dramatic. The "once spontaneous and laughing child adopts the docile, restrained, formal controlled demeanor of his elders."[14] In a word, he becomes Javanese. Suppressed yearning may remain, however, as is revealed by dreams and stories in which the main theme is search for one's lost father.[15]

How, if at all, do reformists deviate from these practices? Javanese values apparently remain strong among reformists. Thus, reformists equaled or even excelled other groups in believing that the child should learn manners and high Javanese, together with the feeling of isin, by age 5.[16] And reformists (by theology and school) reported slightly more sons who do the *sembah* (a kneeling posture of veneration) before the father on the day of Ramadan, an action which suggests formality between father and son. On the other hand, subjectively, the reformists were less likely than the other groups to recall the father as so venerable as to evoke shame *(isin)*; and objectively, they were more likely than the others to pay their respects to

13. H. Geertz (1961 and 1959).
14. H. Geertz (1961, p. 107).
15. Peacock (1968, pp. 106-7, 109).
16. Approximately half of every group believed the child should learn manners and high Javanese together with isin by age 5; other statistics relevant here will be provided in the section on hierarchy in Chapter 3.

him on Ramadan by a simple Muslim handshake. Certainly the reformists have not entirely deleted the father-oriented, hierarchical aspect of becoming Javanese; this retention may partially reflect an Islamic-based patriarchal tendency.

A patriarchal emphasis on law and obedience perhaps is expressed also in reformist responses to HQ II-20, which asked fathers what major trait they thought sons should acquire. Reformist fathers, whether defined by schooling, theology, or membership, strongly emphasized obedience (taat).[17]

A break from the traditional pattern is suggested, however, in HQ II-23, which asked respondents what method they preferred in inculcating traits in their sons. By schooling, theology, or membership, reformist fathers were slightly less likely than any others to prefer the tuturi method (push-pull and continuous instruction).[18] Note also the lack of training by reformists in the dance, a type of instruction traditionally emphasizing kinesic imitation. The reformist fathers were the most likely of any group to "encourage the child to initiate endeavors on his

17. Over 75% of santri groups by schooling, including both reformists and traditionalists, chose "obedience," compared to 60–64% of the others; by theology, 71% reformists vs. 50% syncretists; and by party, 74% reformists vs. 47% syncretists. Whereas Protestantism has been said to encourage independence training by its insistence on understanding the scripture for one's self (McClelland, 1967, p. 49), the Islamic scripturalism of similar type here seemingly correlates with obedience training, which is in accord with Islamic legalism in general. (Muslims in Singapore, too, strongly favor "obedience," in the survey done there.) Note also that the reformist's desire for sons to learn obedience correlates with his choice of the son's school: 77–88% of fathers who send their sons to Muhammadijah schools, vs. 62–69% of those who send their sons to government schools, indicate that obedience is the most desirable trait for the son to acquire. "Friendliness" is desired by 14% of the fathers who send their sons to government schools vs. 5% of those who sent their sons to Muhammadijah schools at the elementary level. Observation suggests that discipline is indeed stricter in the moralistic santri schools whereas the government schools give an impression of more open sociability.

18. By schooling, theology, and party, every group except reformists chose tuturi approximately 50% of the time, whereas reformists by schooling chose it 35%, by party 42%, by theology, 45%.

own,"[19] and they were most likely to regard "keeping the child happy" as secondary.[20] Darol Arqom fathers showed these emphases to an even greater extent than the reformist household heads in our survey.

Neither the reformists nor the others favored the method of rearing by punishment and reward. Indeed, many fathers objected vigorously to this method and said they favored instead moral instruction; the child should be "taught the true morals of Islam," "given understanding," or "given advice." Said one father: "Do not punish him when he is mistaken, but make him understand, point him to the right path." While these comments may border on the continuous-instruction method, they give more emphasis to doctrine than to the stream of discrete stimuli ("put your left hand back, your right out") characterizing that method. At the same time, they suggest that the traditional Indic model of the guru advising his beloved pupil remains more influential in Javanese child-rearing than the Islamic conception of an authority figure who rewards and punishes.

Javanism, Reformism, and Child-rearing

H. Geertz[21] considers that two major traditional Javanese values, urmat (respect, emphasizing hierarchy) and rukun (social cooperation and harmony, emphasizing solidarity) are reinforced by the Javanese pattern of child-rearing. The swaddling, cuddling, and protectiveness encourage passivity, and the push-pull and continuous advice stifle initiative. The passivity and inhibition are necessary, she feels, to instill the restraint needed for maintaining respect and harmony. The specific feature of the child's abrupt distancing from the father contributes to the strong Javanese sense of courtesy and hierarchy.

19. By schooling, almost 50% of the reformists, vs. 33–40% of the others, ranked "initiative" first; by both theology and party, 40% vs. 30%.

20. A third of the reformist schooled vs. a fifth of the others relegated "keeping the child happy" to second place. By theology, the difference was 27% vs. 18%. It is of course tricky to interpret second choices, since they are influenced by first choices.

21. H. Geertz (1961, esp. p. 107).

Despite the numerous linkages left undemonstrated in such a functionalist analysis of the contributions of child-rearing to sociocultural patterning, Geertz' portrayal is persuasive. I would add the notion that the meshing of birth and childhood with the slametan cycles serves to instill a sense not only of social harmony and hierarchy but also of union with the cosmic order that underlies these.

Following this same type of analysis, what is implied by reformist tendencies to deviate from the traditional pattern? Three reformist trends are apparent: (1) Practices such as *gendong* and *tuturi*, that encourage passivity and dependence on the mother, are diminished; (2) independence and initiative are encouraged, along with self-discipline—as in scheduling of ingestion and excretion—and obedience to rules *(taat)*; (3) the ritualization designed to mesh childhood with cosmic cycles is diminished. All of these tendencies would seem to resonate with goals of reformism, which veer from traditional Javanese values of social harmony and hierarchy toward the ideal of the seeker of salvation who is both self-reliant and disciplined and who is motivated by distant objectives rather than enmeshed in the sociocosmic nexus.

LATER CHILDHOOD AND YOUTH

A pattern common throughout Southeast Asia (Buddhist as well as Islamic) is the "lending" of the child to other families for long periods. In Java, the practice of being "lent" is felt to encourage such traditions as refined manners and hierarchy, since surrogate parents must be treated with extra respect. From the child's viewpoint, being "lent" is often traumatic, and the experience may account for the poignancy in Javanese culture of the symbol of the orphan or stepchild.[22] Foreshadowing long-term lending, there is a pattern in early childhood of relatives other than the mother caring for the child for a short time *(momong)*.

22. Peacock (1968, pp. 106-8).

The Jogja survey reveals some tendency of reformists to deviate from both the "lending" and "momong" patterns. Of the 34 eldest sons who were reported by the Jogja mothers as having been lent (HQ III-64), 20 were from the syncretist group, while fewer were reformist. And by schooling and membership (but not theology), reformists' sons were least often *momong*.[23] Were it not that reformists tend to live patrilocally (see later data), one might assume that their lesser reliance on relatives as nurses is due to their lesser proximity. Another explanation is that the reformists feel more personal responsibility for their children; put negatively, they extend their notorious "hadji stinginess" to their children. More positively, one could speculate that being reared by a single set of parents contributes to the development of a Protestant-like personality: a clearer sense of self (because of internalizing identity from parents only, instead of an extended set of adults); a correlated tendency to self-blame, i.e., guilt (because responsibility is located within the self rather than extended to others); and perhaps a disposition toward Tauhid: a concentration of spiritual power in a single entity rather than diffusing it among several, as in the syncretic animism.

Play

As boys and girls mature, they begin to play separately, and certain games are traditionally designed for each. An example is "playing market," which informants of all persuasions assure me is a girl's game; this view doubtless reflects the woman's strong role in the market. Yet a surprisingly large percentage of reformist mothers report (HQ III-59) that their

23. Frequent momong was reported by 54–64% reformists vs. 56–75% syncretists. On possible parallels between Islamic and Christian reformists with respect to lending out of children, cf. Demos (1971, p. 74), who in his study of the Puritans reports a survey of Bristol, England, in 1689 showing 10% of the children "put out" to relatives; this was to learn a trade. In the Malay culture, lending of children *(anak angkat)* is frequent, and reformists in Singapore deviate from this tradition about as often as the Jogja reformists.

sons play market "often" (50%) or "occasionally" (60%); these percentages are higher than those reported by nonreformist mothers.[24] Conceivably, santri commercialism here overrides the traditional dichotomy of sex roles.

Capitalistic play is paralleled by a reformist tendency toward technological play. A striking difference between Javanese and Western childhood is the lack of technological play in Java. Javanese children do not normally play with construction kits (such as Erector sets, Tinkertoys and Lincoln logs) or such toys as building blocks and sandboxes that could be constructed from the environment. Inquiry reveals, however, that Javanese are aware of the existence of building blocks, and the Jogja survey indicates that sons of reformists by party membership play with blocks somewhat more than the others[25]—possibly reflecting a santri concern with technology that jibes with their inclination to become manufacturers (see later discussion of occupation).

Circumcision

Circumcision, the introduction of a boy to manhood by amputating his prepuce, existed in Indonesia before Islam, is practiced in some non-Islamic areas of Indonesia, and is not an official requirement of Islam. Nevertheless, it is widely regarded as a crucial part of the Muslim identity; presence/absence of circumcision critically distinguishes Muslims/non-Muslims in some areas, and degree of Islamization seems to correlate with age of circumcision.

This correlation is suggested by data collected by Schrieke, elaborating earlier work by Wilken.[26] Summarizing briefly the data concerning Java, it is clear that at the time of Schrieke's

24. For "playing market" 26–29% reformists vs. 19–22% syncretists say "often," and 27–33% reformists vs. 15–26% syncretists say "sometimes."

25. For playing with blocks, "often" is reported by 49% reformists vs. 35% syncretists by party, but there is no difference by schooling or theology.

26. Schrieke (1921); Wilken (1912).

survey the average age of circumcision was earlier in the more Islamized Sundanese areas than in the more syncretized Javanese areas. In Sunda the age was between 5 and 9 in one region, before age 6 in another, whereas in the eight residencies of East and Central Java surveyed, the modal age was 12, and the highest ages recorded were in the syncretic court city of Surakarta and environs (12–18 within the city, 15–20 in the villages).[27]

Extending the survey outside Java, the strongly Islamized areas such as West Sumatra, Islamic Bali and Lombok, and South Sulawesi had lower ages of circumcision than syncretic Java.[28] Several early twentieth-century observers also reported that circumcision was becoming earlier than formerly, especially among the santri,[29] but this decrease seems to have been part of the general movement to purify and strengthen Islam in the early part of the century, and has not gone further since.

The Jogja survey carries Schrieke's data further; it shows clearly that both the adult reformers and their sons are circumcised at earlier ages than the syncretists—reformists usually before age 9, syncretists between the ages of 10 and 15 (HQ II-10 and III-55).[30]

27. Schrieke (1921, vol. 60, pp. 410-12).

28. In the Minangkabau area of West Sumatra, the ages were 7–10, according to Schrieke (1921). (Wilken [1912, vol. IV, p. 402] recorded 10–12 for Minangkabau, compared to 12–25 for Javanese.) Muslims in Bali and Lombok averaged 8–11 years—see Boon (1975) on the strong significance of circumcision in distinguishing Muslims from Hinduized Balinese—and Wilken (1912) recorded 12 years for the Buginese and Makassarese.

29. Snouck-Hurgronje (1927a, p. 207); Schrieke (1921, vol. 60, p. 410).

30. Half of the Islamic-educated, compared to less than a fifth of the others, were circumcised before age 10, and similar differences accord with party and theology. At the extremes: 24% of the syncretic party members were circumcised after age 15, compared to a large minority of santri party members by ages 7–8. No more than a sixth of sons of syncretic fathers by party, and a tenth by theology, were circumcised before age 9, whereas over half the reformists' sons by either count were.

Concerning the ideological meaning of circumcision, the attitudes elicited by Schrieke would seem generally to hold today one is neither fully male nor fully Muslim until one is circumcised, and while the amputation is repugnant to some non-Muslims, the santri feel that one is ritually impure until the prepuce is amputated.[31]

The ceremony itself is both traumatic and solidifying. A typical description catches the boy bathing his penis in icy water at dawn, after which he is dragged cold and blubbering to the knife; yet by collectively surviving the trauma the boys gain comradeship, and afterwards they are ceremonially honored by the father and other adults.[32]

31. Thus, Schrieke (1921, vol. 60, p. 470; and 1922, vol. 61, p. 83) notes that the Javanese of Semarang consider the noncircumcised to remain infidels, while some santri consider the uncircumcised impure. Boon's analysis (1975) reveals the other side: the repulsion that non-Muslim Balinese feel about Muslim circumcision. In short, the act sharply defines a Muslim identity.

32. Schrieke (1921, vol. 60, p. 470). The trauma might suggest much to the psychoanalytically inclined. The santri push the age of circumcision back to the alleged point of the oedipal crisis, and certainly the knife might evoke an unconscious fear of castration. Here is the spectre of the father arranging for the son's "castration" at the point when their competition for the mother is at peak. Following a theory like Hagen's (1962, pp. 166-71), one could speculate that the anxiety aroused in the son is later compensated by the santri brand of machismo, exemplified by polygyny, patriarchy, and sexism. Unfortunately for this type of theory, the psychodynamics surrounding circumcision are poorly known and difficult to disentangle; also, the facts point in other directions. While early circumcision has remained among reformists, they have dispensed with polygyny and have moved toward a rather bourgeois, egalitarian relationship of husband and wife. And the santri father's eagerness to circumcise his son (by contrast to the well-known and statistically documented reluctance of the syncretic father) would seem most obviously to be rooted not in the father's desire to deprive his son of his masculinity but to confirm it, by ritually preparing him for entry into the Islamic community of which the father himself is part. Also note that in Indonesia, unlike the Middle Eastern countries, the average age of circumcision never drops below early childhood—5 years, which is the point at which native psychology considers the child

Syncretists and traditionalist santri traditionally subsume the circumcision within a framework of cosmological classification: seating according to the cardinal directions, oppositions of left versus right hand in doing the cut, and dances that oppose male and female teams. The arena may be strewn with syncretic charms, slametans are held, together with performances of the puppet plays, and the boy's mother participates in the ceremony. In reformist circumcisions, the syncretic elements are purged and the affair becomes one solely of males—male speakers, father presiding, and perhaps only patrilineally related male guests. Where syncretic imagery accentuates constancy even at this point of transition, reformist imagery emphasizes the transition. In the syncretic ceremonies, such cosmological oppositions as male/female and left/right that have governed the boy's life since birth remain present even as he moves toward adulthood, and his mother is still there; in the reformist ceremony, such elements are removed, and the ritual seems to stress that now the boy is *moving* into the circle of men.

While the meaning of circumcision most clearly relates to the male-solidarity aspect of Islam, rather than to the rationalist and reformist aspect, one overall implication for the life cycle is apparent: acceleration of the boy's joining the reformist movement and curtailment of his period of immaturity. (Interestingly, a similar speed-up has been noted for the American Protestant Puritans.)[33]

Pesantren

Syncretists most distinctively elaborate the life-cycle culture during the period surrounding birth, at which time the slametan

---

to become acculturated; in the Javanese idiom, to "become Javanese"— it is as though the santri want to insure that circumcision remains an experience of cultural learning.

33. Among New England Puritans, Demos (1971, p. 146) reports, baptism took place soon after birth and conversion by age 6–8—a speed-up of the child's joining the religious group—and children were dressed like adults by age 6–7, so that adolescence was skipped.

cycle is in full force. Santri place comparatively greater emphasis on later childhood, a critical period for instruction in Islam.[34]

In early childhood, the santri boy's mother begins to tell him Islamic stories (see stories reported in the Jogja survey in Chapter 4). By age 7 or so, he begins to learn elementary Islamic doctrine and how to chant passages from the Qur'an. By age 9, his father takes him to the mosque to learn to pray. By age 10 he has been circumcised, and his father may hold a feast to celebrate this event, together with his learning to chant the Qur'an. Between the ages of 12 to 15 he traditionally leaves home to live at one of the Muslim schools known as *pesantren*, for a period varying from a few months to ten years or more. This pesantren education traditionally marks the point of emancipation of the santri from his household and family.

Owing to replacement of the pesantren by modernist religious schools *(madrasah)* and secular-style schools among the Muhammadijans, the pesantren is not central in the life cycle of the emerging generation of reformists; the Jogja survey indicates that virtually none of the reformist respondents are sending or plan to send their sons to pesantren,[35] and a pesantren background appears rare among the younger leaders of Muhammadijah. Yet for some present and past reformists, the pesantren may have been an important element in their education. We recall (Chapter 2) that respondents to the Jogja survey who attended pesantren have become reformists by theology and membership in a larger proportion than has any other group classified by schooling. Biographies of reformists born in the late nineteenth century usually reveal a pesantren background, and

34. For exposition of the general santri pattern, see Kraemer (1952, pp. 177-9); for Java, C. Geertz (1960b, p. 235); for Maudura, Shadily (1955); for Sumbawa, Goethals (1961, pp. 58-59). Parallels in American Puritan education are suggested in Cremin (1970, pp. 121, 129, 156, 377): moralistic parental teaching, memorization, repetition, and the reading of devotional books such as *Pilgrim's Progress* and the *Day of Doom*.

35. Only 3 sons of the entire sample of Jogja respondents were reported to attend pesantren, compared to 34 respondents who themselves attended.

among those sons and daughters who are presently attending the Muhammadijah madrasah, many recall in detail their fathers' attendance at pesantren. Thus, a pesantren education is an element in the background of many reformists. What were the features of this education?

The pesantren was typically in a remote area, separate from village or town. Its walls enclosed a mosque, dormitories, and bathing places for the students (santri), as well as the house of the teacher. Traditionally the students would wander here on foot, bringing only the clothes on their backs, which soon become dirty and tattered under the ascetic conditions of the school. Study focused on the Qur'an and Qur'anic commentaries. There were traditionally no examinations or classes. When a boy had completed learning a given text, he could pass to another school. Emphasis was on form as well as content, on proper pronunciation of Arabic and beautiful chanting of the Qur'an.[36]

The daily schedule was demanding. According to one source, it began at 5 A.M. with prayer and lesson, followed at 7–9 A.M. by classes, then a day of work in the fields, and it concluded in the evenings with practice in Malay karate. There were possibly also mystical chants and meditation, tests of strength, walks through fire and over thorns, and abstention from food and sleep.[37]

While this pesantren milieu of mental and physical discipline has historically been associated with Muslim militarism (as in anti-colonialism during Dutch times[38] and anti-Communist guerilla armies during the 1965 purge of Communists), the recollections of individual santri emphasize that the pesantren forced withdrawal from the world. This type of experience is reported by Muhammad Radjab, who begins his account by depicting himself as a happy, carefree village boy, running

36. C. Geertz (1960a). This sketch applies to pesantren for boys only; pesantren for girls do exist today, but I do not know the patterns there except superficially.
37. Djajadiningrat (1936, p. 21).
38. Djajadiningrat (1936, p. 23).

barefoot and playing soccer. Then his uncle, who is to become his pesantren teacher, comes out of the prayer-house door:

> His body is thin, his face is sour, rather pale from too much thinking and too little exercise, and he always looks angry. He is always indoors reading thick books from Mecca. He has studied eleven years in Mecca and because of that is very fanatical. He commands us boys: "Better to study than to play soccer, which has no religious utility."

The uncle gives the boys lessons by reeling off Arabic passages which he translates into difficult and incomprehensible Malay, and he demands that Radjab study in the prayer house from 8 to 1 each day. Radjab wonders why he must be deprived of his freedom:

> I, who was always free, cheerful, laughing, running and jumping, here and there, wrestling and playing soccer, bathing and sweating, ruddy-cheeked and with a sturdy and healthy body.

In time Radjab became a santri, which he dourly characterizes as not "loving life in this world." Having barely enough to eat, the santri would wear white clothing to the village every Friday to beg. Sleeping together, they became infected with skin diseases which the uncle interpreted as God's punishment, and their hair grew long, thick, and matted. Radjab recounts that

> Gradually my bond to the world diminished. My friends played as before, while I associated with the santri, wore white like them, acted and talked like them, that is to say always lowering myself, had a pale complexion, and if I conversed with a female always looked down, as we were not permitted to look a woman in the face.[39]

In sum, the traditional pesantren was an otherworldly, ascetic, all-male boarding school, which taught toughness and loyalty born of the boot-camp experience of shared hardship.[40]

39. Radjab (1950, pp. 80, 84, 90).
40. Needless to say, pesantren today do not all resemble those of the past. The NU Pesantren in Tebu Ireng, for example, supplements its

There is reason to believe that pesantren experiences of Jogja reformists bore the major features of those depicted: an abrupt break with the family, ascetic discipline, and the incessant drumming-in of the Islamic texts, which become a source of ultimate meaning for the reformist fundamentalist.

Pilgrimage

As is revealed in the biographies of such founders of reformism as K.H.A. Dahlan and Hadji Rasul, the *hadj*—the pilgrimage to Mecca—was a natural extension of the pesantren for the early reformists; a *wanderung* (in Indonesian terminology, a *rantau*) that continued the trajectory away from family of orientation and toward community among male peers who sought greater knowledge of Islam.

The Jogja survey confirms a pattern also suggested by biographies of reformists who began their careers after return from the hadj. The survey reveals that almost all pesantren-schooled individuals took on reformist theology, provided they had also made the hadj; of the 10 who had experienced *both* pesantren and hadj, 8 adopted the reformist ideology. Although the numbers are small, the combination of experiences, pesantren and hadj, looms plausibly as well as statistically as a recipe for a reformist.

The pilgrimage has decreased in frequency among Indonesians, Jogjakartans, and Muhammadijans, and observation suggests that for a devout youth to make the hadj is neither as frequent nor as desired today as it was in the day of the founders.[41] Instead of seeking knowledge on his own through

---

religious subjects with secular ones (including anthropology). For students at Pondok Modèren at Gontor, games replace mystical exercises and students follow a progressive curriculum (Castles, 1966).

41. Despite a tripling of population, only a fifth as many Indonesians made the hadj in 1961 as in 1926. Benda (1970, p. 182) states that in 1926-27 some 52,000 Indonesian and 12,000 Malaysian pilgrims went to Mecca. The Statistical Pocketbook of Indonesia shows only 11,613 Indonesian pilgrims in 1961, no more than Roff (1970, p. 172) cites as having gone in 1895. In Jogjakarta, only 16 made the hadj in 1961, compared to 72 in 1900. Fewer Muhammadijah leaders use the title *hadji* now than at the time of its founding.

the hadj, the youth today is systematically assimilated into the Muhammadijah; he attends the Muhammadijah sequence of schools and is drawn into its sequence of organizations, first for high school (IPM), then for college (IMM), and finally for adults. As reformism has come of age in Indonesia, the adventure of pilgrimage has given way to indoctrination: a bureaucratization of the youth phase of the reformist life cycle.

ANALYSIS OF REFORMIST ORIENTATIONS

Factor analysis (see Chapter 2) suggests that reformist orientation differs according to the life-cycle stage at which it was acquired. Among the Jogja respondents, some are classified as reformist primarily because of family heritage and early childhood experience (a Muhammadijan father and elementary Muhammadijah schooling), some because of youthful experience (intermediate and secondary Muhammadijah schooling, and membership in the youth movement HMI), and others because of present, adult ideology and membership.

Regression analysis suggested, further, that each type of reformist enculturation was associated with a distinctive type of reformist orientation. "Adult" reformists showed affirmative commitment to an Islamic ethic, whereas "youth" reformists manifested their orientation mainly through a negative attitude toward the *slametan* complex, especially the slametans of the life cycle. "Child" reformists failed to strongly manifest any of the dominant reformist orientations.

Why should it be the youthful experience which is most strongly manifested by rejection of the slametan complex? A gross explanation is that youth is in general a time of rejection, rebellion, and protest—and further, that what is being rejected is a ritualization at the heart of the authority and tradition of the family and community, typically perceived by the young as the base of stagnation. The data suggest more specific explanations.

Not youth as such, but youthful participation in reformist schools and reformist movements, is what correlates strongly with rejection of the slametan ritualization. What can be said about these experiences?

Observation of the Muhammadijah intermediate (SMP) and secondary (SMA) schools today reveals that much of the pesantren asceticism has been dispelled. Classes are coeducational, for example, and the Malay equivalent of the hair-shirt—the dirty *sarong*—has been replaced by neat trousers and skirts. Even memory of the pesantren experience is dim among the present students of the Muhammadijah SMP and SMA; very few of the students in these schools claim memory of their fathers' pesantren experience (whereas, as noted, numerous students in the more pesantren-like Muhammadijah *madrasahs* admit such recollections). Given a dilution of the ascetic ideal in the Muhammadijah SMP and SMA, it is perhaps plausible that an adult reformist would be more likely to originate in the pesantren than in these blander schools.

Yet the Muhammadijah intermediate and secondary schools had a more radical attitude in the past than today. To judge from biographical accounts, the movement in its early years centered to a striking degree around the schools, and the teachers and pupils had a strong sense of their opposition to the traditional society, including the traditional pesantren. Indeed, there is even a biographical account of an explicit and radical rejection of traditional life-cycle slametans by teacher and pupils in a new reformist school (in Minangkabau, however, rather than Jogjakarta).[42] Historical materials render plausible the linkage between Muhammadijah schooling in youth and rejection of traditional ritualization in adulthood.

The other part of this factor analysis is that rejection of the slametans is correlated with experience in a youth movement. Here too, qualitative materials suggest some plausibility for the statistics. The Islamic Student Association (HMI), one of the movements that correlate with rejection of the slametan, is the most radical of the large-scale Islamic youth organizations in Java. At the time of fieldwork, HMI activities ranged from extremely controversial pronouncements by its leading ideologue (Nurhalis Matjit) to indoctrination camps that provide

42. Hamka (1957, pp. 81-2). Reformist teacher Hadji Rasul joined with his students in boycotting the funeral slametans of his own father.

instruction in revolutionary tactics. And though less radical than the HMI, the Muhammadijah youth sectors were nevertheless radical by comparison with the adult organization. This "radicalness" is illustrated by a comparison of Muhammadijah youth and adult indoctrination camps, both types of which I attended. Whereas the adult camp devoted most of its instruction to the positive features of Islam and Muhammadijah, the youth camps emphasized more the negative features of opposing cultures. Only in the youth camps, for example, did one hear lengthy and explicit criticism of syncretic belief and ritual. And only the youth camps held the so-called sessions of "mental destruction" that forced the neophyte to admit and purge opposing loyalties.[43]

Linkage between these historical-ethnographic patterns and the factor analysis is loose, but it is plausible. Psychologically it makes some sense to interpret these data as suggesting that something like these *types* of experiences in school and movement contribute to a reformism based on rejection of traditional ritualization.

Less child "lending," more "market" and technological play, earlier circumcision—these are all tendencies of reformist rearing in late childhood. They complement the experiences that come next, in youth. The youthful experiences—whether in pesantren or pilgrimage, in the past, or training camp and school, in the present—signal a certain radicalism in opposition to the surrounding society. The late childhood experiences ce-

43. An example of a mental destruction dialogue (from field notes, not verbatim recording):
Instructor: Is it IMM [Ikatan Mahasiswa Muhammadijah, or Muhammadijah Association of College Students] or HMI that most attracts your loyalty?
Candidate: IMM.
Instructor: Is that simply because your parents are Muhammadijah?
Candidate: No, because my personality fits better.
Instructor: Why do you join the struggle?
Candidate: To seek experience.
Instructor: Wrong! You simply waste our time. The idea of training only to seek experience! Don't you know what struggle means?

ment identity with the Islamic family, especially the adult male. Not being lent means the son remains with the father (lending is often associated with divorce, in which case the son is permanently severed from the father); commercial and technological play encourage identity with the reformist father, who is often a capitalist-manufacturer, and early circumcision accelerates the point at which the son begins to identify with the father, as a worshipper at the mosque and more generally as a member of the male community that dominates Islam. The beginnings of an outline emerge: diminishing of early-childhood practices that encourage dependence on the mother, heightening of late-childhood practices that encourage identity with the father, and a youthful experience that permits a break with both parents and opposition to the larger society. This seemingly plausible recipe for the incubation of the reformer has changed somewhat, however, since the time of the movement's charismatic phase. Where pesantren and pilgrimage encouraged a radical break between youth and family, the bureaucratized modern organization encourages continuity: the son continues to live at home while he attends the governmental-style day school, and his pilgrimage is replaced by participation in training camps and other activities sponsored by the youth wing of the organization of which his father is a member. Here the Weberian shift from charisma to bureaucratization would seem to have the function of discouraging the radical break of youth from home that spurred the movement in its inception.

ADULTHOOD

Work

The syncretist, when he comes of age, ideally becomes a government official (though the majority actually become peasants and proletarians), but the santri tradition is to go into business. The literature amply documents the relation between Islam and trade historically, and also by region,[44] and the

44. The relation between Islam and entrepreneurial activity is analyzed by Castles (1967) for North Java; By C. Geertz (1963) for East

correlation is upheld in more specific terms by the Jogja survey. The survey shows that the santri in general, reformists in particular, are less likely than the syncretists to stem from bureaucrat fathers, become bureaucrats themselves, or aspire for their sons to become bureaucrats (HQ I-51 and 53, with "bureaucrat" defined as government official, clerk, soldier, or government teacher).[45] The santri are more likely to stem from entrepreneur fathers, become businessmen themselves, and aspire for their sons to become businessmen. The differences hold whether the groups are defined by education, theology, or organizational membership, and more specific patterns are suggested by comparing generations.

Beginning with respondents' fathers, the survey confirms our expectation that fathers employed in the bureaucracy send their sons to government schools, which in turn produce bureaucratic sons. The santri send their sons to Muslim schools, which graduate businessmen. And the survey shows that sons of merchants tend to hold reformist theologies, whereas those who are sons of bureaucrats tend to hold syncretist theologies. A more specific link in the chain: A larger proportion of the membership of the reformist organization than of any other are sons of merchants and manufacturers; indeed, most of the sons of

Java; by Kuntowidjojo (1971) for West Java; by Siegel (1969) for Atjeh; by T. Abdullah (1971) for Minangkabau. Hudson (1972) mentions that even in the remote Kalimantan village of Padju Epat, the few traders are Muslim.

45. The typology of occupations used in coding responses to these questions distinguished between self-employed and bureaucracy-employed *(pegawai)*. Cross-cutting this was a distinction between managerial and clerical: Those who termed themselves *kepala* (head), were considered managerial, while those who either specified that their title was less than managerial or simply listed their employer (e.g., saying that they work "for" or "at" some place, as in "pada Bank Tabangan Negeri BNI, Unit V, Djakarta") were considered clerical. These civil servants were in turn distinguished from elected leaders and special types of civil servants, such as village, palace, and religious officials. Artisans *(tukang)* were distinguished from technicians *(teknik)*, and merchants *(berdagang)* from owners of an enterprise *(perusahaan)*, whom I have labeled "manufacturers."

manufacturers as well as the manufacturers themselves (86%) are found in the reformist organization.[46]

This last relationship reflects the long-standing association between Muhammadijah and the *batik*-makers, who comprise the majority of these so-called "manufacturers" in Jogjakarta. Considering the importance of the historical association and the fact that the batik industry is one of the largest indigenous handicraft industries in Indonesia, the Jogja situation is worth examining in more detail.

Hawkins' survey of batik manufacture in Jogjakarta[47] revealed that in 1960 virtually all of the 667 batik firms in that city were owned by santri, usually Muhammadijans. Syncretist

46. Summarizing some statistics documenting the last two paragraphs: Slightly more than 50% of the Javanese schooled have become bureaucracy-employed (officials, managers, clerks, teachers, professors, soldiers), compared to less than 20% of the pesantren schooled and 30% of the Muhammadijah schooled; 18% of the Muhammadijah schooled are manufacturers and merchants compared to 10% and 4% of the pesantren and syncretist schooled in these categories. By party, a third of the Javanese party members are clerks, compared to a tenth of the reformist party members. Theologically, twice as many of the syncretists as santri-oriented are bureaucrats (65% vs. 35%), and three times as many santri-oriented as syncretists are merchants (13–16% vs. 5%). Approximately 20% of the Islamic schooled vs. 10% of the syncretist or Western schooled are sons of merchants, and approximately the same ratio holds by theology. By party, *no* sons of officials, mililtary, or clerks have joined the traditionalist santri party, though some 10% have joined the reformist organizations and 15% the syncretist. Sons of merchants and manufacturers are more likely to take on reformist theologies than any other; 58–67% of them become reformist, 19–35% traditionalist santri, and 11–14% syncretist; the relationship does not imply economic determinism, since these entrepreneurial fathers were also likely to be reformists or at least santri. (Note that reformists are twice as likely to have fathers who made the hadj, just as they stem from entrepreneurial fathers; again, the commercial and pious demeanors go together, and both plausibly influence sons toward reformism.) The majority (35 of 58) of sons of manufacturers also join the reformist party. Some 25% of the Javanese party members and almost none of the others are sons of village officials, and over half of the traditionalist santri are sons of farmers.

47. Hawkins (1961, pp. 12, 52).

prijaji also make batik—but primarily of the hand-drawn type, which is more an art than a business. Most of these santri batik firms are family owned and operated. Most of the present-day manufacturers had parents in the industry, and they attribute their entering it to family influence. The factory usually is part of the household, and more than a quarter of the firms are run by women, presumably as an extension of their household; as firms become larger, they are taken over by men, and they become based more on a regular labor/management organization instead of piecework. But most of the Jogjakarta batik firms, Hawkins finds, lack capital, skilled labor, regular book-keeping, and other rationalized procedures that would make them paragons of the Weberian "spirit of capitalism."

Turning now to the new generation: The majority of the respondents' sons are not yet employed, but of those who are (HQ I-57), almost all who have become politicians, soldiers, or clerks stem from fathers with syncretist or Western schooling, while the merchants come from fathers with Islamic schooling. Reformists defined by theology and membership are producing fewer clerks than the nonreformists, but otherwise do not differ significantly.[48]

Where sons are not yet employed (HQ I-57), the Western-schooled fathers most frequently of all groups aspire that the son be official, clerk, or physician; the reformist schooled that he be merchant, manufacturer, or religious teacher; the pesantren schooled most often say that the choice should be "left to the child's aptitude *(bakat)*"; and the syncretist schooled lead in having no plans at all. Defined by theology and organization, the syncretists aspire that their sons wear the white collar, the santri that he be self-employed.[49]

48. Reformist respondents are producing the smallest percentage (5%) of clerk sons, vs. 23% from syncretist theologies; by party, the differences are 14% reformist vs. 20% syncretist. All sons who are now employed as politicians, soldiers, or clerks stem from parents with syncretist or Western schooling, and none from parents with Islamic schooling. But the Islamic schooled have produced 14-20% of the merchant sons, vs. 10-14% for the syncretist schooled.

49. By party, white-collar occupations total 66% of the syncretist fathers' aspirations, compared to 25-33% of the santri fathers.

Aside from statistics, the phrasing of aspirations is suggestive. Largely among the reformists were found those few fathers who conceived of the son's future not as an occupational *status* but a *function*. One father made this contrast explicit by stating that "my son need not be a civil servant *(pegawai negara)* but *anything* that serves Islam *(faédah Islam)*" (italics mine). All such reformist phrasings in terms of function were Islamic; the son should "serve in the field of Islam" or "be a missionary who is steadfast in service." The only syncretist phrasings in terms of function were by one father who hoped his son would "help society advance" and another who hoped the son would "be creative"; no father aspired for a son to be an artist, dancer, puppeteer or other culturally "creative" role which would seem akin among syncretists to the avocation of religious teacher among santri. The greater santri tendency to imagine occupation as function rather than status accords with other evidence of santri tendencies to think in terms of Weber's "rationalization of means," to imagine life as goal-oriented, a mission, a contribution.

The school survey (SQ 7) elaborates the association between reformism and occupation. Students now in the madrasah have the highest percentage of merchant fathers. Next highest are the government-patterned Muhammadijah schools (SMA), and last are the government schools themselves. Most sons of civil servants and professionals are in the government schools, as might be expected.[50] Less expected was the finding that the majority of children of manufacturers (58% of them, which is to say 32 children) are also found in government schools. Judging from Hawkins' survey, these are probably the children of santri. Here status seemingly overrides religion; by education in the government schools, the rich santri manufacturers of Jogja begin to turn their children into prijaji.

One may wonder if this apparent trend implies an influx of

50. Considering current students, government SMA students are most often sons of managers and officials (7%, vs. 1% for Muhammadijah SMA and 0.4% for madrasah) or clerks (38%, vs. 19% Muhammadijah SMA and 7% madrasah). The madrasah have the highest percentages of laborers' and farmers' children.

bureaucrats into the Muhammadijah. The answer is not simple. An analysis of current Muhammadijah membership lists for sections in Jogjakarta and also other cities in Java, South Sulawesi, and West Sumatra reveals predominantly non-white-collar, pesantren or madrasah schooled among the rank-and-file members. Yet participant observation of the Muhammadijah reveals a predominance of government-schooled non-businessmen among the young leaders. None of these come from the wealthiest manufacturing families of Jogja, and rumor has it that these wealthy children are more likely to join the jet set of Djakarta than the Muhammadijah. These data suggest a stratified pattern: the rank-and-file of Muhammadijah still show its commercial/artisan roots, the leaders now wear the white collar, and the children of its wealthiest patrons have moved out of the organization. There does not remain a simple correlation of reformism and capitalism after the classical Weberian model.

The reformist respondents more frequently went to work early (before age 16) than did other types (HQ II-12).[51] The reason could have been a strong motivation to get into the world of work, though it was probably also the lack of need for a diploma in order to go into business.

HQ I-62 and SQ 15–17 were modeled after an item in Gerhard Lenski's well-known survey of the Protestant Ethic in Detroit.[52] Lenski asked respondents which of several conditions they considered most important in a job: high income, no danger of being fired, short working hours, lots of free time, chance for advancement, and sense that the work is important and gives a feeling of accomplishment. Lenski considered the last alternative closest to Weber's Protestant Ethic value, emphasizing the worth of the work and the personal satisfaction it offers. Jogjakarta informants agreed with Malays with whom I had worked earlier that for them the individualistic dimension of the Lenski scale needed supplementing by the social, so we added two additional conditions: the work's "social contribution" and

51. 8–13% reformists vs. 1–6% syncretists went to work before age 16.
52. Lenski (1963, p. 89).

its "social prestige." In light of Indonesia's extremely low average wage, we also added "enough salary to get by."

When this question was asked of the household heads, most of them (but fewer of the students, doubtless reflecting their lesser domestic responsibilities) did choose this subsistence alternative. Few ranked prestige important, contrary to expectation. Western-schooled household heads tended to place less emphasis on the job's social contribution, suggesting that their education or careers might encourage individualism.[53] Those who were most concerned with work's social contribution were the students[54] and the participants in the Muhammadijah training camp, Darol Arqom—reflecting an idealism that seems to go with both youth and activism.

Asked what method he most often used to increase his income (HQ I-60), the reformist by schooling was more likely than the syncretist to say "with effort that is planned" and less likely to say "luckily an opportunity emerges." And by theology, twice as many syncretists as santri chose "social connections" as the second most frequent method of increase. But this pattern of individualistic activism and planning that Weber would have predicted to correlate with reformism did not hold when the division was by theology; here the syncretists had a slightly higher choice of planning than the reformists. Most frequently mentioned by all types was hard work, which a few Muslims supplemented by saying "Work hard and pray to God." No one mentioned investment or welfare.[55]

Marriage and Family Life

As in many traditional societies, Javanese marriage is arranged by parents; yet this custom of arranged marriage is

53. 12% of Western schooled vs. 19–25% others chose "social contribution."

54. One-third of the students in all groups chose "social contribution."

55. By schooling, 36% reformists vs. 17% syncretists chose "planning," and no reformists vs. 9% syncretists chose "luck." By party, 25% reformists vs. 13–19% others chose "planning," and 12% syncretists vs. 3% reformists chose "social connections." By theology, however, 26% syncretists vs. 23% reformists chose "planning."

challenged by the young, especially when they, in some sense, "fall in love." The Jogja survey shows a slightly greater tendency for the reformist schooled (though not the reformists by theology or membership)[56] to marry for love rather than by parental arrangement (HQ II-15). Reformists were also a bit more likely to marry "early" by educated, urban Javanese standards, i.e., between the ages of 16 and 25 (HQ II-14).

The newlyweds traditionally live matrilocally (with the bride's parents) during the early part of their marriage, but eventually they establish a neolocal, nuclear household independent of any extended kinship group. Even where more than one nuclear family lives in a house or compound, it is strongly felt that each couple should have its own area, an ideal which most attain. Of all groups, the reformist schooled are most likely to deviate from this matrilocal pattern during the first year of marriage, though not in the bourgeois, neolocal direction as do the Western educated, the most neolocal-inclined of any group; the reformist schooled tend rather toward patrilocality (residence with the groom's parents). By theology and membership, reformists' again score high on patrilocality and low on matrilocality, by comparison with the other types.[57]

Even after the Javanese household becomes neolocal, it enjoys frequent visits from kinsfolk. These tend to be the mother's rather than the father's kin, an emphasis which expresses the "matrifocal" patterning of the Javanese family. This matrifocality has two aspects: first, the mother is the link to relatives outside the household, including her parents (when the couple moves in with the bride's parents soon after marriage or her parents move in with them later on), her nieces and nephews (who are the children most likely lent to her household), and her visiting siblings. Second, the mother controls internal domestic affairs; she holds the purse-strings and disburses funds to father and children, she disciplines the children, she is usually the parent who is at home while the father remains relatively aloof

56. The difference was 57% reformist vs. 51% other for "love."
57. Reformists lived patrilocally 41–46% vs. 27–42% syncretists. See H. Geertz (1961, p. 31) and Jay (1969, pp. 40-1) on residence patterns.

from domestic affairs and occupies himself with the outer realm, the wider society.

Informants indicate that this "matrifocal" pattern remains true of santri, and skimpy evidence suggests that in certain respects it may be even stronger among them than among syncretists. Slightly more frequently than other types, the reformist schooled acknowledges his mother as a more important influence than his father in his household of procreation (HQ II-17),[58] a tendency sustained by the Darol Arqom participants though not by reformists through membership and theology. Here the "matrifocal" pattern is shifted up a generation, from wife to husband's mother, whose exercise of influence is compatible with the "patrilocal" residence in that this would place her son and his wife under her roof.

Specifically among those reformist santri who manufacture batik, the wife, mother, or grandmother may have an additional power. Hawkins found that 27% of the Jogjakarta batik businesses are run by women, and 54% by husband and wife together but with wife tending to dominate management when the business is at home.[59] Such a pattern may partially account for the influence of the husband's mother. This mother-influence occurs in the face of a patrilineal tendency reflected in the Muslim law that the son receives two parts of inheritance to the daughter's one; thus, batik businesses (which, as Hawkins shows, tend to be inherited) would tend to pass down through the male line, from fathers to sons. Drawing together these various facts, one might hypothesize a scenario something like this: the son marries, then enters the business (Hawkins' data show that this occurs usually between the ages of 25 and 35, which is after the typical age of marriage reported in our survey); inheriting the business located at his natal family's household, the son moves his bride into that place; in this patrilocal household, the son's mother exercises great influence, partially owing to her management of the business, and in time the son's own wife will take on such influence herself. This

58. Reformists acknowledge mother 39–43% vs. 31–39% syncretists.
59. Hawkins (1957).

configuration obviously differs from the stereotype of the patriarchal Islamic family where all power is in the hands of the males, but it differs too from the bourgeois, Western stereotype of the independent nuclear family.

Also relevant to the question of patriarchal Islamic versus bourgeois Western stereotype were responses to HQ II-35, which asked whether respondents recalled their fathers as "harsh"; it was felt, both on the basis of theories that reformists stem from authoritarian fathers and of reformist life-history accounts of stern fathers, that reformists might come from such fathers more than do others. In fact, numerous respondents from all groups recalled their fathers as harsh, and the only difference was that leaders (i.e., participants in Darol Arqom and individuals who termed themselves religious teachers) had a higher percentage of harsh fathers than did the general sample.[60]

The conjugal relation in Java traditionally differs from the bourgeois, Western romantic ideal. Indeed, conjugality is frequently subordinate to consanguinity. Marriage is hardly considered consummated without children, and even at weddings symbols of fertility announce the expected procreation. Javanese practice "teknonymy," where the parent is sometimes addressed by the child's name rather than his own ("father of X" or "mother of X") a practice which may symbolize the child's importance in binding the spouses. In popular drama, loss of a spouse typically evokes not sorrow about the breaking of conjugality but concern for the children, and this consanguineal emphasis is expressed further in story endings which reveal that relations apparently based on marriage are really bonds of blood.[61]

A certain tendency toward conjugality appears among reformists on the Jogja survey in response to HQ II-34; asked which of a number of figures he seeks for counsel in time of

60. Seven of the eight respondents with the title *kijai* (Islamic teacher) recalled their father as harsh, compared to 21 of 39 respondents with noble titles.

61. Peacock (1968, p. 119).

sadness, the reformist schooled was more likely than others to name his wife.[62]

For various reasons, including perhaps the lack of romanticization of marriage, divorce is frequent among Javanese; approximately half of all marriages contracted dissolve,[63] and it is not unusual to meet Javanese who have been married half a dozen times. Though Muhammadijah informants assert that divorce is less frequent among them than syncretists, statistics on this claim were not collected in the Jogja survey.

Reformism and Adulthood

Freud's "love and work" are the two areas of emphasis here, and the two bear a connection; the survey data suggest that the reformist tendency to go into business is in part associated with family businesses, and that these may be organized patrilocally but with a heightened role for the woman, who manages the business as an extension of the household. Within this patrilocal-matrifocal complex, reformists show a trend toward a bourgeois conjugality, a partnership of husband and wife in that the one seeks counsel from the other more than among syncretists and traditional santri.

These trends in work and family life obviously suggest the bourgeois and capitalistic directions of the Protestant Ethic and the Spirit of Capitalism—tempered, however, by a patriarchalism perhaps derived from Islam and by the traditionalism of business practice rooted in a long history of santri commerce in Jogjakarta. Note that the trend toward identity with the father is continued, possibly (though, as noted previously, less today than in the early stages of reformism) after a break with the

62. 64% of reformists sought their wives for counsel, compared to about half of the other groups.

63. The 50% proportion has been discovered by many studies, e.g., H. Geertz (1961) and Singarimban and Manning (1974). In 1966, the Indonesian Direktorat Urusan Ugama listed 1,096,895 nikah (official marriage registrations) and 512,972 talak (official divorces) for Indonesia as a whole, and 258,743 nikah and 115,489 talak for Central Java.

family altogether for a period in a pesantren or on pilgrimage; this identity culminates in the santri son entering the father's business, a direct link of son and father not available to the syncretist who enters the bureaucracy, which is not the personal property of his father. By entering the family business, the son exercises the values both of independence (the sense of running one's own shop is strong among the santri private enterpreneurs) and of obedience to the father—the two major values of child-hood that differentiate him from the syncretist.

Despite the traditionalization of business in Jogjakarta, it is true even in the Javanese context that the criterion of success in business, i.e., profit, is more specific than the criteria of success in bureaucracy (power, solidarity, patriotism, symbolic effi-cacy, efficiency, and maintenance of a sociocosmic order, all mixed together). This point alone can explain much of the more easily discernible thrust toward rationalization of work among the businessmen than among the bureaucrats. Some sense of this difference is given by the survey data that show certain types of reformists affirming planning versus luck, function versus status, and social contribution.

DEATH

With old age, Javanese turn increasingly toward spiritual concerns; syncretists meditate mystically and cosmologically interpret the *wajang*, while some become santri—praying, stud-ying the Qur'an, and even attending the mosque. A reason for this santri-ization is that only Islam has a coherent doctrine of salvation and life after death; though some syncretists vaguely believe in reincarnation,[64] and perhaps the new Hindu-Buddhists do so strongly, the traditional syncretic view of death is simply a cessation of life.

In the sphere of ritual as well as belief, the santri are better prepared for the afterlife than the syncretists. The Islamic offi-cial is not essential at such transitions as syncretist birth or

64. C. Geertz (1960b, p. 75).

marriage—but, as a dramatic case study demonstrates, the syncretist cannot do without him at death; the Islamic official is required to supervise the funeral.[65] At funerals, the santri give concern to the afterlife, as in the *salat al-djinazah* (prayer for the deceased) and the placing of the body in a grave pointing toward Mecca.[66] They are concerned with assuring the dead a good journey into the next life and in avoiding eternal retribution in Hell.

If santri are more concerned with the salvation of the dead, syncretists have a more elaborated culture for restoring order in the existence of the living. Slametans for the dead utilize special symbols, such as rice arranged in a flattened disc to express calm acceptance of the loss, and relatives of the deceased hold slametans of increasing size at 3, 7, 40, 100, and 1000 days following death, and at the end of the first and second years. According to the Jogja survey, these death slametans are rarely held by reformist santri, especially those whose reformism was sealed in the school and movement experiences of youth; biographical materials suggest that the rejection of funerals is in part a rejection of elders, for whom the funeral cycle is normally held. Whatever the dynamics, this ritualization of death is lost to reformists. The loss is not without significance, since the pattern of a cycle of ceremonies to gradually bring about order between the ultimate and the living is an integral part of Southeast Asian syncretic culture, known throughout the islands, peninsula, and mainland.

Factor analysis indicates that while the "youth" reformists reject the death slametans, "adult" reformists (so defined by their present beliefs and membership) do not. The adults distinguish themselves by their commitment to those pillars of Islam which, among other things, yield salvation. Such is the ultimate objective of most of the elements in the so-called Islamic Ethic, including the prayers, mission for Allah, and desire to be near God at time of death (see Chapter 2, which details these values clustered in the factor termed Islamic Ethic).

65. C. Geertz (1959).   66. Kraemer (1952, p. 210).

Reformism and Death

If salvation is seen as an Islamic end, old age is a logical time to bear down on the means. Indeed, this appears to be the case among reformists. Where the syncretist has more fully elaborated the rituals of birth, marriage, and rituals to harmonize the lives of kinsmen of the deceased, the reformist—indeed, santri in general—appear to give greatest attention to rituals of initiation into the Muslim community (circumcision) and rituals of initiation into the next life (funerals). From an Islamic standpoint, this is rationalization: the streamlining of the life cycle so as to emphasize only those points of transition most critical to the ultimate goal.

LIFE HISTORIES AND PLANS

Autobiography: Past

Are the reformists distinguished not only by specific stages of the life cycle, but also by their overall conception of the life history? Each participant in the Darol Arqom was requested to summarize his life history in writing. Most organized this autobiographical summary by these categories, listed in outline: age; address; religious preference; ethnicity; education, with chronological list of schools attended; and work, with chronological list of jobs held. A few elaborated the outline by adding "hobbies" (e.g., "sports and evangelism"), "ideals" (e.g., "I crave to be a person useful to myself, my family, the society, and the Islamic religion"), and "experience in organizations" (e.g., offices held in Muhammadijah and other associations). Several listed the wife's name (none listed more than one; contemporary reformists are largely monogamous) and names of children, usually in order of birth, giving ages of each. In short, the surface conception of a life history by these reformists was a bureaucratized "curriculum vitae," showing no particularly exotic features; it is typical of written documents throughout the Malayo-Indonesian region, ranging from the Malaysian *Who's Who* to the Indonesian elementary-school biographies of national heroes.

The same form was followed initially by both syncretists and santri when they narrated the life history orally. After this initial oral chronology, however, a difference was apparent. Almost all of the syncretist males (approximately 20) launched into a narrative of a youthful love affair that contrasted favorably with the present (parentally arranged) marriage. None of the santri males (23) gave such an account, and most did not spontaneously mention marriage at all, but instead followed the chronology with an account of their continuing "struggle" for Islam, perhaps then telling about their children's careers and future. The contrast suggests a "future" and "programmatic" orientation on the part of the santri, compared with a "past" and "episodic" orientation of the syncretists.

On HQ II-30c, reformists were more likely to choose "I feel that I must plan all aspects of life in order that I can carry out the command of God," while syncretists were more likely to choose the statement describing remembered childhood veneration of the father. The contrast again is between a future, programmatic orientation and a past, nostalgic one.[67]

Published biographies show a santri/syncretist contrast, in that the santri were the first Javanese to publish full-fledged

67. The "mission" (rather than "venerate") statement was chosen by 85–90% reformists vs. 43–72% syncretists. A methodological issue relevant throughout this study is illustrated by the last two paragraphs. In this comparison of life-history narrations, the difference cannot be attributed entirely to religious creed, for the narrators differ in other ways (social status, context of narration, and so forth). In the comparison of statements chosen—mission versus veneration—the choice cannot be said to reflect psychological disposition independent of religious creed, since the mission statement fairly directly represents a reformist Islamic view. In short, extraneous variables interfere with neat comparisons. Reformism, or syncretism, is a complex which includes features of social status; it influences such matters as context of narration, and is also difficult to separate from the expression of psychology. A paradox of correlational analysis is that one assumes at the outset that variables are interrelated, yet one must differentiate them to some degree in order to analyze this interrelationship. In the present study, this desired differentiation is rarely achieved.

biographies. Since the rise of nationalism, however, syncretists too, in political guise, have published biographies which seemingly differ from the santri works only in cultural content (e.g., nationalist rather than Islamic names) rather than basic form. Impressionistically, syncretist versus santri creative literature give a stronger sense of difference. This can be seen, for example, in the richer imagery and subtler conception of time in the remembrances of the syncretic author Toer, contrasted with those of reformist author Hamka in his *Memoirs*.[68] Similar differences were observed in the spontaneous efforts of santri and syncretist actors to dramatically re-create scenes of childhood, as part of training sessions conducted by the playwright Rendra.

When the comparison is broadened to include all media, a striking difference is the reliance of the reformist on the word. In syncretist culture, the puppet-shadow play has long been the seminal formulation of the life history. As the play moves through the phases of life during the course of an all-night performance, the audience vicariously experiences (as well as conceptualizes) that maturation. In reformist culture, the play is replaced by the book and the sermon, and even Muhammad's life history is subordinated to exemplification of moral principles. Traditionalists fall between the two extremes of play and text. They cherish and chant the Qur'an, but distinguish themselves from reformists by their richness of ritual expression of the life of the Prophet. Their celebrations include the *Maulud* feasts, at which time the *Berdjandji* (story of Muhammad's birth) is sung, and the *Mir'adj*, when they chant how Muhammad passed through each layer of heaven until finally he reached God.

Autobiography: Future

In complement to remembrances of life history elicited from the adults, visions of the future were given by the students in response to SQ 28 ("Imagine how your life will be in the future

68. Toer (1952), Hamka (1966).

... "). These essays, which were occasionally two or three pages long each, have been analyzed only for the madrasah (mualimien and mualimaat) and the government high schools (SMA I and III), since these two types of schools tended to differ most cleanly on other items, while SMA Muhammadijah fell in between. After these two groups of essays (totaling 265) were translated and coded according to a number of categories derived from content analysis, these categories were lumped into several quite broad ones; a computation was then made of what percentage of the madrasah sample vs. what percentage of the government-school sample included content fitting each of these broad categories. Notable differences were these:

Students at the government schools gave a higher percentage (73% vs. 52% for madrasah) of images describing a pleasant state of being: peacefulness, harmony, happiness, simplicity, wisdom, and prosperity; a higher percentage (94% vs. 83%) describing concern with some social collectivity, status, or reward: family, community, co-workers, organizations, society, nation, government, or social status and prestige; and a higher percentage (23% vs. 5%) showing passive relationship to the family. Thus, the government students tended more than madrasah students to conceive of their future in other-oriented images, to be concerned with pleasant states of being, and to describe passive or dependent relationships to the family.

A higher percentage of madrasah students (77% vs. 46% government) conceived of the future in terms of religious categories: the hereafter, pilgrimage, prayers, will of God ("If God is willing"), religious organizations, and religious functionaries; a higher percentage (63% vs. 39%) saw themselves making an active contribution to the family; a higher percentage (63% vs. 50%) were concerned with the family of procreation generally and also (56% vs. 47%) with specific concerns of the family of procreation: aspirations for the children, qualities of the spouse, and family planning. Thus, the madrasah students were more concerned than the government students with religion and the future of the family, matters about which they were activist and ambitious.

Biography of Muhammad

According to Pigeaud,[69] only after the coming of Islam did the Javanese create biography—that is, an entire book devoted to the life of a single individual. Previously they submerged biography within myths of the state. Of central importance, as one would expect, was the biography of the Prophet Muhammad—a form difficult for the Hinduist Javanese to duplicate, since the Hinduist tradition offered no equally central human figure.

Given the importance of biography and especially the biography of Muhammad in the Islamic tradition of Indonesia, it seemed appropriate to include a question on this topic in the Jogja survey. Assuming that the period of youth is vulnerable to influence by biographical models, each respondent was asked (HQ II-8) to give one example of an event in the life story of the Prophet Muhammad which made an impression on him when he was young.

The events recalled were coded in categories of Muhammad's biography that are emphasized in the Malayo-Indonesian area and expressed in the survey data. These categories were the following, with typical examples given by respondents cited in parentheses: (1) The childhood of Muhammad (he was an orphan of lowly origin); (2) Muhammad's life as a shepherd (he led a simple life herding flocks); (3) Muhammad's young adulthood as a merchant (his honesty as a trader attracted the widow Khalidjah); (4) Gabriel (Jibril) brought Allah's message to Muhammad in the cave of Hira (though illiterate, Muhammad was able to write and chant the Qur'an upon receiving its words from Allah); (5) Muhammad fled from Mecca to Medina, a journey called the *Hijrah* (he fled, leaving all worldly things, in order to escape from his enemies the Quairish); (6) Muhammad engaged in the Badr-Uhud Wars for the cause of Islam (he was kindly in that he forgave the conquered and took no revenge on Mecca after its fall); (7) in the miracle known as Isra Mir'adj, Muhammad ascended to Heaven and was shown what would

69. Pigeaud (1967, pp. 133, 179).

happen on Doomsday, and he received the mandate to reduce the fifty daily prayers to five (he was taken up by an angel who himself could not see God, though Muhammad could, which indicates that Muhammad was sacred); (8) Muhammad was diplomatic in handling intertribal conflicts (when the Arab tribes fought over possession of the sacred rock of Ka'bah, Muhammad placed the rock under a cloth of which all the tribes could take hold); (9) Muhammad overcame physical suffering to continue the struggle (he continued to pray even when he was sick); (10) Muhammad showed compassion by forgiving sinners and helping the poor (he arranged for a dying child to receive pardon for sinning against its mother, so that it could die peacefully); (11) Muhammad resisted temptation in order to continue the struggle to spread Islam (his uncle offered him women and riches if he would stop the struggle, but Muhammad replied that even if he were given the sun in his right hand, the moon in his left, still he would struggle to spread the word); (12) Muhammad gave the commandment that all must follow the Qur'an and Hadith'; (13) Muhammad had good relations with his first wife (he was kind to her and never beat her, though he had three other wives too); (14) Muhammad was industrious; (15) Muhammad had great knowledge; (16) Muhammad faithfully did the five prayers; (17) Muhammad's life was miraculous (he was born and died on the same day); (18) Muhammad died (he bequeathed a sermon at his death). In addition to these specific categories, there were three general ones: (19) a perception of Muhammad's total life thrust (he rose from being an orphan to being a prophet); (20) a remembrance of Muhammad not in terms of events he enacted but of moral virtues he manifested (simplicity, honesty, piety, dedication, tolerance, kindness); (21) a claimed inability to recall any events that made a strong impression.

Not surprisingly, it was the santri (by theology and membership) who most often claimed to recall an event in the life of Muhammad as making an impression. Virtually none of the santri by theology and membership failed to give some recollection, whereas less than half of the syncretists by theology and membership did so.[70] Within the sample that gave recollections, reformists recalled the Isra Mir'adj considerably more frequently than did the other groups,[71] and the theologically reformist recalled more frequently than did the other theological groups Muhammad's trading, his Badr-Uhad wars,[72] and his struggle to spread Islam; by membership, reformists most often recalled that struggle.[73] In short, it is the commercial, military, and missionary endeavors of the Prophet that the reformists recall— an emphasis which resonates with reformist values.

The small number of reformists (1%) who recalled the event of Muhammad's birth or death as meaningful is striking, as is the large number of each group (approximately 25%) who chose not to recall an episode in Muhammad's life, but some virtue or moral principle which he manifested, even though interviewers had been instructed to press respondents to recall events instead of abstract traits or principles. One might speculate that a sample of Christians would place much emphasis on the birth and death of Christ, since the theological meaning of these events is at the root of Christian belief. One might speculate further that Christians would be more likely to recall events in place of moral principles, because the Bible is more of a narrative than the Qur'an, which is structured around moral exhortations by the Prophet. Indeed, the whole thrust of Christianity is more dramatic, while that of Islam is legalistic and moralistic. In Christianity the drama of Christ's life is itself the core of the

70. By schooling, the difference was not so pronounced: only 10% of the Islamic schooled, but also only 25% of the Western and syncretic schooled, failed to recall an event.

71. By schooling, 33% reformists vs. 10–14% of the others recalled Isra miraj. By theology and membership, 16–19% reformists vs. 2–9% syncretists (but 23% traditionalists).

72. 7–8% reformists vs. 0–5% syncretists recalled the wars, and 5–9% vs. 0–5% Muhammad's trade.

73. By theology, 10% reformists vs. no traditionalists and 2% syncretists recalled the struggle; by membership, 11% vs. 5% and 3%; by schooling, 7% vs. 19% and 6%. (The last three figures show, again, the power of pesantren schooling to produce reformist concerns.)

systems of meaning, whereas for the Muslim the life of Muhammad, though significant, is not in itself a form of mystical meaning and theological importance; as remembered, Muhammad is more a giver of law than a liver of life.

Conversion and the Legalistic Life History

The Darol Arqom indoctrination camp for branch leaders in which I participated in July 1970 required that many of the participants (23 of 38) narrate their autobiographies to the group. These narrations afforded me an unusual opportunity to witness reformist self-revelation in a natural (as opposed to interview) setting. These narrations, summarized elsewhere,[74] serve in the Islamic context rather like the testimonials that constitute an integral part of many Christian meetings, especially fundamentalist; like the Christian testimonials, Darol Arqom narrators frequently recounted a past bereft of proper belief (e.g., rearing in a syncretist or traditionalist household or village), then testified that present belief is proper (i.e., reformist, Muhammadijan). The Darol Arqom "testimonials" differ in one major respect from the Christian ones, however; they contain no account of a dramatic, emotional conversion experience which incited the transition from past to present belief. In this respect, Darol Arqom contrasts not only with Christian groups but also with charismatic movements in general, which frequently include conversion experiences, as in visions.[75]

Lack of testimony of conversion experience does not deny radical shifts at personal cost that Darol Arqom participants may have undergone. Poignant accounts contrast loyalties to Muhammadijah with affection for family members loyal to the traditionalists or to Communism; such divided commitments led to the killing of brother by brother in the 1965 purge, for example. The so-called "personal introductions" of Darol Arqom trainees complement the "mental destructions" at the

74. Peacock (1975a and forthcoming).
75. Wallace (1956).

youth camps, where neophytes are badgered to confess conflicting loyalties and swear allegiance to the organization. Loyalty is
expressed at Darol Arqom in the assertion that one "loves"
Muhammadijah, expressed by terms ranging from the erotic
tjinta to the maternal *sajang*. Such explicit affirmation, utilizing
the language (if not the nonverbal affect) of strong emotion,
contrasts strikingly with the subdued, low-key participation in
such traditional syncretic activities as the slametan; opting for
the Muhammadijah over family or village, the Darol Arqom
participant shifts not only his membership but his *type* of
personal commitment.

   Yet he does not testify to a conversion experience. Nor do
Muhammadijans outside the Darol Arqom. No such accounts
appear in Muhammadijah autobiographies (in contrast to numerous ones in Christian autobiography), and trusted informants
assured me they had never heard of any Muhammadijan under-
going such an experience. Even in the autobiographical account
of the most radical conversion that I knew, the emotional
experience was apparently absent. Reared in a Catholic, syncretist family and educated a Catholic, this man became, as a
student, a militant and devoted apologist for Islam, one who is
sacrificing health and career to proclaim his message. Yet after
months of close acquaintance, when I questioned him about his
conversion he replied:

> I had no dreams or vision. I simply began associating with
> Muslim students at medical school. Through reading
> books on Islam, I came to see that Islam is a continuation
> of the tradition begun by Christianity. It was easy to
> accept the concept of "One God" over that of "Trinity,"
> but difficult to replace Jesus with Muhammad. However,
> after I had accepted the Prophet, I felt as though I had
> shifted from a difficult to an easy religion, and I felt calm.
> This occurred during my first year at the University. We
> "drink" Bismillah (the statement of the oneness of God);
> Malcolm X said, after his pilgrimage, that the recipe is
> simple: If you believe in the unity of God, you believe also
> in the unity of man. Christianity tells us to search for a
> black cat in a dark room, Islam is like coming into a light.

Tauhid is like coming from darkness to clarity. And with Islam I feel close to my fellow believers; if I meet a fellow Muslim for the first time, I am already a brother.

This individual, whose childhood syncretic and Catholic background is exceptionally well-documented,[76] explains the shift of his commitments entirely as rational choice of a new doctrine and a new group.

The apparent lack of emotional conversion experience would seem to reflect the generally legalistic as opposed to dramatic conception of autobiography in Malayo-Muslim reformism. By comparison with Christians, Muhammadijans believe that man is born good, that he did not commit any "original sin." His dynamism, his struggle, do not, according to the Muhammadijans with whom I discussed the issue, come from a desire to be saved from a state of sinfulness. He should feel not fear but tranquility (tentram) as he struggles, with stoic commitment (ichlas), in continuous conformity with the laws and ritual prescriptions set forth in the holy Qur'an. Certainly he desires salvation, but he moves toward it not by climaxes and bursts of guilt-motivated vision and release but by steadily learning the law and performing the rites. The ideal life is not wasted youth followed by mature conversion (we see nothing of the Christian "wasted youth" idea in either the life histories by adults or in the future visions essayed by students). Instead, it is steady learning from early childhood in the schools to sacrifice for the struggle, which revolves around the schools. From this standpoint, the more relevant biographical model is the methodical, dedicated founder Dahlan rather than the visionary Muhammad; certainly it is not Paul on the way to Damascus.[77]

76. By chance, this man was a subject, at the age of 12 (during his Catholic period), of interviews and Thematic Apperception Tests administered by Hildred Geertz; his TAT stories show syncretic content but also strong moralistic concerns perhaps foreshadowing his conversion to Islam.

77. One Indonesian informant queried about conversion experiences to Islam stated that the only persons he knew to have such experiences were Chinese, who have visions. Interestingly, the one example of an emotional conversion experience that I have been able to discover

Overall Conceptions of the Life Cycle

Biography and the future are significant categories in syncretist as well as santri thought (with nationalism and revolution working a somewhat similar influence for syncretists, as do Islam and reformism for santri), and the Jogja survey does not support a claim that the two hold fundamentally or radically different overall conceptions of the life cycle. Survey and other materials do suggest a more linear, historical orientation for the santri, especially reformists, in certain ways. Reformists tend more to rely on the book, instead of the play and ritual, as an expression of conception of the life cycle, and they intellectualize more, subordinating experience to law and principle. They tend also to emphazise mission, future, aspiration, and activism, whereas syncretists were more likely to anticipate pleasant states of being and to remember rich experiences. Reformists also show a certain legalism in their view of the life history—a tendency reflected in their notion of conversion.

THE REFORMIST LIFE CYCLE

It will be recalled that a major thesis of Max Weber was that a reformist cultural orientation such as the Protestant Ethic implied a rationalization of life so that it thrust more single-mindedly toward an ultimate goal of salvation. Weber did not pursue this thesis to the point of systematically tracing such rationalization through the life cycle of a reformist. The present

---

among Southeast Asian Muslims is by a Christian-educated, of Malayo-Chinese descent (but Chinese cultural identity), convert to the Ahmadiyya in Singapore. This person, whose life history and experience I came to know through long contact (as was also true of the Catholic convert to Muhammadijah mentioned here), recounted during our first meeting a vision in which he dreamed of hearing an explosion and seeing a figure in white, after which he began to pray at a mosque. Something about the Chinese-Christian cultural orientation may encourage such experiences, whereas they may be discouraged by the Malayo-Indonesian orientation (perhaps the combination of Hinduist cyclical and Muslim linear structure of the life history), even among nominal Christians.

chapter has taken a first step in this task. At this point, the difficult question of whether the Jogja reformist's life cycle is more "rationalized" than that of the traditional syncretist will be postponed; however, the analysis can be taken forward by summarizing an overall contrast in pattern in the two life cycles. Simplifying, it is proposed that the traditional life cycle is repetitive, static, and cyclical, compared to a reformist tendency toward a more progressive, dynamic, and linear pattern.[78]

For the traditional Javanese, the child, highly desired, is ushered into life by *slametans* that serve both to shield mother and child against threatening spirits and to subsume the continuous, natural maturation of the fetus and infant under the punctuate, cosmic cycle. During early childhood, harmony between child and milieu is instilled through massage, kinesic teaching, and permissive nurturance by cuddling and suckling. Spread among several nurturant figures by lending and *momong*, the child is taught to harmonize himself to a diffuse "other," probably resulting in a diffusion of his identity. Discipline and rigidity are present not so much in scheduling of natural processes, such as eating and excreting, as in sharp distinction between nature and culture; as when the child is prohibited from crawling, concern here is less with harnessing process (nature) than with maintaining structure (culture).

A significant shift occurs around age five, when distance between father and child is abruptly established—the affirmation of hierarchy. Now the child begins to learn manners, language, and emotion that insure veneration of superiors and maintenance of the cultural order, which is based on values of refinement and hierarchy.

Circumcision and marriage return the adolescent and adult to the cyclical, cosmic complex of slametans which introduced him to childhood. At marriage, childhood themes are repeated,

78. While it may be objected that the metaphor of lineality is unjustly imposed on exotic materials, it should be noted that the image is utilized by the reformists themselves. I have seen a Muhammadijan depict in chalk on a blackboard the "shape" of the movement as a straight arrow, while portraying an opposing approach as a circle.

such as push-pull instruction, physical support during psychic disequilibrium (as when the groom physically leans against his friends during the ceremony), and even more overt themes of childhood (as when the father holds bride and groom on his knees). By signaling the return, transition is defined as constancy. With the help of slametans and other imagery, passage is subordinated to the repetitive structure of the cultural framework.

With old age, some syncretists turn their thoughts toward death and salvation, with the result that they become more like the santri. The majority, however, seek meaning within the cyclical framework of mystical syncretic philosophies. Their death itself is subordinated to a cycle of slametans.

The reformists, being largely Javanese, remain rooted in the traditional culture just sketched, but they also show significant deviation in the progressive, dynamic, and linear thrust of the life history. (See Table 3). The survey shows that reformists tend to break out of the pattern of ushering the child into life at home among kinsfolk and with slametans. They reduce, also, the mother-oriented, bodily mediated training for harmony, as in the gendong, kuloni, and kinesic teaching (for which they tend to substitute moral advice). Diminishing subordination to cosmic cycles, they discipline such processes as ingestion and excretion, suggesting a drive toward voluntaristic control of the natural, rather than an orderly division between natural and cultural orders. Reducing the child's range of parental surrogates, by decreasing lending and momong, they focus the child's identity and perhaps his sense of spiritual focus, as in Tauhid.

The child is circumcised earlier than among syncretists, suggesting a drive to speed his entry into the Muslim community. Reformist circumcision, like reformist marriage, tends to be stripped of syncretist symbolism of cycle and constancy: reformist rites of passage really do mark a passage.

Reducing the ritualization of childhood, reformists elaborate the education of youth. Traditionally, the santri school was the ascetic pesantren, leading to the pilgrimage. While pesantren and pilgrimage have played a critical role in the background of

TABLE 3.
Characteristics of the Javanese Muslim Reformist Life Cycle

CHILD-REARING

Hospital birth

Absence of *slametan* birth ritual

Early cessation of cuddling *(gendong* and *kuloni)*, and early toilet-training

Less veneration of father, and less memory of father as venerable

Emphasis on obedience and initiative

De-emphasis of imitative learning *(tuturi)*

LATER CHILDHOOD AND YOUTH

Less long-term and short-term child-lending

Commercial and technological play for boys

Early circumcision

Pesantren attendance and pilgrimage *(hadj)* by older generation; Muhammadijah school attendance and participation in reformist youth movements by younger generation

ADULTHOOD

Employment in business rather than government bureaucracy

Aspiration for son to serve a function rather than fill a status

Concern with work's contribution to society

Begin working early

Marry early

Reside patrilocally

See mother as dominant domestic influence

Seek counsel from wife

DEATH

Emphasis on single Muslim funeral (facilitating salvation of the deceased)

De-emphasis of multiple *slametan* rituals (which maintain harmony of the living)

OVERALL CONCEPTION OF THE LIFE CYCLE

Autobiographical narration oriented toward future program rather than nostalgic and sensuous remembrance

Media are scriptural rather than dramatic or ceremonial

Young people's visions of the future emphasize religious activity and plans for new family, rather than pleasant state of being and dependence on present family

Remembered biography of Muhammad emphasizes his commercial, military, and missionary endeavors

many reformists, they play little part in the lives of their sons. The sons are educated through bureaucratized school and organization, an upbringing that perhaps resembles that of their syncretist peers more than did that of the founders of reformism. As a result, psychological differences between syncretists and reformists in the present (and future) generations may be less than during the charismatic era of the founding fathers. Factor analysis does suggest, however, that among contemporary reformists, youthful experience of schools and movements has encouraged a radical rejection of ritualization of the life cycle through slametans of birth and death. A complementary but distinct attitude is the Islamic Ethic, held by persons whose reformism is based less on youthful experience than on adult membership and belief: emphasis is less on rejection of cyclical ritualization than on affirmation of the linear, salvation-oriented ritual and belief of Islam.

The reformist's attitude toward death appears to differ from that of the syncretist primarily in his greater concern for life after death and lesser concern for ordering relations between living and dead. As with birth, circumcision, and marriage, death is for the reformist not an aspect of a cosmic constancy or cycle: it is a stark break, marked by a single ceremony and looking forward to Judgment Day.

Autobiographical materials broadly support the notion that the reformists conceive of the life cycle (or arc) in a more linear, progressive, goal-oriented way. When narrating the life history, reformists tend more than syncretists to block nostalgic and sensuous memories and to emphasize ethical prescription and future objectives. Reformist students asked to imagine the future tend more than syncretists to think of their families-to-come, aspirations for their future children, and the hereafter, by comparison to the greater tendency of students in government schools to describe a pleasant state of being. Finally, in identifying their autobiographies with the biography of the Prophet, reformists emphasize struggle in the effort at missionizing: a dynamic, forward-looking concern.

4

Psychological Analysis: The Reformist Character

ANALYSIS of the life cycle approaches reformist psychology diachronically, analysis of character approaches the topic synchronically. Whereas the last chapter endeavored to trace patterns of development as the reformist's life unfolds, the present chapter explores what has been termed "character structure": "the personality's nuclear region comprising broad, organizing value orientations, enduring dispositions, and policy-setting premises that guide an individual in a variety of situations."[1] Such character structure is explored in relation to social values, expressive forms, psychopathology, and motivational dispositions.

SOCIAL VALUES

Hierarchy

Hierarchy is deeply rooted in traditional Javanese civilization, a point that is made quickly by examining terminology and language. *Hormat* (politeness), *sungkan* (respect), *tata-krama* (etiquette), and other terms already mentioned (such as *isin*) are commonly accepted as dominant categories in Javanese life,[2]

1. Honigmann (1967, p. 69).
2. Dipojono (1972, p. 268); C. Geertz (1960b, sect. 3).

and the hierarchical values these terms denote are expressed in such realms as language, posture, and titles with remarkable consistency.

Javanese language is really several languages, arranged in a hierarchy of refinement ranging from the earthy *ngoko* (low language) to the respectfully exalted *krama*, and those of low status must speak krama to those of high, while those of high status speak ngoko to those of low.[3] Through gradations based on this principle, the language gives extremely precise expression to status difference, and to speak Javanese without reflecting hierarchy is impossible. Speech is complemented by posture in accord with the basic rule that elevating the language requires lowering the body; thus a servant may kneel while serving a dish to her mistress, or bow the head at the feet of a master; and lower-status persons still jump off chairs in order not to sit higher than their superiors.[4]

One *is* one's title in Java in a profound sense. To address a person by name without title is less proper than by title without name. And one may be addressed in terms of the title of a person to whom one has a relationship, as when a wife of an official in colonial times might be addressed as "Mrs. Subdistrict officer." The types of titles surveyed in Jogjakarta are those outside the realm of kinship, such as the academic, noble, and Muslim ones, but it should be noted also that kinship titles are frequently used, among both kinsmen and nonkinsmen, and these too are hierarchically patterned. Thus friends and spouses address each other as *mas* (older brother) or *dik* (younger sibling), depending on their age and sex; only in the Indonesian language or low or slang Javanese do they escape from hierarchy by the use of terms such as *saudara* (comrade) or *rek* (buddy; literally "child"). In Javanese, siblings must distinguish seniority by terms, and even uncles and aunts are addressed by different terms according to seniority.

3. For basic description, see C. Geertz (1960b, sect. 3); for detail, see references in Uhlenbeck (1955).
4. Bateson and Mead (1942, pp. 10-11) analyze this type of posture in detail for the Balinese.

Description of hierarchy in Javanese society could be elaborated to include the golden umbrella and the white collar, but the important question is the meaning of this hierarchy. Certainly status does not reduce to power; consider the immense power of Semar, the clown-servant of mythology, or conversely, the alleged impotence (in the sense of ability to move people to comply) of high-status civil servants.[5] The most seminal analysis[6] of the meaning of hierarchy in Java is based on a cultural feature, that the Javanese perceive the universe as teeming with spiritual energy and they crave to concentrate this energy into some form, which may be a status. Such a status then radiates charisma, the *wahju* of the Javanese god-king, the magnetism of a President Sukarno.

Emphasis is on this concentration of energy, whether through meditation, ceremony, etiquette, unifying opposites,[7] or absorbing spirits, and not on its *use*. This is why the civil servant may seem impotent; rather than dissipate his power by applying it, he concentrates and conserves it through heightening the magnificence of his status. When power must be used, the ideal is *perintah alus*, the effortless release of great force, as when the spiritually sublime Ardjuna banishes a raging and leaping monster opponent by a mere flick of the wrist.

The underling craves to absorb the *wahju* of the great one, and this he does not by serving him instrumentally—being *used* —but by a kind of worship. Thus did officials meditate for hours on the greatness of the king of Mataram, and in lesser degree relations of peasant to regent, employee to boss, voter to politician and student to teacher, follow the same worshipful pattern. These relations resemble that of child to father; indeed, they are termed "fatherism" *(bapakisme)*. What the father, the *bapak*, tries to give his literal or figurative child is not training or sanctions, but a diffuse spiritual guidance. Kings instructed subjects by singing moral poems, politicians give speeches that sound like kindergarten sermons, and fathers, as

5. Fagg (1958).   6. Anderson (1972a).
7. Anderson, (1972a, p. 12).

we have noted, claim to raise their children by giving them "advice" rather than through reward and punishment.

Embracing these myriad aspects ranging from spirituality to kinship, the hierarchical relationship in Java is what sociologists would term "multiplex" or "diffuse."[8] Disruption of such a relationship would threaten not only the individuals involved but the whole sociocosmic order. Accordingly, harmony must be maintained, hence *tata-krama*—the elaboration of manner, language, and ceremony—and the tendency to avoid direct application and force.

Reformists and Hierarchy—The Jogja survey generally supports the expectation that reformists place less emphasis on hierarchy than do the others, although in certain areas reformists retain an allegiance to hierarchy.

Fewer reformists, defined by education and theology, use any title (HQ 5), and the titles which have traditionally most strongly expressed hierarchy—i.e., those of nobility—are claimed most often among the Western schooled and the syncretists by theology.[9] *Kijai*, a title of sacral Islamic status, is used more often by the pesantren schooled and traditionalist Islamic party members than by the reformist schooled and reformists by membership.[10]

The term *hadji* (he who has made the pilgrimage) is also used more often by the pesantren schooled and traditionalist party members than by the reformists. Yet persons with the hadji title most often hold reformist *theology*.[11] This pattern

8. Gluckman (1962, p. 26); Levy (1966, p. 304).

9. The highest percentage of reformists to use any title is 30% compared to 50% for syncretists, traditionalists, and Western schooled. More than 50% of the Western schooled hold a "noble" title, compared to less than 10% for any other school group, and 25% of those with noble titles profess syncretic theology vs. 15% who profess reformist theology.

10. The title *kijai* is used by only 5% of reformist party members vs. 25% of traditionalist party members, and the pesantren have produced the highest percentage (13% vs. no reformist schooled) with this title.

11. Among those who profess reformist theology, 20% had made the *hadj*, compared to only 7% who hold traditionalist theology.

suggests that the title hadji carries a triple meaning. First, it is a sacral status revered especially by some traditionalist Muslims and socially useful in conservative circles; hence those who possess it tend to join the traditionalist party.[12] Second, the *hadj* is a phase of education traditionally following schooling at a pesantren—and indeed, those who have made the hadj were educated in pesantren more often than in other schools.[13] Yet, as has been discussed earlier, the experience of making the hadj tends to emancipate the individual from traditional values. Accordingly, it is logical that 8 of 10 persons who have made the hadj should hold reformist theological views even if they are members of the traditionalist party and were educated in a pesantren.[14]

The highest percentage of academic titles is found among members of the reformist organization.[15] While the academic title carries prestige and thus reflects hierarchical values (as when title is used as an adjunct to name: "Will Masjuti M.A. please step forward"), it indicates, too, the high reformist value on education. Academic titles resemble "hadji" and differ from the titles of nobility in that they are achieved rather than ascribed and reflect both deeds and status.

12. By party, 37% traditionalists, 23% reformists, and no syncretists are *hadjis*.

13. By schooling, 45% of the pesantren educated, 23% reformist educated, and virtually none of the Western or syncretist educated bear the title hadji.

14. This reformist influence of the hadj tradition may also extend over generations, as is suggested by the fact that of those whose father made the hadj, 73% (35 of 48) took on a reformist orientation, whereas of those whose father did not make the hadj, only 47% (159 of 335) have done so. Of course, it is not the hadj alone but the type of father (a certain classical hardnosed *hadji*, exemplified by early founders of Muhammadijah such as K.II.A. Dahlan and Hadji Rasul, represented in that generation) which is probably influential.

15. Academic titles are held by 21% of the reformist party members, compared to a maximum of 13% for any other group. Defined by schooling, syncretists and reformists are in this respect equal (23–28%), even though the Muslim schooled are disadvantaged compared to government schooled in getting academic titles.

At first surprising is the large percentage (17.4%) of noble titles claimed by members of the reformist organizations. This doubtless reflects an historical intimacy between Kauman and Kraton peculiar to Jogjakarta; none of the non-Jogjakartan reformist Darol Arqom participants hold noble titles. Observation suggests that though reformists may reveal such titles when asked about them on surveys, few display them in Muhammadijah social circles. In any case, the statistic warns against too simple a dichotomy between *santri* and *prijaji*—or, for that matter, between reformism and hierarchy.

Questions designed to get at hierarchical values included asking respondents if they upheld the value of *andap-ansor* (obsequiousness; HQ II-33). The majority of *all* groups, including Darol Arqom, admitted holding this value.[16] Also, a majority or near-majority of all groups reported conforming to traditional Javanese modes of teaching such values; they believed that the child should be taught *isin* (HQ III-56) and *krama* (HQ III-57) by age 5.[17] This confirms the impression that Jogjakarta Muhammadijans (even, reportedly, the founder, K.H.A. Dahlan) conform to the refined, *alus* hierarchical etiquette of other Jogjakarta Javanese.

The Javanese rite of asking parents forgiveness on Lebaran, the day of ending the fast, expresses, among other things, a deep veneration of the father by the child, who relates to the father formally and hierarchically. Most reformists join the other Jogjakartans in celebrating this rite (HQ III-68). Differences are apparent, however, in its form. The reformist son, by comparison with the syncretist son, more frequently shakes hands with the father *(salaman)*, rather than bowing the head *(sungkem)* and kneeling at the father's feet *(sembah)* (HQ III-69).[18] This appar-

16. All groups had frequencies of over 88% affirming *andap-ansor*, except the Islamic conservative party with a frequency of 80%.

17. From 48% to 63% felt the child should learn *isin* by age 5, and 51–86% felt he should speak *krama* by age 5.

18. 45–53% of the reformists' sons vs. 25–42% of the syncretists' do the *salaman*, whereas 51–67% of the syncretists' sons vs. 39–49% of the reformists' do the *sungkem*. The statistic varies according to cri-

ently lesser hierarchical orientation of the reformist is possibly confirmed by his lower frequency of recalling the father as "a person I venerated with a manner that was so polite that I felt shame when I was in his presence" (HQ II-30c).[19]

In Islam and reformism, a basic premise is that all believers are equal in the eyes of God, which contrasts with the essential inequality of castes in Hinduist ideology. In early Islam, and still in traditionalist Islam in Java, this egalitarianism is diluted by tendencies to venerate the Sajid (descendants of the Prophet), religious teachers, and the Sultan. Yet the veneration of men was subordinated to respect for the Islamic law, the *sjariah*, which was elaborated by various schools *(madzhap)*—primarily, in Indonesia, the Sjafiite. To enforce the law, there emerged religious bureaucrats (the *naib, modin, muezzin, penghulu,* and others)—and though these inclined toward aggrandization, they were compelled to justify their actions by analysis of the law as revealed in the holy scripture. Men should serve the law, Allah was supreme, and the rejection of divinity in the world was reflected in the denial of the god-king: no worldly status could be divine; no human could, like the syncretist's god-king, concentrate the spiritual forces and energies. And where the Prophet was revered as ideal, one respected not a haughty prince but a poor orphan who had risen to become a camel driver, a merchant, and a warrior.

Affirming these equalizing tendencies in Islam and deleting certain hierarchical deviations of the traditionalists, Muhammadijans themselves have observed that they reduce Javanese emphasis on status. They point out, for example, that they do not dress as princes and princesses at weddings, as do the traditional syncretists. And they do indeed behave with considerable

---

terion of religious orientation, but no matter what criterion is used the reformists are higher than syncretists on salaman and lower on sungkem; however, the reformist schooled is more likely to do the *sembah* (13.9%) than the syncretist schooled (6.6%).

19. By party, 15% reformists vs. 32% syncretists chose the "veneration" statement; by theology, 23% vs. 57%; and by schooling, less than 20% reformists vs. 31–35% syncretist and Western schooled.

egalitarianism. They are inclined (among themselves) to use Indonesian instead of Javanese, they avoid employment as servants, they eschew a host of artistic forms that preserve values of hierarchy, and their leaders truly are "men of the people" who ride rickety buses and live in simple houses in the Kauman, while the syncretist politicians boast the "big man" image so well known in the Pacific cultures. Based on the association between their seemingly devout monotheism and this egalitarianism, it appears that these reformists give negative confirmation to the thesis that at least one meaning of power to traditional Javanese is in the striving to concentrate spirituality in a status.

The Status of Women—Weber has stated that "Islam displays . . . characteristics of a distinctively feudal spirit: the obviously unquestioned acceptance of slavery, serfdom, and polygamy, the disesteem for and subjection of women."[20] Slavery and serfdom are not features of contemporary Islam in Java, and the general import of Weber's remark would seem not to apply to the comparison of santri and syncretist cultures in Java.

But what about the subjugation of women? Studies on the role of women in Java have usually emphasized their high status, in the home, in the marketplace, and in the ancient empire and the contemporary nation where certain women are politically quite powerful. For Javanese women, the coming of Islam has frequently brought a loss of status, as in the law of inheritance which in indigenous Java is equal for male and female, but in Islamic law gives two parts to the male for one to the female. And consider such Islamic laws as this one, summarized by Pijper: If women and men pray together, a man must lead, and the worship is worthless if a woman leads men; also it is worthless if a man is led by a hermaphrodite, a hermaphrodite by a woman, or a hermaphrodite by a hermaphrodite, though it is permissible for a man to lead a man, a man to lead a hermaphrodite, a man to lead a woman, a hermaphrodite to lead a woman, or a woman to lead a woman. And men must stand in front, women behind, and hermaphrodites—if any should happen to be available—in between.[21]

20. Weber (1964, p. 264).

What Pijper found striking about Java was the extent to which, despite such Islamic laws, women were prominent in Islamic affairs. He reported that in some areas women were more diligent in fasting and praying and more concerned to make the hadj than men, and the female hadji was respected and pious: "Never does one meet in Java a female hadji who bathes with men in the river."[22] Javanese santri women are diligent in religious studies, at home, in the palace, and in female pesantren. They have built female prayer houses and mosques, and they take part in the mosque services of the men. This participation varies, however, by region; in Pijper's survey, the areas of greatest participation were those which have now become strongly reformist or were then strongly syncretist, whereas the areas which most strongly forbade female participation in Pijper's day have become the strongholds of the traditionalist santri party (NU).

In both east and central Java, women took part in mosque ceremonies celebrating the breaking of the fast and the Prophet's ascent to heaven (Mir'adj), though in some places they were forced to sit behind a screen while doing so. In Jogjakarta, already the center of Muhammadijah, they attended Friday services at the Great Mosque and Paku Alaman. But in the traditionalist santri areas of east Java, few women attended the mosque, and several women who attempted to do so in one place in 1932 created an uproar and were barred. In the syncretist holy mosque of Demak, in a celebration of the syncretist saint Sunan Kalidjaga, alleged creator of sacral elements of Javanese arts and culture, both women and men were in the mosque, older women with breasts uncovered (in contrast to the orthodox Muslim norm that women should cover the body from soles of the feet to hair of the head while praying).[23]

The Jogjakarta survey inquired whether the male Muslim respondent favored a larger role of women in the mosque (HQ

21. Pijper (1934, p. 10).
22. Pijper (1934, pp. 16-18). On the role of women in Indonesia generally, see Dewey (1962), H. Geertz (1961), and Kartini (1921).
23. Pijper (1934, pp. 50, 54).

II-5). Reformists were the most frequent to say yes, traditionalists and syncretists less frequent.[24] The traditionalist and syncretist answers should be interpreted differently, however. Since syncretist males themselves rarely if ever attend the mosque, an answer of "no" from them does not necessarily discriminate against women, since they care little whether anyone, male or female, takes a stronger role in the mosque. What is significant is the reformist yes versus the traditionalist no, since reformists seemingly *already* give women a stronger role in the mosque than traditionalists. Among reformists the role of women in the mosque is already relatively strong, and they are apparently willing to make it even stronger.

Given the patriarchal (as Weber put it, "feudal") thrust of Islam, and given the drive of reformism to perfect the Islamic ideology, why should reformism move toward sexual equality? An immediate answer may lie in the politics of the Muhammadijah movement, in which the women's branch ('Aisjijah) has gained considerable power, accomplished much, and put pressure on their husbands. (During one interview, a Muhammadijan looked at his wife, a leader in 'Aisjijah, and said jokingly that "while mother is here" he had better answer yes to this question about women in the mosque.) A broader answer would point both to the traditionally high status of women in Javanese society and to the general trend in modernizing movements toward egalitarianism between the sexes. In the Muhammadijah, the patriarchal and modernizing tendencies are in conflict, but the modern seems to be winning. The trend is symbolized by the construction of Muhammadijah biographies of early leaders. The old photographs, buried inside, depict these patriarchs with their many wives; the new pictures, on the covers, show one wife with one husband, one son, and one daughter, all walking toward a sunrise (emblem of Muhammadijah), with a mosque on one side and a modern hospital on the other.

24. By the various criteria, the modal santri affirmative answer was 60%, compared to the syncretists' 27%. By theology, reformist santri outdid traditionalist santri 61% vs. 34% on the question of more female participation.

In areas outside the mosque, too, a trend toward a bourgeois, egalitarian relation between the sexes is suggested by the survey. Informants agreed that HQ II-6, alternative 2, accurately depicted the traditional pattern of father remaining exalted and aloof while the mother did the actual work of raising the child; this is the pattern noted in ethnographic studies of Javanese families. Yet 90% of the males of all groups in the Jogja survey claimed to favor deviation from this pattern toward alternative 1: cooperation.

Solidarity

Expressed by such terms as *rukun, gotong-rojong,* and *musjarawah,*[25] the hierarchical axis of traditional Javanese society is cross-cut by the solidarity; these terms emphasize the avoidance of conflict and the maintenance of harmony. The locale of such solidarity tends to be concrete, based on bond to a particular territory (ranging from neighborhood or village to region or nation) or network, such as kinship or friendship. The purpose of the solidarity is solidarity itself; that is, the social relationship itself takes primacy over some higher or further purpose that it might serve, such as developing the economy or upholding the law.

While the first principle, concrete loyalty, is obvious and to be expected where peasantry, regionalism, nationalism, and face-to-face relations are important, the second—solidarity as end in itself—may require illustration. In fights between children, parents are more concerned to restore order than to pin blame; in distributing inheritance, dictates of Islamic law are sacrificed to preserve harmony; in arriving at decisions, whether locally or nationally, the preferred technique is not vote but consensus *(musjawarah)* so that harmony is maintained, even though the mechanics of bureaucracy are violated.[26] In formulations of ideology ranging from the peasant rite to Sukarno's

25. On *rukun,* see H. Geertz (1961, pp. 47-8); on *gotong-rotong,* see Koentjaraningrat (1961).

26. Also see Anderson (1972a, pp. 22-3) on Javanese mistrust of federalism.

grandiose nationalist visions, the emphasis is less on logical consistency than on a kind of symbolic harmonization of such varied and seemingly contradictory orientations as Hinduism, Buddhism, animism, Communism, nationalism, and Islam.[27] In every case, primacy is given to maintaining social or socio-spiritual relationships rather than to conforming to the dictates of some abstract principle, be it justice, logic, bureaucracy, doctrine, or the law.

Reformists and Solidarity—What the Jogja survey suggests concerning reformists, and to a degree santri in general, is that they tend more than syncretists to transcend concern with primary social units, whether based on locale, friendship, or kinship, and that they are more willing to sacrifice primary social relationships for abstract purposes or principles. The survey also suggests that a factor in this "transcendence" is the cosmopolitan experience of the santri, a moving and mixing which unglues particular bonds.

Whether defined by schooling, membership, or theology, the santri were more likely to belong to nonlocalized, non-familial associations such as youth organizations, whereas the syncretists were more likely to belong to village or neighborhood associations (HQ II-42).[28] The nonlocalized membership was paralleled by general attitude, in that the Muslims ranked "building society" as the second most important priority (following the five prayers) in moral action, whereas the syncretists more frequently ranked "building a good family" in this position.[29]

27. This pattern has been noted by observers from Kern (1925) to Dahm (1969) and McVey (1970).

28. For reformist and pesantren schooled, 22% and 18% respectively, belonged to religious youth organizations, whereas the other groups' frequencies were 0–3%. By schooling, 68% of syncretists belonged to communal (village or neighborhood) organizations vs. 50% for reformists; and by party, 77% vs. 65%; but by theology, 51% vs. 63%.

29. By schooling, the syncretist and Western educated ranked "building a good family" most important 11–13% of the time, while 0–4%

When work was contrasted with socializing (socializing being distinguished from social contribution such as "building society," in that emphasis is on the solidarity itself rather than an abstract end), the reformists by schooling more frequently than other groups opted for work (HQ II-26a, and the equivalent question for students, SQ 24a, where "study" was substituted for "work").[30] Likewise, when socializing was contrasted to allegiance to God, reformists were slightly more likely than the others to choose God (HQ II-30b; all of the reformist schooled say they would rather die in God's presence than among friends at home).[31] Reformists, defined by theology and membership, were less likely than syncretists to choose "sociability" as the most important trait to be learned by the son (HQ II-20),[32] and less likely than the Javanese or Western schooled to choose "good social relations on the job" as the most desirable aspect of a job (HQ I-62).[33] The reformists placed less emphasis on friendship than did the syncretists (HQ II-29c; SQ 26b), which recalls the Calvinist's rejection of friendship as idolatry; in place of friendship the reformist chose association with "famous persons,"[34] which may reflect less a hierarchical desire to absorb *wahju* than an interest in the typical santri *tokoh*, the great man of history who leads the struggle.

---

santri gave this ranking; by party and theology, syncretists 25–56% vs. 1–3% reformists. While few of any group ranked "building society" first in importance, 34–39% of the reformists (by the various criteria) ranked it second, compared to 24–29% syncretists.

30. By schooling, 84% of the reformists vs. 78% syncretists chose "work" over "socialize"; 78% of the madrasah students vs. 65% of others chose "study" over "socialize."

31. But 90% of the other groups by schooling also chose God. By theology, 95% reformists vs. 77% syncretists; by party, 96% santri vs. 77% syncretists.

32. 4–6% reformists by the various criteria vs. 17–30% syncretists chose sociability.

33. This difference was slim: 7–9% Western and syncretist schooled vs. 4% reformists.

34. By the various criteria, 36–37% reformists vs. 50–60% syncretists favored friendship.

The lesser frequency of slametans among the reformists can also be interpreted as a lessening of neighborhood and household ties, as well as of concern for harmonizing these sociospiritual realms. Santri replace slametans with prayers. The central place for prayer is not home but mosque (syncretists lack any equally centralized place for their slametans), and the prayers are oriented not to face-to-face relationships but to Allah.

Cosmopolitanism—A cosmopolitanism of the santri is reflected not so much in the gross statistics as in details. Virtually all of the household heads from every faction were born in central Java of parents born in central Java, and most were of Javanese ethnicity (HQ 2, 3, 47).[35] But the few non-Javanese

35. Syncretists by theology and party were 100% Javanese in father's ethnicity, and by schooling 97%; santri were slightly less, 89–95% Javanese. Despite the small overall difference between syncretist and santri ethnic heterogeneity, differences are apparent in details. None of the 3 individuals with an Atjehnese father or the 3 with an Arab father report practicing any of the birth-death slametans, and the 3 with Minangkabau fathers report practicing only one slametan, that given the first month after a child's birth *(selepanan)*. The persons with Sundanese fathers, however (who are culturally and geographically closer to Javanese) report practicing several of the birth-death slametans. All the Arabs and Atjehnese believe in djin, though only one of each believes in one of the spirits *(tujul, memedi, wewe, peri, gendruwo,* and *wedon)*. Only the Sundanese profess belief in sacred relics *(pusaka)*. While all the sons of Arab, Atjehnese, Minangkabau, and Sundanese fathers ask forgiveness on Lebaran (note indications that this is a pan-Malayo-Muslim custom, rather than strictly Javanese), Arabs and atjehnese use the handshake (salaman) rather than the ways of bowing and kneeling to show respect (sungkem and sembah).

In terms of theology, none of these non-Javanese profess the syncretic, Javanese orientation, while 2 profess the traditionalist and 6 the reformist Islamic attitude. The reformist organizations boast as members *all* of the non-Javanese ethnics in the Jogja sample, with the exception of Sundanese. Like ethnicity, birth of self or father outside Java is associated with non-syncretist theology and membership; none of these non-Java-born select the syncretist theology, and all but 4 of the respondents born outside central Java are in the reformist organization. In short, the non-Java-born by ethnicity and birth reject Javanese cus-

(e.g., Sumatrans) and non-Indonesians (e.g., Arabs) who did appear in the Jogja sample were in the santri groups. The significance of this is that contact with even one or two outsiders provides an experience qualitatively different from contact with none, and observation confirms that in santri circles the influence and visibility of the few Arabs and Sumatrans is disproportionate to their numbers. In the schools, cosmopolitanism was more marked than in the household sample (SQ 2, 5, 6);[36] the Muhammadijah schools had more non-Javanese (mostly Sumatran), non-Indonesian (mostly Malay), and non-Java-born (usually in Sumatra) than the government schools.

In sum, the overall pattern of the survey data is to confirm that the santri in general, reformists in particular, tend more than the syncretists to replace primary solidarities and orientations with orientation toward the wider society, the Muslim community, and ultimately God. Certainly the secular forces of socialism, nationalism, and modernization experienced by the syncretic and Western-educated Javanese push toward the same "transcendentalization," and the santri are not immune to these influences; one may conjecture that the slight santri edge over syncretists in this regard can be attributed to the additional influence of Islam. And the Islamic thrust toward transcendentalization is rooted in a history of itinerant trading, ethnic

---

toms and affirm the Islamic. (Note that the ability of the theological/ organizational measures of non-Javanese [syncretic] orientation to screen out the non-Javanese by ethnicity and birth could be interpreted as an added indication of validity.)

36. 25% of the madrasah students, 20% Muhammadijah SMA students, and 15% government SMA students claimed non-Javanese ethnic identity. 13% of the Muhammadijah SMA students, 10% madrasah students, and 4% government SMA students were non-Java-born. In the Islamic school sample, the number of non-Java-born fathers corresponded closely to the number of non-Java-born sons, suggesting that these students are first-generation immigrants. By contrast, the number of non-Java-born fathers (22) is almost triple the number of non-Java-born sons (8) in the government SMA, suggesting that these are second-generation immigrants and likely to be more assimilated into Javanese culture.

mixing, and cross-national union based on loyalty to the pan-
Islamic community.[37] For Indonesia, this history goes back to
the fourteenth century; for Islam, to Muhammad.

A history of cosmopolitanism and mobility, then, together
with the basically transcendental values of Islam, would seem
sufficient to explain at the broadest level these several indications that santri, and especially reformist santri, to a certain
degree eschew the syncretist concern with the harmony and
solidarity of primary and localized groups and relationships. To
those traditions are added today the rationalizing concern of
organizations like Muhammadijah, who talk less about solidarity, cooperation, and consensus than about goals, struggle, and
plans.

Reformist Social Values

Hierarchy affirms an essential inequality among statuses,
expressed in a multiplex stream of rights, obligations, symbols,
and behaviors. The Jogja survey confirms the continuing importance of hierarchy among Javanese, reformist or not. Yet tenets
of egalitarianism and universalism basic to Islam and bolstered
by rationalizing trends common to all modernizing processes
account for the apparent advantage reformists have over syncretists in diminishing hierarchy in certain spheres. Inequality
between men and women remains, owing to basic values of
Islam—yet even here, reformists exceed traditionalists in moving toward a wider role for women in the mosque.

Similarly, the survey suggests that overall, though not always, the reformists in particular and santri in general transcend primary solidarities more than do the syncretists, and they
have moved further from such deeply rooted Javanese values as
cooperation, consensus, compromise, and harmony. This is not
to deny trends in the same direction in syncretism, but the
survey suggests a stronger bent among reformists.

It is interesting to note that this trend is not identical,
however, with that predicted by models of bourgeois, Western

37. Reid (1967) and Roff (1967).

modernization. An example is the survey finding that the reformist is more oriented toward a collectivism—reform of the total society, and association with great leaders—than toward the personalism of bourgeois life, as in emphasis on friendship and interpersonal relationships at work.

EXPRESSIVE FORMS

Given the syncretist tendency to conceptualize the cosmos as icons and images, it is logical that syncretists should feel strongly moved to express their world-view through the arts. The term 'radical aestheticism' has been applied to the Balinese,[38] and it is true of the syncretist Javanese as well, though in a more specialized, less communal way. Both of these Hinduized civilizations are much concerned with the sensuous *surface* and beauty of human action, whether displayed in music, dance, drama, literature, manners, or ceremony. Before comparing certain specific expressive forms of syncretists vs. reformists, it is necessary to sketch some of the broad linkages between world-view and expressive form conceived by these two orientations.

Several studies have shown the central place of dance in the society and identity of the syncretic Javanese,[39] one linkage being the suitability of that form to express the Javanese concern with balance, equilibrium, and harmony. Other studies have shown the relation of music to Javanese conceptions of cyclical time,[40] and analyses of Javanese musical stratification suggestively parallel the Javanese form of social hierarchy. Drama is a highly significant form in Java, and there are many studies on the large number of troupes, the deep penetration of drama into national life, and the rich variety of forms.[41] While suggestive comparisons could be made between the syncretic and santri

38. C. Geertz (1966, p. 56).
39. C. Geertz (1960b, p. 282), Peacock (1968, p. 242).
40. J. Becker, (1974).
41. Brandon (1967, pp. 172-3); Anderson (1972a); Dahm (1969); Emmerson (forthcoming); Kats (1923); C. Geertz (1960b); Pigeaud (1938); Peacock (1968).

118   MUSLIM PURITANS

traditions in the realm of dance and music—for example, the
monotonic, linear Qur'anic chant, as opposed to the hierarchical, cyclical, syncretic *gamelan* orchestra—the contrast between
the traditions of drama among syncretists and literature among
santri is of most relevance here.

Most sacral of the syncretic dramatic forms is the *wajang
kulit*, a play of flat leather figures manipulated by a puppeteer so
that their shadows flicker on a screen. Enacting vast cycles of
Javanized Hindu myths, the wajang expresses numerous values
central to the syncretic culture. In wajang, time is not a linear
plot but, instead, is pulsating; different stories occur simultane-
ously but repeatedly collide through complicated coincidence.[42]
Death is not forever, as characters are reborn; hence there is no
real tragedy. Nor is there true choice, since each character has
his own predestined course; and probably of more importance
than the individual personality is a hierarchical relationship
between low and high statuses, exemplified by clown and
prince. Development of a character is less critical than a ritual-
like restoration of sociocosmic equilibrium, and retribution
comes through cosmic mechanism rather than personal struggle
deriving from a sense of sin and self.[43] Although this sketch is
caricature, and countertrends in the direction of linearity, moralism, and other "Western" values have been noted,[44] the pattern would seem broadly to hold for traditional wajang as well
as for other types of syncretist dramatic forms.

The santri contrast with the syncretists, first, in their lesser
development of dramatic form in general; the form most distinctively associated with Javanese Islam is not the dramatic performance but the written word, which includes the scripture itself
as well as biographies, tracts, and other writings. Originating
with bourgeois, trading classes around 1500 A.D., the santri
literary tradition also exemplifies other trends suggestive of a

42. A. Becker (1974); Mangkunegara (1957).
43. Holt (1967, pp. 146, 148).
44. Emmerson (forthcoming); Anderson (1965); J. Becker (1974);
note parallels to trends in rationalization of the *ludruk* (Peacock, 1968).

shift from the Javanism exemplified in the wajang.[45] Santri have contributed the first true Javanese biographies—i.e., a form devoted entirely to narrating the life story of a single individual (by contrast, syncretic plays and legends subsume individual experiences within the wider sociocosmic order)—and the first chronological histories (syncretic legends were less concerned with chronology than with symbolic and classificatory elements, such as clowns, dualistic divisions between left and right, and wajang mythology—elements which are present but diminished in the santri histories). Other santri literary forms include: genealogies that depict commoners as well as kings and nobles; tales of a messianic king, probably derived from the messiah of Islam, the Mahdi; and romance, which portrays the wandering individual hero, such as Panji, Amir Hamzah, or the young man of Giri in the story of Tjentini. Despite syncretic elements remaining, especially in the older literary forms, santri literature in general shows a trend toward individualistic, linear, rationalizing values.

Our task now is to explore whether these broad historical differences between Islamic and syncretic traditions are reflected in the evidence from the Jogja survey and other localized materials.

Children's Stories

Requested to summarize stories that they told their children (HQ III-62), approximately half of the Jogja mothers chose not to do so, usually on the excuse that the child was too young to listen to stories or that the father did the telling. Half did tell a story, however, and these were classified into five genres: folktale (of an animal or village figure), parable (of a Muslim figure who makes a moral point), legend (of an historical syncretist hero), myth (of a god or goddess), and advice (which states a moral precept instead of telling a tale).

Folktales were most frequently of the Kantjil type popular throughout Southeast Asian folk society (both Muslim and

45. Pigeaud (1967, pp. 97, 133, 139, 179); Poerbatjakara (1940).

Buddhist); these feature the mousedeer, Kantjil, a small animal who tricks large, predatory ones as well as humans in order to get out of difficult situations. Legends starred both Hinduist figures of the wajang kulit, such as Ardjuna, and Javanese heroes of syncretist Muslim kingdoms, such as Djoko Tingkir of Demak. Parables told, for example, of Muhammad's honesty. A myth told of Adam's creation of God and of Eve's creation by Adam's rib. An example of advice was: "The child who is diligent and studies hard will become so clever that he is not easily insulted by others."

Wives of reformists (by schooling) most often told parables or gave advice, wives of the traditionalist schooled most often told folktales, and almost all the legends and myths were told by wives of the syncretist schooled.[46]

Content of all stories was broken down into the following categories: *agent*, agent's *goal*, the *agency* used to achieve that goal, the *outcome* of the goal-oriented striving, and the *setting* in which the action occurs. In these terms, several comparisons are suggestive.

Syncretist mothers (so-called by virtue of the schooling and theology of their husbands) told most of the tales with animals as agents, trickery as an agency, *nafkah* (satisfying the basic needs of life) as a goal, and escape or survival as an outcome; these themes were largely derived from the Kantjil stories. Wives of syncretist or Western-schooled husbands also gave most of the examples of tales featuring magical agents, such as goddesses, whereas santri wives gave none. Raw nature as a setting was found most rarely among the tales told by reformist mothers, who most often set their stories in domesticated nature. In a word, the syncretists were more inclined than the santri to tell

46. By husband's schooling, 20% of women with reformist-schooled husbands vs. more than 50% with pesantren-schooled husbands told Kantjil folk tales; 14% of the wives of reformist schooled vs. 3% of wives of syncretist and Western schooled told parables. Around 40% of wives of syncretist schooled vs. 25% or less for other groups told legends and myths.

literally of a "jungle of magic." The contrasts are not, however, absolute, and the complexity of the story-telling context should be noted; for example, some informants recall that even when their mothers were inclined toward stories of the santri type, the abangan layer was transmitted through the tales told by servants.

Popular Stories

The survey method checks on the narrative recollections of the people by asking them to recall tales they have heard or read; a complementary method is to analyze stories as they are performed or written, placing emphasis on encoder rather than decoder, source rather than response. In carrying out this level of analysis, the reformist source selected was the Muhammadijah magazine *Suara Muhammadijah* (Voice of Muhammadijah), and the sample included all short stories appearing in this magazine during 1968—a total of 12. The syncretist source was the popular abangan drama form *ludruk,* and the sample was all examples of the most popular type of plot I had observed during 1962-63—a total of 10.[47] The comparison is one of form as well as content; as has been noted in terms of the larger syncretic and santri traditions, the former are distinguished by their dramas, the latter have tended more toward literature, and certainly this contrast holds for the two groups among whom my observations were carried out; the Muhammadijans I knew did not perform dramas, and the syncretists in this study did not write short stories. As with children's stories, the contents of the two sets of stories were analyzed in terms of *agent, goal, agency, outcome,* and *setting.*

47. Peacock (1968, pp. 104-25); further ludruk analysis cited here is also repeated from this source. It will be noted that this, as other comparisons between santri and syncretist, involves a contrast between working-class and middle-class culture as well as religious orientation. An attempt to match working-class santri culture with merchant-class syncretist culture would be revealing but not representative of the majority of either santri or syncretist types. I am grateful to Charles Markman for making a preliminary comparison of the tales.

The agent in the Muhammadijan stories is a middle-class male (11 stories out of 12), while that in ludruk is a lower-class female (10 out of 10), played by male transvestites. Though this contrast neatly reflects the bourgeois versus proletarian affiliations of the two groups, the supposed mercantile base of Muhammadijah is not apparent; not a single agent in these stories is a businessman, and usually he is white-collar: clerk, teacher, or student. This pattern probably reflects the rising influence of secularly educated, bureaucratically employed youths in the Muhammadijah organization; indeed, such youths edit the magazine in which these stories appear.

The goal of ludruk lower-class characters is marriage to higher-class characters in order to gain higher status. The goal of Muhammadijah characters is to arrive at a morally acceptable decision or resolution.

The agency by which the ludruk protagonist accomplishes her objective is, in an older type of story, luck, and in a newer type, flirtation. The agency of heroes (usually the narrator) in the Muhammadijah stories is persistence (7 out of 12), whereas that of opponents is power, ruthlessness, and irresponsibility. God's will plays a part in 4 Muhammadijah stories, whereas no ludruk story action is specifically guided by God.

The outcome of the "modern" type of ludruk stories is successful marriage of low class to high, whereas the outcome of "traditional" types is incorporation of low class into high through blood kinship. The outcome of 4 of 12 Muhammadijah stories is punishment of bad characters and reward of good; but more important than this theme of retribution is that of achieving moral understanding, which is the outcome of all the Muhammadijah stories.

The setting of the ludruk stories at the end is always collective, whereas that of the Muhammadijah stories is individualist. Ludruk stories end in typical comic fashion with a plurality of characters onstage who celebrate their newly achieved solidarity. The Muhammadijah stories take place in the memory of a single individual, alone both at the beginning and at the end as he reflects on the moral issues exemplified by his experience. More than any other feature, perhaps, this pattern of individual reflection versus collective celebration reflects the short-story versus stage-play form; and of course the story is read alone, while the play has an audience.

Muhammadijah plots expressing these themes are illustrated by the following: "The Last Man," in which the narrator discovers too late that a dying author has been mistreated by a society that failed to recognize his true worth; "Annual Meeting," in which a father's adult children realize they have wronged their father's new wife; "Coming and Going," in which a young man realizes he has returned to his village too late to help his dying grandmother; "Within the Evening," in which a husband realizes he has falsely accused his wife of prostitution, when in fact she was receiving money from her mother to supplement his own inadequate salary; and "Haunted by Shadows," in which the hero realizes he has tortured his wife cruelly, leading to her death:

> Tortured by guilt, he shouted, "I'll go, that's all." He watched his mother. Her face was wet with tears. Her sobbing tore his heart. He stepped outside. Outside he was absorbed into the mysterious and sorrowing grip of the dark night. His native countryside seemed to stare at him. He didn't know his future. In the darkness he could see Bariah's [his dead wife's] smile, which was transformed into sharp jaws yearning to tear him to pieces. . . .

With one exception, these stories end too late to correct the wrong, and the narrator can only weep, pray, and reflect.

Clown and Transvestite[48]

Endeavoring to probe a third realm in the repertoire of Javanese expressive form, it is suggestive to examine two seminal symbols which cut across the literary, dramatic, and musical genres and express categories of belief and value bearing on

48. The following is elaborated in Peacock (in press).

124 MUSLIM PURITANS

the question of psychopathology. These are the clown and transvestite, figures which are beheld differently by syncretists as compared to reformists.

Transvestitism is deeply rooted in the pre-Muslim, pan-Indonesian cosmology, as is revealed by the sacral meaning of transvestite shamans, priests, and kings in cultures as varied as those of Kalimantan, Sulawesi, and the lesser Sundas and Sumatra; the sacrality seems to derive essentially from the tendency of archaic Indonesian mythology to divide the cosmos into male and female divisions, which transvestites mediate and unite.[49] In Java, sexual dualism has ceased to dominate worldview, and the transvestites have generally lost their sacral function, though they retain in imagery and form remnants of the old dualistic meanings; now they are aesthetic and erotic, appearing on the stage and street as actresses and prostitutes.

The clown is less pan-Indonesian, more distinctively Javanese; but like the transvestite, the clown is of sacral status linked to pre-Islamic dualistic cosmologies. Visible on temple reliefs as old as 800 A.D., the clown, like the transvestite, appears in drama. Representing the indigenous Javanese, he plays the servant or underling to some elite type who represents the foreign invasions of Java: the Hindu, the Muslim, or the Westerner. Though a servant, the clown is also a god, superior even to Kresna.[50] Omniscient, omnipotent, he can, whenever he desires, control those he serves. The clown and the transvestite are ironically complementary, in that the transvestite who plasters himself with rich clothing and pseudo-aristocratic roles onstage is of lowly status in life; the clown who plays lowly roles onstage has a sacral cultural status.

Both figures pervade Javanese dance and drama, and fascinate the public. While psychogenetic explanations may partially explain their appeal,[51] cultural analysis would emphasize instead

49. Schärer (1963); Hoek (1949); Needham (1960); Matthes (1872); Holt (1939); Noteboom (1948); Cunningham (1965); de Josselin de Jong (1960); Ras (1973).
50. Kats (1923, pp. 40-1).
51. Amir (1934); Peacock (1968, pp. 71-8).

their linkage to the cosmological and classificatory scheme of Javanese theatre. As Pigeaud has noted, Javanese drama is "imbued with the idea of classification,"[52] and in both classical and popular forms, various clues point to the role of these figures not merely as characters in plots but as symbols in cosmological systems.[53]

What is the cosmology that these figures express? Without delving into the great complexity of the Javanese beliefs or arguing that these figures represent ancient dualisms, one may note two dominant axes in much Javanese syncretist classification: the high/low and the male/female dichotomies, both of which are subsumed under the distinction between culture and nature, as in the terminology *alus/kasar*.[54] High status is more cultural or *alus*, exemplified by the god-king, and low status more natural or *kasar*, exemplified by the peasants in their fields. Male status is more securely linked to the alus realm of spirituality and public culture, females to the body and the home.

Statuses within each opposition, high/low or male/female, are normally conceived as segregated. But under the special circumstances of the sacral, comic, and licentious ritual-dramas, or even commercial plays, integration is permitted. Spectators seem excited by the transvestite's mixing of maleness and femaleness (and of culture and nature, as he constructs feminine illusion atop masculine biology), and they laugh as the clown cleverly reduces high and to low, plays a counterpoint to the high, or proves that actually low is high, in that the servant is a

52. Pigeaud (n.d., p. 236-7).

53. See Peacock (1968, pp. 7-8, 205) on the symbolic as opposed to narrative function of these figures. Compare Holt (1939) and Peacock (1968, pp. 168-9, 205) on the similarity of form between the priestly-related *wandu* of Makassar and the *ludruk* transvestites; and Peacock (1968, p. 207) and Chabot (1950) on their rigid classification. Ling (1968) discusses their conceptualization of self as symbolically female, despite examination proving biological maleness.

54. On the high/low or *alus/kasar* dichotomy, see Peacock (1968, pp. 7-8). On the male/female classification, see Rassers (1959, pp. 126-31).

god.[55] One explanation for the charge the Javanese get from these figures is that in mixing normally segregated cosmic oppositions, they demonstrate an underlying cosmic unity—a condition which, through mysticism and ceremony, the Javanese seek continuously. At a simpler level of interpretation, mixing categories—clowning or transvestitism—*is* syncretism.

Reformist Disapproval—The notion that clown and transvestite are distinctively expressive of syncretism is supported by the negative case; anti-syncretist reformists condemn them.

Historically, one may correlate the extent of santri opposition to these figures with the extent of reformism. Traditionalist santri enjoyed plays featuring clown-servants; Marmaya and Marmade were clown-servants in Menak versions of the Amir Hamzah stories, and the Javanese santri even replaced the warrior uncle of the Prophet with a clown. But Pigeaud regarded such an "element of classification" as less in these Islamized plays than in the Javanized Hindu Ramayana and Mahabharata.[56]

Traditionalist santri also performed plays with transvestites, though Pigeaud confirms that the figure is rarer among santri than among syncretists as an element of importance in himself rather than simply a character in a story.[57] Outside of drama, transvestites also played in santri dances which Pigeaud considers to contain elements of the syncretic "dualism."[58]

Pigeaud believes that staunch santri opposition to transvestitism began in the late nineteenth century, the time of the rise of reformism.[59] Certainly there is evidence of opposition today. Chabot traces the decline of the Makassarese transvestite priests to persecution by Muslims, and a similar fate befell the

55. Peacock (1968, pp. 176-80, 198).

56. Pigeaud (1938, p. 227).

57. Pigeaud (1938, p. 258, and personal communication). Rejection of the transvestite singers reflects aesthetic as well as sexual ideology of santri; see Snouck-Hurgronje (1927b, p. 288) on santri rejection of syncretist aesthetic forms.

58. Pigeaud (1938, p. 479).

59. Pigeaud (personal communication).

Makassarese transvestite in general.[60] Transvestites of the ludruk tell of being chased from home by angry santri fathers.[61] One might imagine that transvestites of santri origin would share the feelings of a homosexual patient described by Adikusomo; he felt that his perversion was a great sin *(dosa)* which would subject him to the punishment of hell, and he felt "suspected, slandered, and persecuted" by the Muslims.[62] Though life histories of transvestites reveal santri origins of some, they make their place not in santri society but in the syncretist theatre, in syncretist communities, and on the street and in the market as prostitutes; I have never seen a transvestite within the circles of the Muhammadijah.

As for the clown, santri opposition is by no means so decisive. Yet owing to their long-standing avoidance of syncretist amusements in general, the reformists give considerably less attention than syncretists to the clowns such as Semar, Petruck, and Gareng. The clown himself is sometimes seen as opposing the spirit of Islam; as one reformist groused, in explaining his hatred of the ludruk: "Islam is not funny." For its part, the syncretist comedy delights in caricature of the stiff and stern Muslim.

Why the opposition between reformist Islam and syncretist clowns and transvestites? Explanations can be given at many levels, beginning with the doctrinal condemnation by Islam of homosexuality and the mixing of male and female through transvestitism. Doctrine does not, however, suffice to explain the reformist suspicion of clowns. A comprehensive explanation views this opposition as grounded in the reformist world-view.

The syncretic symbols, clown and transvestite, derive meaning from a classificatory scheme whose categories they "syncretize" so as to maintain a unity which is imagined as eternal, a permanent reality that underlies the flux of action and is discoverable by mystic meditation. The distinctively santri literary figures are heroes of history—prophet, warriors, and

60. Chabot (1950, p. 153, 20).   61. Peacock (1968, pp. 19-20, 203).
62. Adikusumo (1969, p. 70).

missionaries, whose meaning derives not through expressing eternal unities but through harnessing temporal means to such ends as holy war. The syncretist world-view is classificatory, and its essential unity is demonstrated by the symbolic mixing and inversion of transvestites and clowns. The reformist world-view is rationalizing, and its rationalism is threatened by the outrageous creativity of these symbols.

Comedy, Tragedy, Melodrama

HQ II-31b and HQ II-32 endeavored directly to ask respondents about their choice of certain expressive forms. Our guiding hypothesis was that syncretists would opt more frequently for comedy and melodrama, reformists for the serious and the heroic. The hypothesis was not confirmed. In the first opposition (31b), it was not syncretists but reformist students and reformist leaders (Darol Arqom) who liked comedy the most. In the second opposition (32), the maudlin, stepchild melodramatic plot summary was selected more frequently by the Darol Arqom participants than by anyone else.[63] While a process of compensation could be suggested—that reformists opt for comedy in art because they deprive themselves of it in life—it is also possible that the questions were confusing or the opposition too simply put.

PSYCHOPATHOLOGY

Linearity, egalitarianism, future orientation, and other values have been explored in this study in relation to reformism in numerous spheres. What is the use of exploring these values further through expressive forms and psychopathology, especially when the relation between the values and the expression is tenuous? A first answer is that the expressive forms and psychopathological symptoms reveal emotions that surround these

63. 34–53% syncretists, 36–58% traditionalists, 29–36% reformists, and 44% Darol Arqom chose comedy. 86% Darol Arqom vs. 70–80% of the others chose the maudlin plot.

values. Thus, in the depressive psychoses and in the short stories of the *Suara Muhammadijah*, a sense of guilt is seen to flow from the reformist moralism; this type of feeling has not been expressed so clearly by the other materials.

A second justification, illustrated by the first, is that these materials are distinctly useful in plumbing the depths to which a cultural orientation reaches. If, for example, the values of moralism in reformism are reflected in lip-service ideology or explicit pronouncements alone, one would suspect a shallower psychological penetration than if these values are also reflected in expressions not fully controlled by conscious doctrine—as in the total plot structure of a story, the pattern of narrative characterization, the structure of the relations between clown and transvestite, the symptoms of deeply troubled patients. Because the relation of such expressive areas to a cultural formulation is oblique, the relationship is difficult to demonstrate; for the same reason, its analysis is of value.

Diplomacy and ethics forbade any direct survey inquiry about a respondent's possible psychiatric symptoms. The survey did try to ask indirectly about feelings of sin and guilt (HQ II-28a), suspicions that others are against one (HQ II-28b), and self-pity following passive acceptance of parental decree (HQ II-30a, alt. 2). The direction of reformist response was slightly in the direction expected, toward guilt and paranoia and away from self-pity. Obviously these responses could be interpreted as reflecting *doctrine*, realistically assessing the situation (santri have been something of a persecuted minority), and in other ways expressing patterns other than the psychopathological.

In an effort to get more directly at psychopathology, a brief questionnaire was given to a Javanese psychiatrist at a psychiatric hospital, asking him to estimate roughly the number of santri and syncretist patients who, in his experience, had suffered from each of several conventionally defined psychoses such as depressive disorder, paranoid delusion, and schizophrenia, as well as the distinctive *latah* (see below). In conformity with other censuses of patient population in Indonesian hospitals, however, he could recall virtually no instances of either depression or latah in either category.[64] The survey thus gave no information bearing on the hypothesis that seems plausible in light of the general patterning of Javanese culture—that latah would tend to go with syncretism, depression with Muslim beliefs.

Given the paucity of relevant cases in the hospital population, the next step was to comb the literature and categorize all cases of either latah or depressive disorder according to the patient's cultural affiliation as santri or abangan, where this could be determined.[65] This survey found that all latah cases were among syncretists, all depressive cases among santri; numerous instances of the former were discovered, but only a few of the latter.[66]

Latah

Latah has been the subject of extensive research in the Malayo-Indonesian region, and is found elsewhere too, but in

64. Dr. Triman Prasadio of Karamindjangan hospital, Surabaja, Java, estimates that in 1971 there were 84 male and 79 female syncretists and 20 male and 21 female santri under his care in the psychiatric division (this proportion corresponds with my own impressions during two months of work at Karamindjangan in 1963). Dr. Triman estimates that 2 patients, one of each religious type, were "depressive"; one santri and 5 syncretists (4 female) "paranoid," and the majority of the rest various types of schizophrenia. The proportions correspond to Pfeiffer's (1967) classification in a Sundanese hospital of West Java. I am grateful to Dr. Triman for his kindness in providing the estimate, and to Dr. Thomas Maretzki for his help in arranging it.

65. This search was intended to be exhaustive through 1973, and it included several dozen articles discovered through checking the literature on transcultural psychiatry, the Indonesian and Dutch-language journals dealing with Indonesian psychiatry, and use of a computerized system (MEDLAR) for cataloguing medical references.

66. Concerning the identification of latah and syncretism, H. Geertz (personal communication) has stated that every one of the latah subjects that she discovered in Java (H. Geertz, 1968) was abangan, and examination of relevant portions of her field notes, which she graciously supplied, confirms this statement. Survey of the available literature on

Java it can be interpreted as directly linked to the syncretist ideal conception of self. An obsessive imitation of the speech of others, latah is stimulated by a loud noise. There are no associated delusional or fantasy symptoms, and several researchers suggest a parallel between latah and the Malayo-Indonesian trance in that both actions are outside conscious control. The Javanese latah outbursts include obscenity, usually genital rather than anal. The latah subject is usually an older woman, typically employed as a servant; in Java she is always of Javanese ethnicity and in Malaya of Malay ethnicity, but in neither place Chinese, Arab, or European.[67]

How does latah express the abangan ideal self? While Hildred Geertz provides a telling answer to the question, a similar but more elaborate analysis has been given independently by Setyonegoro, himself a Javanese psychiatrist.[68] Setyonegoro begins by noting a difference between the latah subject and the obsessive-compulsive. The latah's actions are stimulated by shock from outside (note later discussion of the strong Javanese fear of *kaget*, shock which disturbs equilibrium), the obsessive-compulsive's by inner anxiety. Latah is thus interpreted as a response to milieu rather than to inner urges, and Setyonegoro outlines the cultural aspect of that milieu in terms precisely parallel to those set forth already: the Javanese emphasize etiquette, status, indirectness; they are tranquil and patient; and their highly stratified language expresses great concern for hierarchy.

Setyonegoro considers specifically the position of the Javanese house servant in the colonial Dutch Indies—the typical latah. He suggests that such a woman, becoming conscious of her oppressive situation around the age of fifty, protests through

latah, including Yap (1951, 1952, 1962, 1967, 1969), Swettenham (1895), Ellis (1896, 1897), and Van Loon (1927), gives an impression that where a latah subject's religious orientation can be identified, it is syncretic rather than santri.

67. Aberle (1952); Opler (1956, p. 133); Setyonegoro (1970); Provencher (1974, p. 2); H. Geertz (1968, p. 556); Yap (1952, p. 550).

68. Setyonegoro (1970). Cf. H. Geertz (1968).

latah. The outburst is easily excused in the Javanese milieu, because it stems from shock, which is assumed to evoke confusion and violence. Her protest in *ngoko* language is full of obscenity, a mockery of the proper respect through *krama*. Thus latah mocks the Javanese ideals of hierarchy, tranquility, and formality.

Accepting Setyonegoro's analysis, we note also other cultural syncretic elements, for example the push-pull, kinesic training of the child in etiquette and dance. Such social rearing, one would imagine, increases the disposition to imitate bodily motions of another. A second point is that latah is not found in mental hospitals, but instead provides entertainment to bystanders and may even be identified with popular clowns, whose imitative mockery it resembles. Thus, latah is part of the syncretic public culture; as the Javanese poet Rendra termed it, it is "our national disease."[69] Though expressed only by a single sex, class, and religious type, the tendency would seem to mirror broad characteristics of Javanese character.

Depression

The great psychiatrist Kraeplin was struck by the apparent lack of depressive disorder in Java.[70] A half-century later, Pfeiffer draws the same conclusion; he claims to have found only one case in Java of what he terms *schulddepression* or "depression based on guilt," though he also found 8 additional patients who had some sense of having "sinned against God," and these were all either orthodox Muslim or Chinese.[71] The one case of "depression based on guilt" was a santri believing deeply, Pfeiffer states, in the Islamic morality. This patient felt that he had wronged his parents during youth and was untrue to his wife. Failing to believe and obey God, he felt that he had been thrust from Him—the apparent reason for his depression.

A search of the literature revealed two other cases of Indonesians suffering from depression owing to a sense of sin, and these were also orthodox Muslims singled out by an Indonesian

69. Peacock (1968, pp. 242, 160).   70. Opler (1956, p. 464).
71. Pfeiffer (1971, p. 95).

psychiatrist because of their religious preoccupations.[72] The first case was a 30-year-old male who feared that he had syphilis which would affect his pregnant wife's unborn child. A medical examination revealed no trace of syphilis, but the psychiatrist discovered that the patient's Islamic education had taught him to feel strongly that one's sin becomes one's "flesh and blood." He felt his adultery was sinful, and that he as well as his offspring would suffer from it by infection.

The second case was a 40-year-old male, a pious santri merchant who felt so sinful he could not work. The psychiatrist traces this to the patient's powerful, religiously prescribed feeling of obligation toward his parents. When his father became sick in bed, the patient secretly wished him dead, and his depression stemmed from a deep sense of guilt about this.

At present, then, evidence for a relation between reformism and depression is suggestive but scanty.

PERSONALITY

The Ideal Self[73]

Central to the traditional Javanese ideal of self is the concept of harmony. One should remain secure *(slamet)* and calm

72. Aulia (1960). Cf. Honigmann (1967, p. 403) on the cross-cultural association of depression and Christianity for reasons similar to those that engender an association here between depression and Islam: a sense of guilt and sinfulness, deriving in part from religious doctrine or outlook. It is not clear, however, that "sin" *(dosa)* carries a Christian-like meaning even for those under the Islam reformist influence. A prostitute who claimed she was the daughter of a santri, educated in a Muhammadijah school, told me that while she was working as a prostitute she did not pray because she felt unclean, but she planned to resume prayer after she had retired from the trade. Here a wrong action is seen as polluting temporarily rather than as a permanent flaw in character which can be erased only by grace or similarly drastic action, as in the Christian definition of sin. Ritual pollution does not necessarily imply continuity of self through a life history, whereas sin does. This prostitute is obviously an extreme case, however, and certainly not a typical devout santri. Among Aulia's and Pfeiffer's patients, the feelings of guilt seem deep-seated, and the short stories analyzed earlier show a strong sense of guilt for earlier wrongdoings enduring in memory.

73. This analysis follows C. Geertz (1960b, sect. III) and other

(tentram) so as to sustain both an inner and outer harmony, order, and equilibrium. To be avoided is shock *(kaget)*, which causes confusion *(bingung)* and consequent loss of the desired slamet.

While disruption may originate from an outside shock, it may also spring from within. The personality is perceived as balanced between a kind of aestheticized superego and an id, the *alus* and the *kasar*. The alus characterizes the refined, civilized Javanese culture which, when internalized, should ideally control the kasar: the base motives, such as *hawa nafsu* (greed or lust) and *pamrih* (ambition). Though the kasar is controlled, it is never dispelled; in the metaphor of the shadow play, though Ardjuna defeats the monsters they always return.

Should greed, lust, or ambition goad one recklessly toward a goal, the result is either frustration or delight. In syncretist philosophy, both are to be avoided, since they represent disequilibrium. Both ups and downs ruffle the surface of the psyche, thereby opening it up to penetration by spirits, which results in sickness, insanity, or death. Instead of desiring avidly, one should be accepting *(nrima)* and patient *(sabar)*.

It should not be supposed that this passivity represents weakness. On the contrary, it permits the concentration of spiritual force; thus does the *wajang* hero crystalize his rock-hard spiritual shell that repels the leaping monster. This force is mobilized gradually, through meditation and orderly movement. A traditional metaphor is that of the caterpillar creeping over the water; a modern one is Sukarno's Spirit of Revolution, slowly accelerating like an engine building steam, placing emphasis on education rather than industrialization, on symbolic rather than instrumental action, to prepare spiritually for gradual completion of the order.[74]

Pigeaud suggests that the lack of lyric poetry in traditional Javanese literature expresses a lack of individualism,[75] and many

---

sources such as Dipojono (1972), Anderson (1972a), and Mulder (1975), as well as personal observation.

74. See Peacock (1973b, pp. 29-30).

75. Pigeaud (1967).

have stereotyped the Javanese as a collectivist culture with no place for the individual. This view is too simple, as is proved by the rich Javanese vocabulary for self-description and the Javanese powers of introspection apparent in spheres ranging from the mystical to narration of the life history. These powers have gained expression perhaps not in traditional Javanese poetry but certainly in the lyricism of Javanese poets writing in Indonesian, such as Rendra and Toer.

What does seem to hold, however, is the idea that the Javanese self is integrally part of the sociocosmic framework. Notions such as *tjotjok* (harmony) and *petungan*, *kebatinan* (mysticism) and *slametan*, remind us of the Javanese ideal of coordinating self and cosmos. Identity of self and society is exemplified by such practices as changing name when changing status. Through mysticism, ritual, etiquette, the arts, and daily life, the harmony of the sociocosmic order is maintained, and through this the tranquility and security of the self.

If Clifford Geertz' *alus/kasar* opposition suggests polarities in the syncretic ideal of self, Siegel's equally schematic contrast between *akal* (rationality) and *hawa nafsu* (instinct) highlights a similar polarity in the santri conception.[76] *Alus* controls *kasar* by imposing a static, tranquil surface atop animal impulses that gurgle underneath. *Akal* controls such instincts by harnessing them to a dynamic process of rationalizing means to achieve ends, in practical spheres, such as trade, as well as in knowledge. The contrast is illustrated by an exposition I heard (and saw) by a syncretic mystic and a Muhammadijan, both using colored charts. The mystic represented instinct as black, and cultured demeanor as white, emphasizing that instinct is disruptive: "It explodes the atomic bomb." The Muhammadijan represented instinct as colorless, and culture (depicted as both rationality and morality) as blue, and he emphasized that instinct can be harnessed: "It can fire a rocket." The Muhammadijan sees culture and instinct as in a means–end rather than oppositional relationship, as instrumental rather than categorical. The reformist conception is akin to Weber's rationalizing of means in

76. Siegel (1969).

relation to ends, as in Calvinist-capitalism. The syncretist philosophy is more akin to Weber's Hinduism, an asceticism for the sake of sheer spirituality, to suppress animal desires and escape into a spiritual order, there to concentrate sacral energies.

The santri ideal resembles the syncretist, however, in its ritualism. Instinct is not sublimated merely to rationality but also moralistically controlled by the Islamic law (sjariah, especially in its ritual aspect, ibadat). Fasting, praying, adhering methodically to those norms which he is continuously rationalizing into a strict ethical code, the santri necessarily suppresses those sensuous impulses which do not fit.

Motivation

Given these generalized and idealized conceptions of the syncretist and santri selves, how are they expressed in motivational dispositions of the individual? The question is difficult to answer partly because of the difficulty of separating the ideological from the motivational; in asking respondents questions, it is difficult to distinguish expressions of "genuine feeling" from statements of what is culturally proper. The Jogja survey certainly did not achieve any sharp differentiation between the ideal and the motivational; but questions most directly related to the "self" could be grouped along a continuum. At one extreme were questions that asked explicitly about cultural ideals, using the native terms by which these are labeled. At the other extreme were questions that described concrete motives and behaviors. In between were motives and behaviors concretely portrayed, but known to directly reflect ideological prescriptions.

The majority of all groups, reformists, traditionalists, and syncretists, affirmed allegiance to traditional "Javanese" terms that explicitly describe concepts of the ideal self, including nrima (passive acceptance), sabar (patience), ichlas (stoic dedication).[77] Reformists differed from the other groups only in their

77. Around 90% of all groups affirmed ichlas and sabar, while over 80% of household heads and 70% of students affirmed nrima. For an effort at analyzing similar Javanese values by survey method, see Koentjaraningrat (1969 and n.d.).

slightly greater tendency to disavow nrima and (by Darol Arqom respondents) to accept ichlas. The emphasis on ichlas was also manifested in another response to HQ II-31a, where reformists by membership and in Darol Arqom led all others in their claim to accept "with a heart that is ichlas" the theft of their goods. This reformist emphasis was not originally anticipated; ichlas was at first interpreted in the meaning that it seems to have among syncretists, as rather like *nrima* in denoting a passive letting-go, an acceptance of loss.[78] In interviews and various writings, however, it became clear that ichlas has a different meaning among the santri, and one that is integral to their Islamic subculture. For santri, ichlas denotes not so much passive acceptance as a stoic, steadfast, sincere fulfillment of obligation, whether to one's cause, teacher, or duty. If one is acting with ichlas, misfortune or loss is easier to bear—but this bearing of loss is not the primary meaning of the term.

HQ II-26 through 32 and SQ 24 through 27 endeavor to express basic personality dispositions through pairs of statements. Each pair was designed to contrast a rationalist orientation (in terms of Weberian theory adapted to Javanese society) with a traditionalist one. These oppositions were, as some respondents observed, not logical oppositions; instead, they were designed as oppositions of emotional attitude.

We should first note, and for psychological analysis rather discount, the pairs where the choices seemingly express Islamic ideology rather than motivational disposition. These items would seem to include the view that one's life is a plan in accord with God's commandment (HQ II-30c); the desire to die in a desert, close to God (30b); a belief that drinking alcohol is always sinful (27c); and a professed concern for mother rather

---

78. This is the meaning given *ichlas* within a syncretist or general Javanese context by C. Geertz (1960b, p. 240) and Koetjaraningrat (1969, p. 43). But Anderson (1972b, pp. 5-8) and Iskandar (in his Malay language dictionary) give it more the santri meaning of sincere and steadfast devotion, as in a statement I heard by a Muhammadijan: "After preaching one night in Garoet, the next night in Tasik Malaju, I felt not fatigue but *ichlas*." Muhammadijans emphasize this meaning of steadfast devotion.

than father (27a). The explicitly Islamic basis of the first three choices is obvious; and reformists, whether defined by education, theology, or membership, did tend more frequently than other groups to select these.[79] And factor analysis showed that, of the personality pairs, these responses most highly correlate with the "Islamic ethic" complex. Motive is difficult to separate from doctrine here, since Islam explicitly teaches that one should obey God, have faith in Him at time of death, and avoid alcohol. The fourth statement, concerning the mother and father, may also reflect doctrine, since several respondents mentioned that they chose "mother" because in the Qur'an, Muhammad called the name of his mother three times before uttering that of his father.

Other choices would seem more likely to reflect motivational dispositions rather than direct doctrinal prescription. The reformists by schooling more frequently than any other group preferred work over socializing (HQ II-26a); were more concerned about planning (29a-1) than about the opinions of kinfolk, neighbors, and friends (29a-2); resented interruption (30a-1), in contrast to feeling self-pity upon passively accepting parental dominance (30a-2); and were more apt to feel guilty and sinful (28a).[80]

Reformists by theology desire association with famous people more than intimate friendship (29c-2), and more than other groups they express willingness to pull up stakes and move if profits are high elsewhere (28c).[81]

Reformists by membership tend more than others to see

79. 84–90% reformists, 77–87% traditionalists, 43–72% syncretists selected the "life as plan" statement; 90–100% reformists, 85–95% traditionalists, 77–92% syncretists chose to die alone but with God; 80–88% reformists, 65–91% traditionalists, 27–61% syncretists believe drinking always sinful; 17–26% reformists, 13–33% traditionalists, 8–16% syncretists would satisfy mother.

80. Work over socializing was chosen by 84% reformist schooled vs. 67–78% others; desire to plan, 87% reformists vs. 77–80% syncretist or Western schooled; dislike interruption, 96% reformists vs. 75–71% others; feeling sinful, 78% santri vs. 64% syncretist and Western schooled.

81. By theology, 62% reformists desire to associate with famous

themselves as stubbornly defending their opinions in favor of keeping smooth relations (26b). This "stubborn individualism" was even more frequently claimed by the Darol Arqom participants, who were the only respondents to choose this alternative more often than "good relations." The Darol Arqom participants were also more apt than the other groups to stress calmness of heart (a reflection of an aspect of ichlas?) over rewards or prestige (26c); to hold a paranoid attitude (28b) rather than homesickness; to emphasize planning all of one's activities (29a); to prefer to go hungry rather than beg (31c-1); and to continue a project even if someone else disapproved (31c-2).[82]

---

people vs. less than 50% syncretists, and 77% reformists vs. 63–65% others are willing to move for profit. Also, 83% reformists by theology oppose drinking, vs. 27% syncretists; 78% reformists vs. 45% syncretists feel sinful; 95% reformists vs. 77% syncretists choose to die in the desert; 77% reformists vs. 43% syncretists believe life is a mission.

82. By membership, 36% reformists vs. 25% others defend their opinions; 87% reformists vs. only 36% syncretists regard drinking as absolutely wrong; 81% reformists vs. 54% syncretists feel sinful; 85% reformists vs. 68% syncretists see life as a mission.

In light of the argument that Muhammadijan informants have themselves expressed to me, that the madrasah is more rationalizing than other types of Islamic schools, it is interesting that within the student sample only the madrasah students exhibited distinctive tendencies in choice of ethos statements. They prefer study to socializing (78% of them vs. 65% others); they feel sinful (84% vs. 71–75% others); they prefer famous people to close friendship (46% vs. 17–33% others); and they prefer comic to sad stories (75% vs. 58% others). These madrasah students' tendencies are all in the santri / reformist / "rationalist" direction as expressed by the household or Darol Arqom sample.

Similarly, in comparisons between adult respondents who have been educated in madrasah as opposed to pesantren or Dutch elementary schools, madrasahs were generally associated with the more rationalistic, reformist, and Islamic orientations. For example, compared to the pesantren educated (31 respondents), the madrasah educated (26 respondents) were 96% (vs. 84% pesantren) for carrying out God's commandment; 92% (vs. 63%) opposed to being interrupted; and 52% (vs. 29%) claimed to have married for love. Compared to the Dutcheducated (110 respondents), the madrasah alumni were more likely to oppose drinking (95% vs. 53% Dutch schooled), and were more likely to have been circumcised before age 10 (38% vs. 18% Dutch schooled).

This rationalizing tendency of the madrasah is suggestive not only

Reformists defined by any single criterion—schooling, theology, or membership—did not always have the highest frequency of "rationalist" motivations for all questions, but reformists defined by one or another of these criteria had the
highest frequency of such choices on 12 of the 16 "personality"
pairs (HQ II-26 through 31, excluding 31b, which was considered with respect to "expressive form"). No other single group—
syncretist, traditionalist, or Western—had so high an overall
"rationalist" score.[83] There seems to emerge, then, a kind of
rationalist or "Protestant" ethos among the reformists: a sense of
mission, loyalty to God, individualism, feelings of guilt, paranoia, openness to mobility, inclination toward sustained action
(resentment of interruption), and emphasis on planning. Two of
the four exceptions (26c and 31a) to the expected "Protestant"
ethos could be explained by the distinctively Islamic emphasis
on ichlas. It should be noted, however, that on virtually all
questions, *all* groups veered more toward "rationalist" than
"traditionalist" responses, and the reformists simply show a

because Muhammadijans themselves single out the madrasah as superior to their government-style (SD, SMP, SMA) schools in producing
such values, but also in light of the earlier query (Chapter 3) about the
distinctive contribution of Muhammadijan schooling to the reformist
orientation; the madrasah is closer than other schools to the pesantren,
which has been found to engender a "radical" attitude later expressed by
reformist ideology.

83. In explaining the overall rationalist rather than traditionalist
tendencies, one should consider whether "demand characteristics" of the
schedule perhaps biased respondents toward giving the reformist or
rationalist rather than syncretist or traditionalist values; traditionalist
stereotypes may be denied as applicable to oneself when stated explicitly, though observation would reveal applicability in many circumstances. Also note that, unlike observation, the survey method is poorly
designed to take account of context; there are doubtless contexts within
which syncretist values would be affirmed by the syncretists and
contexts where they are suppressed, and these "ethos" items ask for
simple affirmation or denial. Despite these drawbacks, however, it must
be noted that overall differences do appear between the syncretists and
santri types.

slight but consistent edge in the rationalist tendencies that generally characterize the Jogjakarta sample.

THE REFORMIST CHARACTER

The traditional syncretist personality should ideally be calm
and orderly, avoiding both external shock and internal drives
that disturb order, lead toward ups and downs, and open the self
to penetration by spirits. Though conceptualized by introspection and terminology, this identity is not differentiated from a
sociocosmic order that defines self as status and status as cosmology; through speech, posture, and manners, the entire psy-
cho-sociocosmic complex is maintained. Syncretic psychopath-
ologies negate this ideal, as in *latah*. Initiated by shock, latah
mocks precisely those values of orderliness, tranquility, manners, status, and hierarchy that characterize the proper syncretist self and maintain its sociocosmic framework.

The reformist substitutes *akal* for *alus*—that is, replaces the
syncretist refinement with a certain rationality. The two categories operate similarly: to control disruptive motivations.
Where the syncretist rarifies these drives through glossy cultural
surface (language, etiquette, arts), the reformist tends more to
channel them toward goals. Yet for the santri reformist, *achlak*
(morality) is as dominant as akal, and he also represses his
drives by a heavy moralism which, as is revealed in his short
stories and his mental illness, as well as in the "ethos" questions
on the Jogja survey, evokes feelings of sinfulness and guilt.
While maintaining some commitment to such central ideals of
the Javanese character as *sabar*, *ichlas*, and *nrima*, the reformist
also leads in a motivational thrust toward a certain rationalism
common to all of the Javanese, expressed in emphasis on work,
planning, and sustained effort rather than sociability. (See Table
4). This rationalizing tendency at the level of motive is part of a
reform of the sociocosmic structure in the direction of egalitarianism, transcendence of primary solidarities, and the cultural
purification of animism, ritualism, and the repetitive-cyclical
framework already described.

TABLE 4.
Features of Javanese Muslim Reformist Character

SOCIAL VALUES

Less hierarchical:
   Fewer noble and traditional Islamic titles, more academic titles
   Less veneration of father, and less memory of father as venerable
   Favor a larger role for women in the mosque

Less communal: *(local)*
   Fewer village or neighborhood memberships, and more nonlocal,
      nonfamilial memberships
   More cosmopolitan regional and ethnic experience
   Less practice of *slametans* (in household), and more prayers (in
      mosque)
   Attitudes emphasizing work, study, and God over socializing; pref-
      erence for association with famous figures over friendship, and
      for building society over building the family

EXPRESSIVE FORM

Textual, biographical, and historical (more than dramatic, ceremonial,
   and mythical) traditions
Children are told parables more than folktales, myths, and legends
Popular stories emphasize personal reflection on moral dilemmas
   (rather than striving for high status through marriage)
Clowns and transvestites (as symbols of classificatory world-view)
   are negated

PSYCHOPATHOLOGY

Less *latah*
More depression

PERSONALITY

Islamic Ethic:
   View life as a mission in accord with God's command; desire to die
      in desert close to God; condemn drinking of alcohol; concerned
      with mother more than father

Reformist Ethos:
   Emphasize work over socializing, and planning over opinions of
      kin, neighbors, or peers; resent interruption; feel guilty and
      sinful; willing to move where profits are higher; stubbornly stick
      to own opinion; dedicated and stoic *(ichlas)*

5

Singapore

WHAT are the geographic boundaries of the reformist psychology detected in Jogjakarta? While Jogja remains the heartland of reformist culture, the Malay areas outside Indonesia are now on the edge. What has been the fate of reformist culture and psychology here?

During our brief treatment of this peripheral region, several related factors should be kept in mind: first, the role of culture and history (Malaya and Indonesia are culturally similar, but have undergone different histories since the early twentieth century when they shared in the advent of Islamic reformism); second, the role of organization (a strong Islamic organization is present in Malaya and lacking in Singapore); third, the role of urbanization (Singapore is urban and the Malay sample is more rural).

The larger objective is simply to explore the reformist psychology in a different milieu.

MUSLIM ETHNIC GROUPS IN SINGAPORE[1]

The island-nation of Singapore covers an area of approximately 217 square miles and boasted a 1970 population of some

1. See Chua (1964), Tan (1967), and the Yearbook of Statistics, Singapore (1967) for census data; Baginda (1959) on the Baweanese (colloquially known as Boyanese); Johar (1961) on the Javanese; Wahie (1959) and Loh (1963) on the Arabs. Unfortunately, the major published

143

2 million, the majority (1,427,000) Chinese, but a large minority (est. 350,000) Muslim. Most of the Muslim population are Malay (276,000 in 1966), plus an estimated 5,000 Arabs and the Muslim portion of some 156,000 Indians and Pakistanis. The so-called Malay group includes numerous immigrants from Indonesia, notably some 35,000 from Java, 20,000 from Bawean (a small island near Java), and smaller numbers from other islands. The "true" Malays originate from the peninsula, and can usually be distinguished from the immigrants by such features as their traditional dress, while other features distinguish the immigrants from each other. But all of these groups share cultural traits (Malayo-Indonesian) and an economic status (low) which place them in opposition to their Muslim brothers from the west —the Arabs, Indians, and Pakistanis.

Originating from Southern Arabia (Hadramaut, Yemen, and Mecca), many of the Singapore Arab families are now fifth or sixth generation. Owing to intermarriage with Malay and Indonesian women, the Arabs have absorbed local traits and genes, but they retain a strong Arab identity. In part, this is because the intermarriage is traditionally between Arab males and local females, so that the family name and title ("Sayed," descendant of the prophet) is retained as it passes from father to son (an Arab woman, known as "Sherifa," should ideally not marry a non-Sayed). Based on this patriliny, the Arabs differ notably from the Malays and Indonesians in that they boast great and powerful families dominant in the economy and Muslim community. They have donated mosques and dispensaries and built religious schools—the two most notable being the Alsagoff Madrasah, built in 1912 and now for girls, and the Aljunied Madrasah, built in 1927, for boys. Arabs founded the All-Malaya Muslim Missionary Society, which is a center for study and worship in the Singapore Muslim community, and they are a force in the "council of Islamic religion" (Majlis Ugama Islam) which is the Singapore government body empowered to oversee Muslim affairs.

---

work on Singapore Indians, Arasaratnam (1970), de-emphasizes Muslims, focusing instead on Hindus.

Like the Arabs, the Pakistani and Indian Muslims tend to be wealthy leaders in the Islamic community, though they have not founded such prominent dynasties. Both the president and the secretary-treasurer of the All-Malaya Missionary Society were, in 1970, Pakistani. In the Singapore Muslim community of 1970, the Malays (including Indonesians) held the few official government offices (*kathi*, president of the sjariah court, president of the Majlis Ugama Islam, and *mufti*), while the Arabs and Pakistanis held power and prestige in the private spheres of economy and religion.

REFORMISM IN SINGAPORE[2]

Origins

Singapore in 1901 was a city of 228,555 persons, of whom 72 percent were Chinese. The stable Muslim population included some 23,000 peninsular Malays, 12,000 immigrants from Indonesia, 1,000 Arabs, and 600 *jawi peranakan* (children of marriages between Malay and Indian). Itinerant Muslims included sea-going Malay and Indonesian traders, the 7,000 or so Indonesian pilgrims traveling to Mecca annually via Singapore, and agents who shuttled between Singapore and Mecca, guiding the journeys of the pilgrims. Then as now, the Arabs were the elite of the Singapore Muslim population, owing both to wealth and to alleged kinship to the Prophet. The *jawi peranakan*, who dominated Malay journalism and publishing, ranked next to the Arabs. The menially employed Malays ranked at the bottom, an economically depressed and educationally inferior class largely of rural origins in the midst of an urban milieu dominated by aggressive and alien peoples.

In 1906, a new periodical in the Malay language entitled *Al-Imam* (The Leader) was published in Singapore. *Al-Imam* confronted the cause of Malay disorientation and deprivation and proposed a cure: Muslim reformism. Corruption of Islam by Malay syncretism must cease, and understanding must be

2. Roff (1967) is the major source for this section, but see also Bador (1964) and Zaki (1965).

sought through self-analysis of scripture *(idjtihad)* rather than from dictates by teachers representing the medieval schools of law. Madrasahs should replace pesantren (known in Malaya as *pondok*), and a general modernization and upgrading of Malayo-Muslim society must take place.

Spreading onto the peninsula, this reformist or Kaum Muda ideology met resistance from two sources. The first opponent was the extensive bureaucracy for governing Islam which by the early twentieth century had been established in the Malay states. Most states had a religious council of some description, had placed the practice of Islam under the authority of the sultanate, and employed such officials as *kathi* and *mufti* to represent both orthodox (syncretic) Islam and the established hierarchy of society. These court-centered, state-governing religious officials prevented Kaum Muda teachers from acquiring government positions and generally curtailed their activities.

The other major opposition to Kaum Muda derived from the village religious official *(ulama)*. Typically pondok-educated, serving as prayer leader and teacher, organizer of local mystical cults, overseer of slametan-like life-cycle feasts, and allied with the local spirit-doctor, the rural ulama was the pillar of traditionalist (Kaum Tua) Islam in village Malaya. With the arrival of a madrasah-educated, Singapore-exposed Kaum Muda teacher, schism was inevitable and frequently divided entire villages. These disputes seem to have reached their climax in the twenties and thirties. After that, the Kaum Muda became politicized and the impetus of Malay change moved out of the sphere of Islam and into the hands of nationalists.

Reformism in Singapore in 1970

Soon after arrival in Singapore in July 1970, I visited the Pakistani secretary of the All-Malaya Muslim Missionary Society, and in the course of the interview inquired about the Muhammadijah in Singapore. He replied:

It is an offshoot of Muhammadijah in Indonesia, which is opposed by NU there. It has Malay leadership here, unlike other organizations which have mainly Arab-Pakistani leadership.

A visit to the Muhammadijah office confirmed the "Malay" leadership, in the person of an elderly man of Sumatran descent, and the Malay settlement location (inside a complex of small houses behind an alley leading from a row of Chinese stores on the road to the airport at Paya Lebar). The branch has no formal affiliation with Muhammadijah in Indonesia, although it draws on the literature of that organization and professes its essentially Kaum Muda philosophy. A major difference between the Singapore and Indonesian Muhammadijah is the lack of businessmen among the reported 200 or so Singapore members.

Aside from Muhammadijah, the other major Muslim "reformist" organization in Singapore is the Ahmadiyya. Unlike the Indonesian-based Muhammadijah, Ahmadiyya has branches all over the world, with headquarters in Pakistan. Because Ahmadiyya claims that its own founder, Ghulam Mirza Ahmat, replaces Muhammad as prophet for this age, many Singapore Muslims consider the movement outside the fold of Islam; certainly its doctrine is not of the core Kaum Muda, although the concept of reform of Islam is central. Like Muhammadijah, its membership is reportedly around 200, only 30 or so of whom appear at any one service in the tin-roofed mosque.

By generous estimate, then, no more than 1-2% of the Singapore Muslims belong to Ahmadiyya or Muhammadijah; in the random sample of Muslim male household heads to be considered shortly, the percentage of members was precisely 1%. Nor do these or other reformist organizations equal in influence that of the more traditionalist Muslim organizations of Singapore: Majlis Ugama Islam, the sjariah court, or the All-Malaya Muslim Missionary Society. In short, Islamic reformism is not prominent as an organized movement in Singapore today.

Yet there exist, largely among the religious teachers, Singapore Muslim *individuals* with well articulated reformist ideology. And owing perhaps to Singapore's reformist history and crossroads location, the majority of Singapore Muslims seem

aware of the broad meaning of the opposition between reformism and traditionalism; this was indicated both by informal
interviews and by survey response.

THE SINGAPORE SURVEY

The domiciles of the Malays who comprise most of Singapore's Muslims are concentrated in certain areas of the island.
The method of carrying out a survey of Muslim male household
heads in Singapore was to select a number of points within these
Malay areas, and to instruct each interviewer to walk from a
starting point assigned him, calling at every house until the
quota for that walk had been achieved (the quota for each walk
being 6 interviews with Muslim male household heads over
twenty years of age, married, with wife present and available for
interview). This sampling procedure was carried out until 400
Muslim males and their wives had been interviewed. Each
interview lasted approximately one and a half hours, guided by
a schedule (see Appendix C) comparable to that used in Jogjakarta but shorter, with questions adapted to the Singapore
milieu and in the Malay language (except for some Pakistanis
and Indians, who were interviewed in English).

As in the Jogjakarta household survey, the Singapore survey (and also the Kedah survey to be discussed in the next
chapter) focused on the male household head; only questions 37-
58 on part III of the Singapore Household Survey schedule (see
Appendix C) were directed to the wife. Accordingly, except in
the case of these questions which focus on child-rearing, the
responses noted come from male household heads.

The interview schedule was constructed with the aid of
Muslim informants, after approximately four months of fieldwork, pre-tested through interviews with Malay, Indian, and
Arab Muslims carried out by myself as well as others, and
administered by Muslim interviewers. A comparison of the
survey statistics with censuses of the total population of adult
Singapore Malays suggests that the sample and the population

are similar in ethnic, occupational, educational, and age characteristics.

A short version of the interview survey was administered as a questionnaire (Appendix D) to Muslim students in the three types of Singapore schools that Muslims attend: "integrated" (largely Malay language), English, and the madrasah.[3] As in Jogjakarta, for each type one commonly acknowledged the "best" school, plus one other, was chosen. The prestigious English school selected was the central-city Raffles Institute, the other was suburban Siglap Secondary. The boys' madrasah selected was the Aljunied school, the girls' madrasah the Al-Ma'arief. The prestigious "integrated" (Malay-oriented) school selected was the Sang Nila Utama, while the other was Pasir Panjang. In the English schools, the Muslims formed a minority of students at the time the questionnaire was administered (in the spring term of 1970, Raffles Institute had a total enrollment of 1883, which included 99 Muslim boys and 2 Muslim girls; Siglap Secondary had an enrollment of 1667, of whom 617 were Muslims). The enrollment of the Malay schools was overwhelmingly Malay and Muslim, as was that of the two madrasahs. The total sample of Singapore Muslim students surveyed was 481, divided into 257 English school pupils, 119 Malay integrated school pupils, and 105 madrasah pupils.

In Singapore, neither schools nor prominent organizations explicitly profess the reformist orientation; hence the primary classification of extent of reformism of household heads was not by schooling or organizational membership, but by theology. Theological attitude was indicated by questions II-2 and 3 on the Singapore schedule, which were almost identical to HQ II-2 and 3 on the Jogjakarta survey schedule. Those who chose alternative 2 on either 2 or 3, or on both, were classified as traditionalist; those who chose alternative 1 on both 2 and 3 were classified as reformist. The reformist category includes only those individuals with a pure or consistent commitment,

3. Concerning the Islamic school system in Singapore, see Hussain (1965-6), and on the other schools, Hussain (1969).

whereas the traditionalist category includes both the consistently traditionalist and the "syncretists" who indicate divided loyalties between traditionalist and reformist tenets.

Students were classed as reformist or traditionalist according to whether they gave the reformist or traditionalist response to SQ 17 and then according to school presently attended, since madrasah students almost unanimously gave the reformist response on this question.

Of the household sample of 400, 65 were theologically reformist and 324 traditionalist. Of the school sample of 481, 280 were reformist and 201 traditionalist.

Cultural Orientations

The Singapore Muslim's beliefs are essentially like those of the Jogjakarta santri's: God is omnipotent, Muhammad is His Prophet, the Qur'an is sacred, and the five pillars are ideally obligatory. The mosque (of which there were 62 in Singapore) and the prayer house are the centers of worship, and they differ from those of Jogja in appearance, the lesser frequency of women present, and the greater tendency to be built on sacred land donated by rich Arab, Pakistani, and Indian merchants. A round of celebrations rather like those of the traditionalist santri of Java centers around the mosque; these include the chanting of the Kitab Berzanji on The Prophet's birthday and narration of His ascent to heaven (Mir'adj) on the 27th day of Rajab (seventh month of the Muslim calendar). The year climaxes with the day of ending the fast, which has been celebrated for a month by an extra prayer, Terawih. Other celebrations are the paying of tithes on Idul Fitri, distribution of meat to the poor on Idul Adha, and Hari Raya Hadji, when families gather at the docks to bid their goodbye to relatives departing on the pilgrimage.

Beneath the Muslim layer, the Singapore Malays retain to. varying degrees animistic customs that broady resemble those in Java and elsewhere in Southeast Asia. Spiritual energy *(semangat)* is everywhere. When captured or contained, it can produce a holy shrine *(kramat)* that promises blessings; when floating loose, it is dangerous and manifested in ghosts or spirits *(hantu)* that enter the body of the vulnerable, perhaps stimulated by a sorcerer and cured by the medicine man, the *bomoh* who is like the Javanese *dukun*. Singapore Malays are quite aware of the distinction between their *adat* (custom) and their *ugama* (religion).[4]

Like the Jogjakartans, virtually everyone in the Singapore sample (99%) claimed to believe in heaven and hell (HQ I-65), thus establishing themselves as part of Islam; and most ask forgiveness on the day celebrating the ending of the fast (HQ II-11), thus establishing their commonality with other Southeast Asia Muslims. Another commonality among the Singaporean and Jogjakartan Muslims is the view that performing the five prayers is the most important moral action. (In Singapore, the question HQ I-66, was phrased negatively: Which omission is the worst sin?) Both reformists and conservatives report great regularity in performance of this daily affirmation of Muslim identity (HQ I-70).

In Jogjakarta, deviants from this prayer-pattern were the syncretists; in Singapore, they are the English schooled, who resemble the Dutch schooled of Jogjakarta in being the most likely of any group defined by schooling to consider faith in God or spiritual communication with God more important than the daily prayers (HQ I-66).[5] Singapore reformists were more likely than traditionalists to veer toward this "Western" direction of

4. On Islam in Singapore, see Djamour (1966) and Kechik (1961). On Malay Islam in general, see S. H. Al-Attas (1963a, 1968a), Kessler (1974), Wilder (1968), Winzeler (1970), and Zaki (1965). On Malay *adat* in general, see Banks (n.d.), Benjamin (1974), Endicott (1970), and Skeat (1967).

5. 52% of the Malay schooled and 59% of the madrasah schooled ranked the "five prayers" first, compared to only 38% of the English schooled. 14% of the English schooled vs. 5–6% of the madrasah and Malay schooled considered "not spiritually communicating with God" the worst sin, and 48% of the English schooled considered "not having faith" worst. Cf. Tamney (n.d.), whose survey found the experience of close contact with God greater among Southeast Asian Protestants than Muslims, but also greater among Sumatrans than Singaporeans of any faith.

ranking failure to communicate with God as the worst sin,[6] and they also differed from Jogja reformists by their stronger emphasis upon "praying to God when desired" (HQ I-66, II-4).[7] Thus, the Singapore reformists tend more than the Jogjakarta reformists toward a "Protestant Western" pattern of devotionalism and away from the ritualism of orthodox Islam. The devotionalism perhaps reflects the fact that Singapore reformism is not an organized movement but a personal philosophy. And Singapore is, after all, a more cosmopolitan, industrial, Western milieu than Jogjakarta.

While the Singapore survey did not provide for a detailed check on whether the reformist is more prone than the traditionalist to reject particular beliefs in animism, one can infer that since a defining characteristic of reformism is the desire to purge Islam of animistic adat (HQ II-2), this is the case.

In the Singapore sample, only a minority of persons in any group recalled an event in Muhammad's biography that had made an impression on them when young (HQ II-8). The lowest percentage of recall was from the English schooled (17%), the highest from the madrasah schooled (36%). The categories of event recalled were rather like those abstracted from the Jogja responses, even though the two sets of responses were categorized by different coders.[8] The Singapore categories were: (1) Muhammad's childhood; (2) Muhammad's writing of the Qur'an dictated by Gabriel; (3) Muhammad's flight from Mecca to Medina (Hijrah); (4) Muhammad's hiding in a cave during that flight; (5) God's turning day into night in order to prevent Muhammad's pursuers from capturing him; (6) the Badr wars;

6. 12% reformists vs. 4% traditionalists considered "failure to communicate" worst.

7. The ratio of favoring fixed over spontaneous prayer was 77 to 23 for reformists vs. 89 to 9 for traditionalists.

8. I myself coded the Jogjakarta data, while a Singapore Malay coded the Malay data. Dr. Hind Khattab, the Egyptian daughter of a Muslim religious teacher in Cairo, independently coded the Malay responses (which had been translated into English) and arrived at virtually the same categories as the Malay coder, which in turn resembled my own categories for the Jogjakarta data.

(7) Muhammad's ascent into heaven (Isra); (8) his approach to God to ask him to reduce the prayer from fifty to five (Mir'adj); (9) Muhammad's being threatened by an enemy murderer whom he forgave; (10) Muhammad's missionary activity; and (11) Muhammad's miracles, such as opening his chest and washing his heart.

The reformists in Singapore resembled those in Jogja in that they were more likely than the traditionalists to recall the Hijrah and the Badr wars—a focus which accords with reformist evangelism and struggle.

Social Orientations

Malay culture is generally less hierarchical than the Javanese, at least in Singapore. The Malay language is not as stratified, manners are not as formal, and the Hinduization has never been as strong. Nor are the royalty and sultan who provide an aristocratic overlay on the peninsula visible in Singapore, where the old sultan's palace at Kampong Glam has become a tenement slum overrun by chickens, beggars, and peddlers. The difference between the two cultures, Javanese and Malay, remains even among those who have long resided in Singapore—exemplified in kinship terminology. Singapore Javanese children designate the age status of parents whenever they use kinship terminology: a cousin who is a younger sibling to one's parent is *adik sapupu* instead of simply *sapupu*. The Singapore Malay would simply address the first cousin as *abang* or *kakak* (brother or sister), and a second cousin as *abang saudara* or *kak saudara*, distinguishing sex but not age.[9]

Given the rather egalitarian stream in Singapore Malay culture, Islam in some ways adds hierarchy instead of equality. An example is the use of the term *Sayed* for descendants of the Prophet; traditionally and even today, Malays, to a greater extent than is true in Java, have venerated the Arabs who hold such a title. A second example is the status of women, who traditionally have been more subordinate among the patrist Arabs and Pakistanis than among the Malays and Javanese. This

9. Djamour (1965, p. 28).

situation may help explain a reversal of relationship in Singapore and Jogja; while the majority of both reformists and
traditionalists favored a larger role for women in the mosque
(HQ II-6), the Singapore reformists were less open to this change
than the traditionalists,[10] whereas the reverse was true in Jogja.
The difference could be associated with the generally more
patrist orientation of the reformists in Singapore. For example,
they were more likely than traditionalists to see the father as the
strongest influence on their domestic life, whereas the relatively
matrist Javanese reformist was more likely to see the mother as
the dominant influence. And this patrism in turn may reflect the
greater influence of the Arab and Pakistani model in Singapore
reformism.

The Malay and Javanese both idealize communal solidarity,
personified by the village, the *kampung*. Even in urban Singapore, Malays prefer to live in their kampung settlements of small
houses rather than in the cheaper high-rise apartments. While
these neighborhoods are not formally organized units of the
government in the fashion of Jogjakarta, they do tend to be
ethnically homogeneous and centered around a mosque. At
higher levels, the Malayo-Muslim identity (which, as we have
seen, embraces in certain levels of contrast the Arabs, Indians,
and other Muslims) is maintained within the pluralistic society
of Singapore by a kind of communalism foreign to the Javanese
society of Jogjakarta. This communalism[11] identifies ethnicity
and religion *(bangsa lan ugama)*, which is to say Malayness and
Muslimness.

In 1970 the Muslim/Malay identity upheld by the political
party PKM (Partai Kesatuan Melayu) stood in contrast to the
Chinese-oriented Singapore party. The identity between Islam
and Malayness is suggested by a visit to PKM headquarters
reported in my field notes.

10. 17% of Singapore reformists vs. 7% traditionalists were against
women's roles becoming stronger.
11. On Malay communalism, see Ratnam (1965, esp. p. 159) and
McDougall (1968).

The office is on the third floor of a building erected on land donated to the party, apparently at the time of Singapore's incorporation into Malaysia. The bottom story is rented to various Chinese establishments, including a restaurant and a business college. The PKM office includes a bulletin board on which are posted schedules of Islam study courses, an auditorium with a stage, mats (on which girls in white uniforms are praying), and a reading room filled with cheap romance novels, some magazines, and an ethnography of a Malay region, *The Minangkabau of Negri Sembilan* by de Josselin de Jong.

PKM meetings that I attended included favorite santri lamb dishes, Qur'an chanting, and speeches by NU teachers from Indonesia. These combinations reflect a combination of Malayness, Muslimness, and (as suggested by the NU teachers and such elements as the Qur'anic chanting) a certain traditionalism. The relationship between *bangsa, agama,* and the traditionalism on the one hand, and ethnic heterogeneity and reformism on the other, is borne out by the Singapore survey.

Singapore reformists are slightly more likely than traditionalists to have Indian or Pakistani fathers, and since 18.2% of the reformists' fathers and only 9.1% of their mothers are Pakistani and Indian (HQ I-3, 4),[12] it appears that about half of this group are of *jawi peranakan* parentage (Indian/Pakistani father and Malay/Indonesian mother). Historically such figures have played a significant part in the rise of Singapore reformism— reflecting, no doubt, the stimulation of cultural clash within a family.

Reformists were more often born in Singapore (63%), traditionalists in Malaya (47%) and primarily in the two states nearest to Singapore, Johore and Malacca (HQ I-47). This, too, suggests a relation between heterogeneity and reformism, since the Malay states are more dominantly Malay, while Singapore is

12. Approximately half the rest of the Singapore sample were Malay and one third Indonesian (largely Javanese and Baweanese) in ethnic descent.

a Chinese-dominated pluralistic city. In Jogjakarta, cosmopolitanism and heterogeneity came from travel (the non-Javanese
ethnics and non-Javanese-born having come from elsewhere into
the reformist arena in Jogja); in Singapore, it is there.

THE LIFE CYCLE

Birth and Infancy

As among Javanese, the Singapore Malay child is greatly
desired, since fecundity is prized and the bond of parent to child
is regarded as one of the most precious of life's gifts.[13] As in
Java, the mother's mother is traditionally involved in the birth.
She oversees a slametan for the mother and fetus when her
daughter is 4 months pregnant, she contacts the midwife, and
she provides her home as a place for the mother to give birth. In
this latter feature, which is part of the complex including the
others, the reformists deviate from tradition more than the
traditionalists (HQ III-37 and 38); they are slightly more likely
to give birth to the eldest son in a hospital, rather than in the
house of the mother's mother or another relative of the mother.

Traditionally the family makes offerings to insure the
child's smooth delivery, and when it is born it is wrapped in
clean clothes and placed on a large tray near the mother. On the
tray are placed such items as grains of rice and coins, which are
covered with seven sarongs, on top of which rests a pillar for the
child's head. The items resemble the charms of syncretic Java,
and the meanings may be similar, too.[14]

About a week after birth, there is held a ceremony known
as the "washing of the floor," when a cock is offered to a boy
baby, a hen to a girl—actions which, after the fashion of the
Javanese slametan, ritually determine future courses of the life
cycle. At 44 days after birth, there is traditionally held the *lepas
hari* or *mandi tolak bala*, an important ceremony which signals
the end of taboos that mother and child have followed during
the early days fraught with danger.[15] Before this day, the mother

13. Djamour (1965, p. 88).   14. Djamour (1965, pp. 90-2).
15. Djamour (1965, p. 92).

has been forbidden to pray or read the Qur'an, but now the religious teacher or the father reads a prayer.

During this period ending 44 days after birth for the Malays, the Singapore Javanese will have gone through the cycle of slametans like those of Jogjakarta Javanese, beginning at 7 months of pregnancy and ending at 7 months after birth, when the child is permitted to touch the earth. Though details differ, the Baweanese and Arabs seem to follow a similar pattern in the broad sense that before, after, and during birth, child and mother are restricted by taboos and protected by ceremonies to usher them through this vulnerable period.[16] Since these customs concern animistic traditions (adat) one may assume that reformists—who by definition desire to purge religion of adat—have been prone to cut down; but the Singapore survey does not provide specific information on this point.

Children are indulged freely with the breast; scheduled feeding is considered cruel. They are reportedly weaned at about 6 months, but are occasionally suckled even after they can walk and talk.[17] There is little difference between reformists and traditionalists in age of weaning.

Wearing no diapers, the child is laid on a mat or mattress to protect the floor. For 3 to 5 months after the time when the umbilical cord drops off, the infant is wrapped in a piece of cotton cloth (bedong) from head to foot and placed in a soft but constricting hammock (buaian kain) suspended from the roof; these customs parallel those in Java of kuloni and gendong, but the survey indicates differences in pattern. The majority of Jogjakartans both kuloni and gendong the child, and the majority of Singaporeans bedong the child, but only slightly over half use the buaian kain. In Jogjakarta, reformists terminate kuloni

16. Information on the Baweanese comes from Baginda (1959), on the Arabs from Wahie (1959), on the Javanese from Johar (1961), and on all of these and the Malays from Djamour (1965) and Shamsudin (1957).

17. Djamour (1965, pp. 34-5, 92) indicates weaning at 6 months normally; the Singapore survey showed an average age of weaning of 2 years.

and slendang faster than other groups; in Singapore, reformists
get the infant out of the bedong more quickly than the tradi-
tionlalists (by four months), but out of the buaian kain more
slowly (after a year or more). Singapore reformists swaddle the
baby and use the hammock less frequently than traditionalists
(HQ III-40).[18]

After about 2 months, the baby is occasionally laid down
and permitted to play by itself outside these soft constraints, but
siblings and especially the maternal grandmother constantly
pick it up and carry it about; presumably the separation from
maternal grandmother suggested by the greater frequency of
hospital births among reformists lessens this type of cuddling.

Training

Djamour has depicted Malay toilet-training as permissive
after the fashion of the Javanese; sphincter control is unimpor-
tant and may not be learned until 4 or 5 years of age.[19] Shamsudin[20] claims, on the other hand, that the training begins as
early as 3 months, that it builds discipline, and that results are to
be seen after 1 year. The survey accords more with Shamsudin
than Djamour, which may suggest that it gives the minimal age
boundaries claimed by native idealists rather than the full range
seen by the observer; the survey finds Singaporeans speedier in
toilet-training than the Jogjakartans; by age 4, 38% of the
traditionalists' sons were still untrained in Jogjakarta and only
18% in Singapore, and 21% of the reformists' sons in Jogja, only
12% in Singapore. These figures also indicate that reformists in
Singapore toilet-train their sons earlier than traditionalists, as do
figures that show slightly more of the reformists' sons toilet-
trained by 18 months.[21]

Reward-and-punishment training is rare among the Malays,
says Djamour; they learn by trial-and-error. Shamsudin again

18. 90% of the traditionalists vs. 78% reformists bedong, and 63%
vs. 58% buaian kain.
19. Djamour (1965, pp. 92, 34-5).
20. Shamsudin (1957).
21. 9% reformists vs. 4% traditionalists toilet-trained by 18 months.

gives a stricter picture, stating that some parents lock the child up as punishment and tell it threatening stories.[22] HQ III-49 paraphrases Djamour in its first alternative, which asks if a child who crawls near the fire or plays with a knife is taught by letting him feel the heat or cut himself a little and then remarking "Hot, eh?" or "Sharp, eh?" and making a disapproving face. Alternative 3 was composed as parallel to the traditional type of child-rearing among the Javanese, which is neither punitive (after the fashion of Shamsudin) nor experimental (following Djamour), but instead gives constant advice. The majority of mothers did, indeed, claim to follow alternative 3, whereas reformists (23%, vs. 8% traditionalist) deviated most from this pattern by letting the child learn by experiment (alt. 1), which would seem to encourage initiative and independence.

As in Java, it is more often the mother than the father who punishes the child. Malay fathers indulge young children by constantly giving them pocket money which the child uses to buy sweets—a pattern similar to the Javanese child's constant snacking.[23] While little difference between reformists and traditionalists could be seen in such permissiveness, the English schooled were more prone to it than the Malay and Islamic schooled—possibly because of greater wealth.[24] The Malay father does not seem to withdraw from the son so abruptly and severely at age 5 as does the Javanese father—a difference probably associated with the lessening of hierarchy and formality among Malays by comparison with the Javanese.[25] The continuing relationship between father and son is shown by the noticeable tendency of Malays, especially reformists, to see the father as influential in the household (HQ II-17).[26]

22. Djamour (1965, pp. 103-6); Shamsudin (1957).
23. Djamour (1965, p. 103); cf. H. Geertz on *djadjanan* (1961, p. 99).
24. 40% English schooled vs. 20–30% others indulged the child with sweets.
25. I am indebted to Robert Jay, who has worked among both Javanese and Malays, for suggesting this point in conversation.
26. 37% reformists vs. 25% traditionalists see the father as more influential.

Later Childhood and Youth

Circumcision has no legal religious significance; praying in the mosque can begin before it, and learning to chant, after. Yet the event signals an important step toward incorporation into the community of adult males, and it is often celebrated by a feast attended only by adult males. (Malay girls also undergo a clitoridectomy at around 4 to 6 years of age, and Singapore Javanese girls on the 35th day of birth, but these events are not much celebrated.) Ethnographic observation indicates that circumcision is at 12–13 years among Javanese and Malays, at 9–10 among Arabs; the survey makes the split between reformists and traditionalists, showing more reformists circumcised before age 9 and more traditionalists after age 10 (HQ II-10).[27]

Adoption, temporary or permanent, is as frequent among Malays as among Javanese; 34 of 391 respondents in Jogjakarta, and 43 of 400 in Singapore, reported that the eldest son had been adopted by a relative (HQ III-56).[28] There was little difference between Singapore reformists and traditionalists in frequency of having the son adopted, but reformists were more likely to give the son to the father's relatives, while traditionalists gave him to the mother's relatives (HQ III-57);[29] again, reformism goes with a certain "patrism" in Singapore.

In Singapore as in Jogjakarta, reformists were less likely than traditionalists to briefly "lend" children (HQ III-51);[30] the tendency may, as was suggested for Jogjakarta, reflect a greater sense of personal responsibility and ownership among reformists, though other explanations include the possibly greater wealth of this type, which relieves them of the need to lend the child out.

Only upon reaching the age of 16 and over, according to

27. 30% reformists vs. 17% traditionalists were circumcised before age 9, and 80% traditionalists vs. 65% reformists after age 10.

28. Djamour (1965, pp. 95-7) reports on adoption, confirming the survey pattern.

29. 83% of reformists' sons vs. 46% traditionalists' sons who were given away were adopted by father's kin.

30. 55% traditionalists vs. 39% reformists briefly "lent" children.

Shamsudin, is the son allowed to eat with the father; the Singapore survey (and interviews as well) suggest more informality, since over half of the Islamic and Malay schooled sons eat with the father all along, or so it is claimed. Respect for the parent is shown by most respondents by the son's custom of asking forgiveness on the day of ending the fast; the Arabs reportedly ask forgiveness on other holidays as well.

Education in Islam begins when the parents tell the child about doomsday, the afterlife, and the punishment of sinners by God, as well as Muhammad's kindness to animals and other virtues. By age 6 or 8, the child is taught to chant the Qur'an, by age 8 to pray, by puberty (among the Malays, age 8 among the Arabs) to fast. In pursuing his formal education, he may, if his parents are especially pious, enter a madrasah; there are no *pondok* in Singapore, though small schools and mosque classes offer religious instruction in the mornings and evenings, when the child is not in regular school. Many parents favor the English schools, which offer greater chance of occupational success, but some favor the Malay (integrated) schools, which offer a Muslim majority and no threat of conversion to Christianity. Boys with an English school certificate would be advised to become clerks or technicians in government or business, while those from Malay schools will more likely become laborers, packers, drivers, or soldiers and, if they do well, teachers in the Malay system. The better madrasah students may proceed to an Islamic university, as in Cairo or Kuala Lumpur, then become religious teachers.[31]

Occupation

Concerning the relation between reformism and occupation, Singapore parallels Jogja in that reformists tend to be associated with business (HG I-51, 53, 55, 57). Singapore reformists more frequently come from businessman fathers, traditionalists from farmer fathers. Reformists also include the highest

31. This sketch of education comes from observation as well as Hussain (1965-6), Shamsudin (1957), and the works on the specific ethnic groups.

percentage of clerks, officials, and businessmen—high-status positions—while traditionalists include the highest percentage of laborers, drivers, and policemen. Reformists were slightly more likely to aspire for their sons to become doctors, lawyers, engineers, and businessmen. Consonant with these patterns, reformists tend more than traditionalists to have come from English schools.[32]

Despite marked differences in milieu, Singapore thus resembles Jogja in showing a reformism/entrepreneurial relationship. The two places differ, however, in that Singapore reformists tend to hold high-status jobs, entrepreneurial or otherwise, whereas in Jogja individuals who hold non-entrepreneurial, white-collar, high-status jobs tend to be found in the syncretic theological group, which does not exist in Singapore.[33] Occupationally, reformism is more status-linked in Singapore, more function-linked in Jogja.

In his career, the Singapore reformist is more upwardly mobile than the traditionalist, to judge from a comparison of "first" and "present" jobs for respondents of each group. Reformists are more likely to move from a blue-collar first job to a white-collar present job, such as bureaucrat or entrepreneur.

Singapore reformists tend to leave home early (by age 18) more often (HQ II-13), to start working earlier (by age 17) more often (II-12), but not to marry earlier (II-14) than traditionalists.[34]

32. The English schooled included the highest proportion of clerks and businessmen (33% of each), compared to almost none for the Malay and Islamic educated, who tend more to be laborers, drivers, policemen.

33. S. H. Al-Attas (1968b) found that 100% of his Malay student sample preferred government service, showing the general Malay desire for white-collar jobs. An analysis of the Singapore telephone directory classified section revealed only some 400 Muslim names (out of an estimated Muslim population of nearly 400,000) in business, though many small businessmen would not be listed.

34. 42% reformists vs. 23% traditionalists had left home by 18, 44% reformists vs. 34% traditionalists had started work by 17, and 42% reformists vs. 47% traditionalists had married by 21.

Marriage

Marriage among the Malays of Singapore is traditionally arranged by parents, even if it is the child's choice of mate. The sequence is proposal, formal engagement, wedding, consummation, and then a formal visit by the couple to their parents—a frame which tends to enclose conjugality within consanguinity. Djamour reports that Singapore Javanese are especially concerned with matching the status of bride and groom.[35] Whatever the reasons for parental concern with arrangement, the survey shows (HQ II-15) a slightly higher incidence of arranged vs. love marriages in Singapore (60% vs. 40%) than in Jogja (50% each). Reformists differed little from traditionalists in this ratio.

Ties to parents are traditionally maintained after marriage through either matrilocal or patrilocal tendencies in residence. A matrilocal tendency is seen in the bride's parents' provision of the wedding bed, though a wedding celebration may be held at the groom's parents' house. Further indications of continuing ties between father and son are the greater use by males in Singapore than in Jogja of *bin* ("son of") before the family name (there is also greater use by females of *binte*, or "daughter of"), and the alleged preference of a parent to live with his son rather than his daughter, on the grounds that his son is the household head—whereas in Java the ideal is to live with the daughter, on the grounds that she controls the household affairs. On the question of whether the couple lives matrilocally or patrilocally, the survey shows that they are most likely to settle neolocally (HQ II-16);[36] however, reformists are more likely than traditionalists to settle patrilocally, to see the father rather than the mother as influential in their household affairs, and to be desirous of pleasing the father rather than the mother (II-27a).[37] The survey also supports Shamsudin's claim that the father is

35. Djamour (1965, p. 70).
36. 29% reformists vs. 18% traditionalists reside patrilocally, but almost half of each group resides neolocally.
37. 37% reformists vs. 25% traditionalists see the father as most influential, and 24% reformists vs. 10% traditionalists desire to please father rather than mother.

more likely than the mother to visit his son, at least among reformists. All of this suggests a more patrist, patrilineal, and patrilocal tone to reformist life in Singapore than in Jogja, which jibes with patterns discussed earlier in relation to the view of women's role in the mosque.

Divorce is about as frequent among Singapore Malays as among Javanese in general—approximately 50%.[38] Following divorce, the woman usually returns to her mother and her matrilineal kin, who provide warm support throughout life.

Later Life

The pious Singapore Muslim looks forward to the pilgrimage as a sacred event of middle or old age. A survey of Singapore hadj-goers found that most were over 56 years of age (observation of the aged passengers creaking on board the ship supports this figure), and the aged are said to secretly hope to die in the holy land so as to attain extra blessing in the afterlife. The hadj confers such a mantle of purity upon the pilgrim that he is supposed to change name and demeanor after his return, and contemporary youths would prefer to have their fling before they burden themselves with such restrictive sacrality.

Funerals among Singapore Muslims include chanting the tale of Muhammad's birth and carrying of the bier by the deceased's Muslim association.

CHARACTER

H.B.M. Murphy, a psychiatrist doing research on the ethnic groups of Singapore, summarizes the personality of the Singapore Malays by saying that they place little value on wealth, success, and commercial aggressiveness, "while the most highly valued probably is the rich emotional relationship between parent and child."[39] Djamour emphasizes their desire for tranquility: "When a Malay contemplates a change of residence,

38. Djamour (1965, p. 139).
39. Murphy (1959, p. 295). In confirmation, note that on the Singapore survey virtually all groups affirmed that caring for the child was

marriage or divorce, or the exercise of a profession, the primary
consideration is not so much the material advantages to be
gained as the serenity of mind which the new type of existence is
likely to yield."[40] These images of serenity and noncompetitive-
ness—rather the opposite of the "Protestant Ethos"—are typical
not only of professional but also popular assessment of the
Malay character; indeed, the Malays themselves tend to express
the same self-image.

Reformist Differences

One of the Singapore survey's aims was to probe the extent
to which reformism is associated with a deviation from this
traditional personality. Considering responses to questions HQ
II-26 through 32, the following tendencies were notable: Reformists were more likely than traditionalists to feel tension
about planning all of life, rather than to think of hedonistic
pleasure (27b); to feel tension in dividing life from work, rather
than to dissolve tension into festivity (29b); to be willing to
move if it is profitable (28c); to be concerned about God's
command of their lives, rather than with nostalgic veneration of
the father (30c). Again reflecting patrism, reformists were more
likely than traditionalists to strive to satisfy the heart of the
father rather than the mother (27a).[41] In short, the reformists of
Singapore do appear broadly to resemble those of Jogja in
differing from traditional personality dispositions in a somewhat
Protestant-like direction: toward individualism, asceticism, mobility, and sense of mission.

---

pleasant, not burdensome (HQ III-48), which Djamour (1965, p. 100)
reports as typically Malay. Lenski (1963, p. 221) did not find this to be
at all typical among American Protestants.

40. Djamour (1965, p. 144).

41. 86% reformists vs. 73% traditionalists chose planning over pleasure; 76% reformists vs. 62% traditionalists chose tension in dividing
life from work over festivity; 74% reformists vs. 60% traditionalists
would move for profit; 67% reformists vs. 43% traditionalists were
concerned with God's plan for their lives; 90% traditionalists vs. 76%
reformists preferred to satisfy mother.

Psychopathology

A survey of Muslim patients was made in the national hospital of Singapore (Woodbridge), relying on patients' charts and on interviews. Distinctions between reformists and traditionalists appeared of little concern to most patients. What was discovered was a general configuration of types roughly like that in Indonesian hospitals and a link, at least in some cases, between depressive and paranoid tendencies and strong religious concerns. As in the Indonesian hospitals, the majority of the patients surveyed (156) were schizophrenic, while only 22 showed paranoid syndromes and 11 depressive.[42] No one was hospitalized for *latah.*

While the depressive patients were too few to be statistically significant, a few examples illustrate the interweaving of religion and these syndromes. Patient A, who is listed on his chart as "depressive," complains that he feels sinful and thinks about the devil, even though he has prayed five times per day. He claims that he has done evil and wants to die. He relates that upon visiting the house of a woman he felt guilty and depressed, and heard a voice say, "You must be punished at this girl's house." His chart notes that he is constipated.

Patient B compulsively washes his hands, constantly quotes the Qur'an, and claims that Allah will harm him for not praying. He fears the staff will beat him. Patient C, the son of an imam, keeps hearing people saying, "This road goes to heaven, and this to hell," and hears voices challenging him to fight. Patient D, who also has strong Islamic concerns, relates the reason for his illness as adultery, which he explains as a sin against God. Patient E unravels an elaborate delusional system revolving around his purported effort to emancipate himself from what he sees as a repressive Islamic religion; in its place, he has created his own system of prayer and fast.

42. Statistics for Indonesia appear in Pfeiffer (1967). Statistics for the Singapore national hospital (Woodbridge) were derived both through a count of psychiatric labels used on patients' charts and by examining cases; the two methods yielded roughly the same statistics. Over 200 charts were examined and several dozen patients were interviewed.

THE SINGAPORE SCHOOL SURVEY

The school survey suggests that students currently in the Malay or English schools have been in that stream since the beginning, whereas the madrasah pupils have a more heterogeneous educational experience, since they frequently come from English or Malay elementary schools.[43] Regionally, too, the madrasah is most heterogeneous (as is true also in Jogjakarta). Most first and second generation Indonesian immigrants are found in the madrasah; half of the students and 90% of their fathers were born outside Singapore, whereas the majority of the English and Malay pupils were born in Singapore.[44] Most Arab, Indian, and Pakistani Muslims, however, are found in the high-status English schools.

As in Jogja, the percentage of merchant fathers is higher in the madrasah than in other schools—though it is a low percentage (8%)—and the madrasah tends to attract the children of blue-collar workers and of fathers who had a *pondok* (pesantren) education (23%, precisely the percentage reported by pupils in the Jogja madrasahs).

In short, Singapore madrasah students fit the classical image of the mobile, working-class or mercantile person of pious Muslim background. These students were overwhelmingly reformist in theology (96% of the pupils in the boys' madrasah, 75% of those in the girls'), compared to less than half the English or Malay pupils. This reformist orientation cannot be attributed to an official position of the schools, since interviews with the heads of each showed them to favor moderate or somewhat traditionalist views that accord with their Arabic backgrounds.

43. 20% of the madrasah students have had previous Malay schooling and 73% previous English schooling, compared to virtually no Malay students with previous English schooling, and virtually no English students with previous Malay schooling.
44. Almost 90% of the English and Malay school students were born in Singapore, whereas 14% of the madrasah students were born in Malaya, 8% in Sarawak, 4% in Brunei, 4% in Indonesia, and 1% in Saudi Arabia. 23% of the madrasah students' fathers come from Indonesia, 24% from Malaya, 9% from Sarawak, and 5% from Brunei.

Probably the most revealing reformist-related trait of the madrasah pupils was their strong concern with social contribution. This came out on both SQ 13, which inquired what attribute they considered most important in a job, and 19, which asked them to imagine their future life.

Over 30% of the Singapore male madrasah pupils and 23% of the female madrasah pupils ranked the job's "social contribution" first, compared to only 7% of the Malay school students. When written-in responses were analyzed, it was discovered that 13% of the male and 6% of the female madrasah students, compared to none of the Malay and 1.9% of the English pupils, stated that the most important job attribute was "service to *agama* (Islam) and *bangsa* (the Malay ethnic group)." The English pupils were most likely of all groups to emphasize interpersonal and personal relationships, that a job should have "pleasant social relationships," fit one's personality and offer emotional satisfaction, while the Malay students most frequently of all groups ranked "high salary" first. Madrasah pupils show a greater concern with wider social contribution; English and Malay school pupils with material, personal, and interpersonal concerns.

The sketches written in response to SQ 19 ranged from a few words to a couple of pages. Themes were categorized, and the percentage of contribution by pupils from each type of school was calculated; it turned out that for every category, the English students contributed the most content (owing to their longer essays), the madrasah students contributed only 2–10% of the content, and the Malay schools the rest. Despite the constancy of thematic contribution among the schools, the variations are worth noting. The highest percentage of madrasah content (10% or more) is in the categories of social contribution and religious organization, while the lowest madrasah contribution (3% or less) is in the story content describing fatalism, education, and family life. Again, the madrasah pupils show greater concern for socio-religious contributions, and less —by comparison with the government school pupils—with imagining their future careers and private, domestic bliss.[45]

45. In more detail, these categories were composed of the following images: *Family* images included imagining the self in the company of

AUTOBIOGRAPHIES

Some 50 life histories were collected by interview from Singapore Muslim leaders, to whom an early version of the Singapore survey schedule was also administered. These serve for Singapore as the Darol Arqom autobiographies did for Jogjakarta: to reveal something of the phenomenology associated with the statistics.

Based on these narrations, the following generalizations can be hazarded: Most of the reformist interviewees had a father of

---

parents and siblings or in the future, with one's family of procreation; future aspirations for one's child; helping one's natal family; envisioning marriage; envisioning the ideal wife; mentioning the number of children desired; wanting one's children to take care of one when old; mentioning relatives. *Education* included imagining a career as a secular teacher; talking about the value of education; and describing travel. *Fatalism* was scored if the student prefaced his vision of the future by the phrase "If God is willing" or "If I live long enough." These images were emphasized by non-madrasah students.

Religious organization included imagining the self as a religious teacher; making the pilgrimage; doing a prayer; marrying a devout wife; and "contributing to the religion and the ethnic group" *(ugama lan bangsa)*. *Social contribution* involved imagining one's child's role in society; "contributing to the race and religion," to society, to the needy, the country, the government, the world; also, to "get along in society, especially with people of other ethnic groups, and work with society." These images were emphasized by madrasah students.

Also fairly high, but below the 10% level (9%), were the madrasah students' subscriptions to a rather "unprogressive" set of future images: seeing the self in a subordinate job (clerk, laborer, policeman, fireman, farmer); seeing modernity as bad; imagining that one would be the same later as now; and not describing hours in the daily routine.

I am grateful to Barbara Brick for writing English translations of the students' essays and doing most of the labor of content analysis and coding them.

Nash's (1974) analysis of students' images of the future in Kelantan, Malaya, schools shows parallels to these of the Malay students in Singapore. Nash found that the madrasah pupils gave higher rank to contributing to race and religion *(bangsa lan ugama)*, were more optimistic about the future, and aspired not to have wealth personally but (presumably) to contribute socially. The madrasah appears to encourage a view of the future significantly different from the government-style school. (Cf. the parallel Jogja school findings.)

the entrepreneur, *hadji* type, usually of Indonesian (rather than Malay) ethnicity. He is described as "harsh," and he often held a religious position, such as prayer-leader or teacher. Most of the traditionalists, by comparison, describe their father as a civil servant, and they emphasize a somewhat bureaucratic career, beginning with his Malay education, to the point of obtaining proper certification. Describing his own career, the traditionalist also emphasizes bureaucratic status, listing offices held, whereas the reformist places more emphasis on the functional, listing activities organized.

Comparison of these 50 leaders' responses to standard questions reveals a pattern rather like that seen in the larger Singapore sample. Reformists show a Protestant-like subjective relationship to the ultimate; 79% of the reformists, compared to 37% of the traditionalists, ranked "lack of faith" the worst sin. Asked when their greatest religiosity occurred, all of the traditionalists cited ages between 15 and 37—i.e., the family-rearing period—whereas half of the reformists named ages either before 15 or after 40. This difference suggests that the reformist concern with faith may reflect a religious belief grounded in a life-period of personal search, as compared to the traditionalist link between faith and established family leadership. Yet none of the reformists reveal an emotional conversion experience (the one emotional conversion reported to me was by a Chinese-Malay Christian convert to the radical sect Ahmadiyya, and he did not score "reformist" on HQ II-2 and 3).

In ethos, the reformists among these 50 interviewees gave responses similar to the Singapore sample in general: they were more likely than the traditionalists to claim not to procrastinate and to express concern with ordering life rather than with being snubbed by neighbors, with planning rather than festivities. They see life as a mission, would choose to die in the desert close to God, prefer to satisfy the mother. In child-rearing, they are more likely to toilet-train the child early, control the snacking habit, and consider the child a burden. In accord with the patrist tendency of reformists in the general Singapore sample, only 47% (compared to 82% of the non-reformists) favor increasing the role of women in the mosque.

Within the category "reformist," as defined by responses to HQ II-2 and 3, the autobiographical materials suggest three subtypes, which could be termed a "classical" reformist, a "secularist," and a "modern" type. The classical reformist finds his inspiration in the original Near Eastern reformist tradition, the modern reformist finds his in the Muhammadijan adaptation, and the secular reformist is less concerned with religious than with social reform. These are perhaps best illustrated by brief comparison of three cases; names are pseudonyms.

Syed lives in a somewhat rundown but middle-class (non-Malay) type of house in a good neighborhood. Wild-haired, gangly, and animated, his autobiographical narrative skips childhood and begins with his adventures in Singapore after migration from the strongly Islamic Indonesian island of Atjeh. Syed portrays himself as cast by fate into a series of situations (a radio speaker for the Japanese, a lecturer for the All-Malaya Missionary Society, an employee of a cousin's import-export business), all of which he considers as opportunities provided by "God's will," to which he responded energetically. He does not portray his career as self-directed and planned. Syed is a "classical" reformist in that he traces his ideology to the writings of Muhammad Abduh and other early Egyptian or Arab reformist scholars.

Ahmat is a "secularist" reformist in that, while he cites the tenets of *idjtihad* and purification, his primary concern is not with religion as such but with social and educational reform. He lives in neither a Malay nor a non-Malay section but in an apartment adjoining a neighborhood social service center by which he is employed. Ahmat is bald, well-knit, with measured speech; his narrative is more descriptive and methodical than Syed's. For instance, he states how many children he has, then accounts for each, whereas Syed mentioned four and then accounted for only two in his narrative. He describes his career as orderly and deliberate, progressing from a technical to a social employment. Ahmat is English educated. When asked to describe meaningful events in Muhammad's biography, he states that Muhammad shows how ambition yields success, whereas Syed described the Prophet's episodic, xenophobic war against heretics. On child-rearing items of the survey, Ahmat is uniformly rationalist, whereas Syed deviated toward the traditionalist on several items.

Imam is a "modernist" reformist in that he traces his inspiration not to the classical Near Eastern figures but to self-study of the Qur'an and to the Malayo-Indonesian organizations, especially Muhammadijah. He lives in a Malay neighborhood and identifies himself as a Malay (of Indonesian extraction). Educated in a madrasah, he is a religious teacher and organizer. On survey items of ethos and child-rearing, he falls neatly between Syed and Ahmat in extent of "rationalism."

These vignettes serve to illustrate the diversity of ideology and life style that surrounds the simple definition of reformism as alternative 1 on both HQ II-2 and 3. For Syed, Ahmat, and Imam, this "reformist" response reflects an outlook that fits into the life and ideology of each. For Syed, reformism is in part a way of signaling his superiority through identity with Near Eastern origins. For Ahmat, reformism is compatible with his generally methodical and rationalist orientation, expressed through his social activism. For Imam, reformism represents a carefully studied approach to scriptural interpretation, exemplified by Muhammadijah. It is true that reformism has a variety of psychological meanings here, but the range of personality types is not infinite; for example, it does not include a conservative elitist bureaucrat or a fatalistic passive peasant, to mention two stereotypes of the Kaum Tua. And the responses do not lack plausible relationship to the psychological dispositions of the respondents. Limited though they are in psychological depth, the autobiographical materials suggest that for most of the fifty subjects interviewed, the response to HQ II-2 and 3 reflect a cultural and psychological orientation identifiable as reformist in an historical and phenomenologically meaningful sense.

SINGAPORE REFORMIST PSYCHOLOGY

The psychological tendencies of the Singapore reformist differ from those of his traditionalist counterpart in the same

TABLE 5.
Characteristics of Singapore Muslim Reformists

RELIGIOUS ORIENTATION

Definitional: Belief in *idjtihad* (rational personal interpretation of scripture) and purification of tradition

Associated: Emphasis on faith in God and communication with God

SOCIAL ORIENTATION

Cosmopolitan experience: Born in Singapore melting-pot of ethnically mixed family background (if adult respondent); immigrant from Indonesia (if student respondent)

LIFE CYCLE (in contrast to traditionalists)
Child-rearing:
  Less use of swaddling and constraining hammock *(bedong* and *buaian kain),* and earlier removal from *bedong* if used
  Earlier toilet-training
  Teaching by trial-and-error instead of continuous advice
  Earlier circumcision
  Less lending of children for short-term, and son given to father's relatives if adopted

Adulthood:
  Employment in business or bureaucracy
  Mobility from low-status to high-status jobs
  Leave home early and start working early
  Patrist domestic values: patrilocal residence; see father as dominant domestic influence; concerned with pleasing father more than mother

Overall Conception of the Life Cycle:
  Chief memories of biography of Muhammad are flight from Mecca and fighting in Badr wars
  Young people's vision of future emphasizing job's social contribution, specifically serving religious and ethnic group, rather than private domestic life, salary, or pleasant social relations at work

Ethic and Ethos
  Tensions about planning and about differentiating life from work; willing to move for profit; see life as a mission for carrying out God's command; strive to satisfy father

direction found in Jogjakarta. Points of similarity include a reformist tendency to accelerate and streamline the life cycle, as in speeding up child-rearing, while conceiving of life as a mission and generally being more progressive, dynamic, and future-oriented than is regarded as proper for the traditional Malay character.

Differences between Singapore and Jogjakarta can be partly explained by the merging in Singapore (but not in Jogjakarta) of reformism with elite status, Western schooling, and Arab and Indian models of life style. Thus Singaporean reformists tend more toward a "Protestant" style of direct communication with God, high-status white-collar employment, and patrist (patri-local, patrifocal, and patrilineal) family patterns.

6

Malaya

THE Malay-language Singapore household questionnaire, slightly adapted for the Malay context and pre-tested with
Malay informants, was administered by interview to 200 Muslim household heads in both rural and urban areas near Alor
Setar in the state of Kedah, Malaya. Sampling and interview
method were identical to those used in Singapore, but the
research differed in that I was unable to carry out "participant
observation"; accordingly, the context for the Kedah survey is
pieced together from documents.[1]

1. Lacking a visa from the Malaysia government, I could not do
ethnographic research in Malaya. Nor could I pre-test the schedule in
the Kedah context. Since ethnographic research—see Kuchiba and
Yoshihiro (1968)—confirms survey results at points of overlap, the
survey does seem to reflect ethnographic realities.

The Kedah interviews, administered by the Far Eastern Research
Organization in Alor Setar, were carried out in the area near Alor Setar,
divided as follows among five *mukims*: 62 in Yen, 64 in Sala Besar, 42 in
Sungei Daun, 20 in Dulang, and 12 in Sing Kir. Within each unit, house-
holds for interview were selected by walking from a starting point, as in
Singapore.

Ethnographic information concerning Kedah is skimpy by comparison with that available on the similar state Kelantan (Kedah rather than
Kelantan was chosen for the survey because the FERO office is in Alor
Setar). Accordingly, the Kedah sketch can be elaborated by perusal of
information on Kelantan; note especially these items in Roff (1974): an
account of the Majlis Ugama, the Religious Council (pp. 102-52);
Winzeler's survey of such basic rural Islamic elements as the pilgrimage,

Kedah

Though Kedah was for a time a Siamese state, its essentially Malay structure remains, in the opinion of Sharom Ahmat.[2] Kedah is a sultanate, under the control of a sultan known as Yang di-Pertuan, "He who is made Lord"—an exalted personage who traditionally boasts the usual attributes of the Malay sultan in ceremonials, clothing, polygyny, and the privilege of being addressed in a special language. He also traditionally had total control of the state purse.

Under the sultan was a hierarchy of ministers, usually of the royal family, who could collect taxes and tributes. Whereas the sultan controlled the state, these ministers controlled districts. The subdistricts were ruled by officials who were religious and moral in their functions: to prevent activity sinful to Allah, maintain orthodox practice of the five pillars of Islam, and stop such crimes as stealing and cock-fighting. The lowest political unit was the village.

Embracing 3,648 square miles, Kedah is a flat area ideal for rice cultivation, long the occupation of the majority of its occupants.[3] Until the twentieth century, land was not usually owned by these peasants but by the sultan and members of the royal

---

schools, officials, and reformist teachers; Kessler's provocative explanation of the appeal of PMIP as opposed to UMNO; Salleh's account of a reformist theology; and Nash's analysis of student aspirations.

2. Ahmat (1969).

3. Ahmat (1969, p. 28) states that in 1911, of the 88,491 Kedah Malays in agricultural occupations, 88,121 were rice farmers, mostly subsistence. See also Annual Report (1936), and Kuchiba and Yoshihiro's (1968) study of Padang Lalang, 8 kilometers northwest of Alor Setar. Though the majority of the Kedah reformists surveyed are farmers, the percentage is higher among the few traditionalists (67% vs. 76%), while more reformists are skilled laborers (13% vs. 3%). Similar proportions hold for respondents' fathers (80% vs. 93%, and 11% vs. 3%). In contrast to Singapore, in Kedah first and present job proportions for reformists are the same (showing no mobility). Aspirations are in sharp discord with actualities, as reflected in the 62% of employed sons of Kedah reformists now working as farmers, vs. only 1% of reformists who *aspire* for their not-yet-employed sons to be farmers.

family; labor too was the possession of the sultan, in that he could force the peasantry to work on his projects, exceptions being made only for mosque officials and Islamic notables— the *Lebai, Sayed,* and *Hadji.* Between 1905 and 1911, however, the sultan lost power to the colonial government, which created a state council and a financial adviser. Forced labor ended, and subsistence farming was gradually transformed into cash.

Where Singapore is a melting-pot, Kedah is ethnically homogenous. Surveying the situation at the beginning of the twentieth century, Ahmat[4] states that more than 195,000 of the total Kedah population of 219,000 were Malay, and the others were largely Muslim. These included the Indian Muslims who had married Malays, Indonesian Muslims (primarily Atjehnese), and the *Sam Sam,* who were mixtures of Malay, Chinese, and Siamese—mostly farmers, some of them Muslims. Around the turn of the century, non-Muslims—Chinese and Indian Tamils —began to arrive; by 1911 there were 35,746 Chinese, who were not easily assimilated. Today Kedah remains one of the states of heaviest Malay concentration. According to the 1970 census report, Kedah's population is approximately 70% Malay (some 670,000), 20% Chinese (some 180,000), 8% Indian (some 80,000), and 16,000 others.[5]

Cultural Orientations

A 1968 report, *Laporan Kemadjuan Islam Kedah* (The Progress of Islam in Kedah), confirms that in basic respects the pattern of Islamic life in that state resembles that in other Malay states, and, indeed, in the Muslim society in general. At the apex of the religious bureaucracy is the sultan (Sultan Abdul Halim Mu'azzam Shah). Under him are an Islamic religious council and a religious bureaucracy, which includes such divisions as the Department of Religious Information for the State of Kedah, which oversaw publication of this brochure.

The *da'wah* (evangelism) so prominent in Muhammadijah is discussed as a central mission, and a report describes these

4. Ahmat (1969, p. 8).
5. Chander (1972, p. 32).

missionary activities.[6] *Ichlas* (stoic dedication), so central to the ideology of Islamic struggle in Indonesia, is here, too; the sultan's preface expresses the hope that the department will continue its work "with honesty and ichlas."

Kedah inhabitants make the hadj (2,662 did so in 1968, which is considerably more than those who did in Jogjakarta, out of a comparable population). They hold classes for the chanting of the Qur'an (attended by 1,224 in 1968), they celebrate Maulud (the birth and death of Muhammad) and they hold slametan-like feasts *(khenduri)*. The women wear head coverings, the men black caps, just like the Javanese santri, and they uphold the five pillars.

One of the two Malay states famed for its *pondok* (pesantren, the traditional Islamic schools), Kedah has 82, with 7,248 pupils and 278 teachers, that are subsidized by the religious bureaucracy from the tithe, plus 30 that are not subsidized. There are also madrasahs, with 1,458 students, and "people's religious schools" *(Ugama Ra'ajat)* that give instruction to students enrolled full-time in other schools.

Political Parties—The two most important politico-religious organizations in Kedah would seem to be UMNO and PMIP. Established nationally in 1951, PMIP (Pan-Malaya Isamic Party, or Persatuan Islam Sa-Melayu) strives to unite Muslims in a common front to realize the requirements of both democracy and Islam. PMIP united reformism and traditionalism by seeking the basis of action in the Qur'an and traditions, though attending to the opinion of the teacher as well. Considering religious law all-embracing, it opposes separation of state and religion. Zaki claims that PMIP "avoids all points of dispute between the Kaum Muda and Kaum Tua," and therefore "Both reformists and conservatives are to be found side-by-side in the party organization." Zaki states further that PMIP draws examples and models from both the traditionalist NU and the reformist Masjumi parties in Indonesia. Certainly the reformist theme is strong; the party organ translates Egyptian and Indonesian writings of a reformist cast, and the first Qur'anic verse

6. Penerangan (1968, pp. 7, 32).

which the leader, Dr. Burhanuddin, quotes in his pamphlet "Our Struggle" is reformist: "Allah does not change the condition of the people until they change themselves."[7]

PMIP is a nationalistic Malay party for the Malays; it has no Indian Muslims in its hierarchy, it opposes Malaysia because of the advantage it gave the Chinese, and it considers the British *harbi*, the national enemy.

More moderate politically, UMNO draws members from all ethnic groups. Yet it does have a strong Islamic element. Zaki states that where UMNO has gained the support of the official *ulamas*, PMIP has the free-lance ulamas, such as pondok teachers.[8] UMNO also has a religious section led by reformists.

In the Kedah sample of 200, 37% reported membership in PMIP and 44% in UMNO. These percentages contrast with the mere 9% of Singapore Muslims who reported membership in any of the Malayo-Muslim parties—PMIP, UMNO, or PKM. While the difference could reflect the Singapore fear of reporting membership in a minority party, only 1% reported membership in the dominant one (PAP); it appears that the Kedah Malays are more politically active than those of Singapore.

Schooling and Beliefs—The Kedah Malays have also had more Islamic schooling than the Singapore Malays: 84% of the Kedah household heads attended a religious school (*ugama kampong*, which could include either pondok or folk-school), compared to only 9% of the Singapore Malays; and 87% of the Kedah respondents report that their fathers attended such a school, and 53% say that their sons are attending one, compared to no Singaporeans on both counts. (Some Singaporeans did, however, report that their sons attend madrasah; and 23% of the current madrasah students—only half of whom, however, are of Singaporean origin—report that their fathers attended a pondok.)[9]

7. Zaki (1965, pp. 397, 415).
8. Zaki (1965, p. 396).
9. On the *pondok* in Malaysia, see Kumton (1957). 87% of the Kedah reformists vs. 67% traditionalists had 10 years or more of religious schooling; 90% had fathers with religious schooling, compared to 70%

On the question of reformism vs. traditionalism, Kedah respondents showed an interesting division. Asked baldly (HQ II-36) whether they were Kaum Muda or Kaum Tua, 99% replied, "Kaum Tua." Yet on the indirect questions (II-2 and 3) used as criteria in the Singapore and Jogja surveys, these Kedah Muslims opt strongly for reformism (99% on *idjtihad* and 70% on purification). Why should they reject the reformist label while accepting the reformist belief? The answer may lie in the bad image that the term "Kaum Muda" has come to have in the Malay states, where it connotes factionalism and even Communism. Yet in belief, the Kedah sample would appear to be strongly reformist.

On basic questions such as belief in heaven and hell (HQ I-65) and asking forgiveness at Lebaran (II-11), the Kedah respondents are as unanimously affirmative as those of Singapore and Jogja. They were also similar in desiring a larger role for women in the mosque (II-6),[10] and in other explicit points of doctrine or ideology. A more subtle indication of attitude concerns memory of the life of Muhammad (II-8); this provides a test of religious interest, in that the respondent must actively recollect his experience rather than answer yes or no to supplied platitudes. By this standard, the Kedah Muslims are more interested in the Prophet, for where 79% of the Singapore sample claimed that no event had made a strong impression, only 53% of the Kedah respondents made this claim. Coded in the same categories as the Singapore sample, the Kedah Malays had a much larger percentage (53 of the 201) who remembered events concerning Muhammad's war and missionary work—an activist orientation consonant with *da'wah*.

---

among the few traditionalists. Otherwise, little difference in educational level was shown between Singapore and Kedah, or between reformists and traditionalists in Kedah. However, 54% of Singapore respondents' sons are in English school vs. 22% in Kedah; and 53% are in religious school in Kedah vs. none in Singapore.

10. However, in Kedah more reformists (80%) than traditionalists (58%) favored the woman's larger role.

Social Orientations

In social respects, the Kedah Malays fit the traditional mold more than do the Singaporeans. Most of the reformists are less upwardly mobile than those of Singapore. The majority of the men in Kedah are farmers whose fathers were farmers and whose sons are farmers. And this agrarian life style is within the framework of the sultanate.

The Kedah sample is more homogeneously Malay (94% have both Malay father and mother) than the Singapore sample, which includes a large proportion of non-Malays and mixed-ethnic marriages. The Kedah reformists were almost all born in Kedah of fathers born in Kedah, whereas many of the Singapore Muslims were sons of immigrants.

Compared to the Singapore reformist, the Kedah reformist is a traditionalist in family affairs and child-rearing. Kedah parents place more emphasis on the son's getting along well with others (HQ II-20), try more to "keep him happy," and are less apt to use a punish-reward (II-23) or trial-and-error (III-49) technique of training.[11] They more frequently use the *bedong* and *buaian kain*, and use the *bedong* longer. They toilet-train their sons later (usually between 2½ and 4 years, whereas in Singapore it is more often before 2½),[12] wean him later (in Singapore more often before age 2), circumcise him later. The Kedah parent is less likely, however, to lend the child briefly or

11. Among reformists, 36% in Kedah vs. 13% in Singapore thought friendliness was the most important trait for the son to acquire; 23% Kedah vs. 5% Singapore favored keeping the child happy as favorite method of rearing; 9% Kedah vs. 20% Singapore favored the punish-and-reward method; and 1% Kedah vs. 23% Singapore favored the trial-and-error method, while 94% Kedah vs. 72% Singapore favored constantly telling the child what and what not to do.

12. 89% Kedah reformists vs. 56% in Singapore use the *buaian kain*; while 89% Kedah vs. 78% Singapore use the *bedong*, and only 60% Kedah vs. 90% Singapore have the child out of bedong by 4 months. Almost 80% Kedah vs. 50% Singapore toilet-train sons between 2½ and 4, only 13% Kedah vs. 42% Singapore before 2½. (However, Singapore and Kedah traditionalists differ little on training.)

have him adopted.[13] When the Kedah mother tells the child stories, virtually all are folktales of Kantjil, the mousedeer.

The Kedah reformists were circumcised later than those in Singapore, over 93% at more than 10 years of age.[14] They started working later (usually between ages 16–20, fewer than in Singapore before age 16), lived at home longer (more Singaporeans left home before age 18).[15] However, they married earlier (at 19–21, compared to more of the Singapore reformists at or past age 25),[16] and their marriages were more often arranged by their parents (87%, vs. 61% for the Singapore reformists). (This survey finding is confirmed by ethnographic observations in a Kedah village near Alor Setar, which shows a pattern of arranged marriage—probably following segregation of the sexes —with the modal age for males being 18–20.)[17]

After marrying, the Kedah Malays live more often in independent households, whereas the Singaporeans are more often matrilocal or patrilocal soon after marriage; on the other hand, the Singaporeans more often set up households one mile or more from their parents.[18] These facts led to a suspicion that the Kedahans were not really living independently but as part of agrarian compounds, with parents and children farming joint

13. 24% Kedah reformists (but 41% Kedah traditionalists) vs. 52% Singapore reformists lend the child briefly, and 10% Singapore vs. 2% Kedah reformists put the son out for adoption.

14. However, Singapore and Kedah traditionalists differ little on age of circumcision. Similarities between traditionalists and differences between reformists in the two places suggest that the differences are not simply of place but in the role of reformism. In Kedah, 9% of reformists vs. 17% traditionalists were circumcised after age 15.

15. 69% Kedah reformists vs. 58% in Singapore started working between ages 16–20; 29% Singapore vs. 19% Kedah started before 16. 46% Singaporean reformists vs. 12% in Kedah left home before 18.

16. 42% Kedah reformists vs. 17% in Singapore married between ages 19–21, whereas 59% Singapore reformists vs. 29% Kedah reformists (but 43% Kedah traditionalists) married at 25 or later.

17. Kuchiba and Yoshihiro (1968, p. 156).

18. 65% Kedah reformists vs. 45% in Singapore lived neolocally; but 33% Kedah vs. 14% Singapore lived one mile or less from the parents.

land. This was confirmed by ethnographic studies which show that, indeed, residence is normally neolocal and in nuclear family units, but that two-thirds of the households are in compounds that include parents' households while children cultivate their parents' land.[19]

Marriage among the Malays of Kedah, as in Singapore, includes both the *nikah* (the Islamic ceremony) and the *kawin* (the *adat* ceremony). The 1968 Religious Department report showed 3,286 *nikah* and 1,554 divorces in Kedah, which is approximately the same 50% rate as in Singapore and Java.

Kedah Character

Despite his traditionalist socio-ecological and life-cycle patterns, the Kedah Malay reformist comes out even more strongly rationalist on the "ethos" questions (HQ II-26 through 32) than the Singapore reformist. The Kedah reformist is more inclined to: resent interruption (30a); feel tense about separating life from work (29b); feel that he would work hard, sacrificing tranquility (26c); veer toward paranoia rather than homesickness (28b); feel that he should carry out God's plan (30c); feel compulsive about scheduling everything in life (29a); feel that he would rather die in the desert close to God than among friends (30b); go hungry rather than beg for favors (31c); and feel sinful (28a). In three respects, he inclines more toward what would seem a Western Protestant Ethic than Islamic attitudes: less inclined to *ichlas* (31a); more inclined to treat drinking as a relative sin to be evaluated according to consequences (27c); and more interested in friendship than in association with prestigious figures (29c).[20]

19. Kuchiba and Yoshihiro (1968, p. 156).
20. 79% Kedah reformists vs. 67% in Singapore resent interruption rather than feel poignant memory of a sweetheart; 98% Kedah vs. 76% Singapore have conflict between work and life vs. seeking jolly relations; 64% Kedah reformists vs. 29% in Singapore choose to "work hard" rather than "be calm"; 32% Kedah vs. 18% Singapore are "paranoid" vs. "homesick"; 91% Kedah vs. 67% Singapore follow God's plan rather than venerate the father; 93% Kedah vs. 56% Singapore desire to die alone with God rather than conform to group

TABLE 6.
Characteristics of Kedah Muslims

RELIGIOUS ORIENTATION

Definitional: Belief in *idjtihad* (rational personal interpretation of scripture) and purification of tradition

Associated:

Membership in Malayo-Muslim parties

Muslim rather than English schooling

SOCIAL ORIENTATION

Ethnic homogeneity

Agrarian

Low occupational mobility

LIFE CYCLE (in constrast to Singapore reformists)

Child-rearing:

Child swaddled and constrained (in *bedong* and *buaian kain*) more and longer

Toilet-training, weaning, and circumcision later

Child told stories of folktale type

Emphasis on son's sociability; parents try to keep him happy, use continuous advice rather than trial-and-error or punishment-and-reward training

Less short-term or long-term lending of child

Adulthood:

Start working later and leave home later

Marry earlier, marriage arranged by parents, reside near parents

ETHIC AND ETHOS

Resent interruption; feel tense about separating life from work; sacrifice tranquility for work; "paranoia" rather than homesickness; commitment to carrying out mission commanded by God; prefer death near God in desert to intimacy of friends; feel the need to schedule everything; prefer planning to expensive clothes; view drinking functionally instead of absolutely; inclined to procrastinate; inclined to be hardheaded rather than *ichlas;* favor friendship over association with famous figures

OTHER "REFORMIST" VALUES

Memory of the Prophet's evangelism and participation in wars

Favor larger role for women in the mosque

KEDAH REFORMIST PSYCHOLOGY

The discrepancy in Kedah between the traditionalist complex of ecology, community, family, and life cycle and the reformist ethic and rationalist ethos is striking. The agrarian, ethnically homogeneous, provincial, parent-oriented, dependency-rearing Kedah life style all fit the traditional model of the rural Malay. Yet in religious orientation the Kedah respondents are almost unanimously reformist, and in personality disposition they deviate strongly from the traditional Malay stereotype—toward individualism, asceticism, plans, schedules, hard work, paranoia, and a sense of mission. Indeed, they are much more reformist and psychologically rationalist than the Muslims of Singapore. Whence came these attitudes? Likely sources are the parties and schools, the UMNO, PMIP, and pondok in which they participate heavily—much more so than the Singaporeans.

Why the lag in such spheres as child-rearing? One might speculate that one reason is the control of this realm by mothers and grandmothers. Grandparents own the land on which parents farm, and while grandfathers, sons and grandsons work the fields, grandmothers, mothers, and granddaughters keep house. In the house occurs most of the early child-rearing, including *bedong, buaian kain,* suckling, and the like; here the influence of the older generation probably preserves tradition. Meanwhile, the males are emancipated from the household as

---

pressure; 22% Kedah vs. 59% Singapore show *ichlas* more than hardheadedness; 83% Kedah vs. 61% Singapore view drinking functionally rather than absolutely; 84% Kedah vs. 71% Singapore desire friendship rather than association with the famous. On only one item did the Kedah reformist appear less "rationalist" than the Singaporean: 54% Kedah vs. 82% Singapore favor working on schedule to procrastinating. Differences between Kedah reformists and traditionalists on the ethos items resemble the differences between Kedah and Singapore reformists; reformists are 70–80% on hating interruption (30a); being mobile (28c); and taking an instrumental morality (27c); while traditionalists are 42–48% on these. Reformists are 86–91% on favoring plans (29a) and God's plan (30c) vs. 70% traditionalists.

they enter the male-dominated schools and parties. The situation may resemble that in Indonesia's Minangkabau, where Islamic dynamism emerged forcefully in male-dominated movements freed of female-dominated domesticity.[21] The Kedah respondents who have expressed the "dynamic" and "rationalist" ethos are, after all, male.

21. Abdullah (1966 and 1971).

7

Conclusion

THIS study began, it will be recalled, with a hypothesis derived from Max Weber: Religious reformism is associated with psychological rationalization. This hypothesis has been explored with respect to several groups of Southeast Asian Muslims, primarily the Javanese, but also Malays and other Muslims in Singapore and Malaysia, insofar as data bearing on the hypothesis were available.

In assessing the validity of the Weberian hypothesis for Islamic Southeast Asia, a sequence of questions must be answered. First, is the definition of "reformism" utilized in this study valid within the Southeast Asian Islamic cultural context? If so, does such reformism correlate with a distinctive psychological pattern? And if this is so, in what sense can this pattern be termed "rationalization"?

REFORMISM AS A CULTURAL CONSTRUCT

The three interview-surveys—Jogjakarta, Singapore, and Kedah—utilized the same definition of reformism as a cultural, i.e., ideational, construct. A reformist by theology or ideology was defined as any respondent who selected alternative 1 on HQ II-2 and 3. This choice in 3 is taken to indicate that one favors personal analysis of the Qur'anic scripture, rather than teachers, spirits, or mystical insight as a source of authority and guidance;

187

in 2, it is taken to indicate that one favors purification of religious tradition to fit the ideals of Islam, rather than maintenance of impure practices in order to preserve tradition. This choice identifies the essence of religious reformism as it is generally understood, while the other identifies that particular basis of authority, known as *idjtihad,* emphasized by the "scripturalist" reformists who are the dominant type in the reformist movement of Southeast Asian Islam.

To what degree is this reformist construct valid or useful? Does choice by a respondent of these two items mean anything —and if so, what?

It is true that these two tenets have been identified as the basic platform of Southeast Asian Muslim reformism. It is also true that HQ II-2 and 3 were confirmed by informants as making sense. These points are basic, but the real test of the validity and utility of these two criteria is whether they correlate with a pattern of responses that could plausibly be expected for a proper definition of reformism. Do those who define themselves as culturally reformist in terms of these two responses also give other evidence of reformist orientation?

Affiliations

An obvious evidence of reformist orientation is membership in a reformist organization. Are the theologically reformist, as defined by these two responses, also organizationally reformist? They tend to be, and in a plausible pattern. For the general Jogjakarta sample, the majority of those who professed reformist theology were also members of Muhammadijah, though not all were. For the more selective sample, the highly indoctrinated branch-leaders participating in the Darol Arqom training camp, the correlation between theology and membership was total: 100% of the Darol Arqom participants professed reformist theology on these two questions.

In Singapore, there was no prominent organization of reformists; hence there was no membership correlate to theological orientation. Kedah, too, lacked an explicitly reformist organization such as Muhammadijah; but PMIP and UMNO have a strongly reformist aspect, and it is logical that membership in these political parties correlates with profession of reformist theology. In Kedah, a large majority of respondents report membership in PMIP or UMNO and also profess reformism; in Singapore, very few report membership in such an organization, and only a minority profess reformist theology.

Education

Schools provide both institutional affiliation and ideological indoctrination. Thus it is plausible that in both Singapore and Jogjakarta, the pupils now in madrasah should score high in reformist theological orientation. In Jogjakarta, the madrasahs are generally acknowledged to be the staunchest educational upholders of the spirit of Muhammadijah. In Singapore, the madrasahs do not explicitly profess a reformist ideology, but they teach the scripturalism that is its basis; note that for Singapore students, reformist theological orientation was defined by positive response to the *idjtihad* item (3) alone, and it is this which would be encouraged tacitly if not explicitly by the scripturalist education.

When educational *background*, as opposed to present attendance, is considered, the relationship to present theological or organizational predilection becomes more complex. Learning wears off, and influences intervene between schooling and adulthood. Thus it is plausible that reformist schooling background may not predict reformist theological orientation so strongly as does present school attendance. Nevertheless, those who once attended reformist schools tend more strongly to profess reformist than other theologies on these two questions.

Aside from parties and schools, which have been discussed previously, it should be noted that reformist theology also correlates strongly with residence in particular neighborhoods. Residents of such well-known Muhammadijah neighborhoods as Kauman and Karang Kadjèn score strongly reformist on HQ II-2 and 3, while those in known syncretic neighborhoods score strongly syncretist in theology. Because schools and parties are more explicit than neighborhoods in their reformist orientation,

these units were emphasized in the present study; but neighborhood residence gave similar patterns of correlation.

Other Correlations

Turning now to the individual personality, this was explored largely through life histories, which have not been detailed here. The vignettes of Singapore reformists Syed, Ahmad,
and Imam illustrate the type of pattern discovered. Less frequently in Singapore, more frequently in the more highly organized and indoctrinated Darol Arqom sample of Java, the type
of person who scores reformist on our two basic criteria turns
out to be a devout scripturalist, highly aware of the theological
and social meaning of the reformist doctrine and committed to
applying it in his own life and through evangelism. Imam is of
this type; Syed and Ahmat illustrate other variants. Ahmat is
aware of the religious implications of the reformist tenets, and
he is committed to them as opposed to the alternatives, but his
main concern is less with religious reformism than with social
reform. Syed has sporadically acted like a reformist in his political and religious activities, and he understands the historical,
Near Eastern roots of the Kaum Muda. But his sometimes
eloquent espousal of reformist tenets and his selection of the
reformist responses do not indicate a thoroughgoing reformist
attitude in all aspects of his religious life and ideology. Nevertheless, even Syed is more validly typed as a "reformist" than as a
traditionalist.

An interesting relationship between the reformist tenets articulated in HQ II-2 and 3 and the actual process of reformist
thought is provided by comparison of the Darol Arqom camp to
another, in which I also participated, for neophytes. Throughout the entire two weeks of physical training, lectures, seminars,
and discussion in Darol Arqom, the two tenets of purification
and *idjtihad* were never directly mentioned. By comparison, the
two tenets were elaborated in the opening lecture of the neophyte camp. From this, one concludes that the tenets are too
elementary to warrant attention in an advanced camp such as
Darol Arqom; here issues more current in the organization were
emphasized: for example, the threat of Christianity, strategies of

organization, and points of ritual and belief that were controversial. The 100% affirmation of the two tenets by the Darol
Arqom participants confirms that they are aware of them.

Finally, affirmation of reformist theology on these two
questions correlates strongly with other cultural orientations, at
least in Jogjakarta. The reformist is considerably more likely
than the syncretist to reject the various animistic beliefs and rites
of Javanese tradition. This detailed list of rejections (see Chapter
2) shows consistency, in that the respondent who chooses the
tenet of purification reflects this choice by rejecting each individual item: *slametans*, the various spooks and spirits, and
petungan. He is also consistent with the tenet of scripturalism in
that he does not reject *djin*, the only spirit affirmed by scripture.

In sum, our definition of reformist theology as espousing
purification and scripturalism appears to have validity and utility across the Singapore, Kedah, and Jogjakarta samples. As
noted, the Jogjakarta survey definition of reformist includes not
only the theological aspect but also membership and schooling;
all three aspects are used in the Jogjakarta analyses.

Another issue can be raised. Even if the construct "reformism" correlates meaningfully with other indications of a reformist orientation, this does not confirm that reformism is an independent cultural configuration. Could this so-called "reformism"
mask some more fundamental category? Such a question is
typically posed from a materialist standpoint; it is suggested that
a cultural construct such as reformism is "really" an expression
of ethnicity, demography, or economic status. The question can
also be raised from a more general standpoint, however, as
when it is suggested that reformism is simply an expression of
world trends toward modernity, that the reformist is simply a
modernist or progressive, and that the specifically Islamic features of his orientation are secondary. What all of these questions imply is that the specifically religious character of reformism is not critical, that this cultural content is reducible to some
more secular category defined by social science theory.

One answer to these alternative analyses is phenomenological. We simply note that the reformist himself defines reformism as having a status separate from questions of ethnicity,

demography, or modernity, and we accept his word for it. Unfortunately, this answer is not adequate for the present study. The present study is both "emic" and "etic": It is "emic" in that its point of departure is a definition formulated by its subjects, the Southeast Asian Muslims, themselves; it is "etic" in that it has attempted to utilize this definition to elucidate categories that relate to general theory (Weberian) and cut across several cultures (Singapore, Indonesia, Malaysia) in a way not always defined by the reformist himself. The basis for this "etic" analysis is correlational, and this same method can address the question of whether reformism is reducible to an external category.

   Ethnicity—Ethnicity does, indeed, correlate with reformism in Jogjakarta. As was noted, ethnic heterogeneity is greater in reformist than in non-reformist circles. Furthermore, those few ethnic minorities (i.e., non-Javanese) represented in the Jogja sample were almost all reformists. In a different pattern, the Singapore data also confirm the relation between reformism and ethnic heterogeneity. For Singapore, the reformists were more likely than non-reformists to be children of ethnically mixed marriages and to be born in an ethnically diversified milieu. These correlations between ethnic diversity and reformism are plausible in *"Verstehen"* terms, since reformism logically implies rejection of traditions, whether Javanese or Malay, of the ethnic majority composing the Muslim group in question, whether Jogjakarta or Singapore. Such rejection would seem most likely for the person whose experience includes alternatives.

   Ethnic diversity, however, is neither identical with reformism nor a necessary and sufficient condition for it. The Kedah survey shows reformist orientations much stronger among an ethnically homogeneous rural people than among the ethnically heterogeneous urban Singaporeans, taking the two samples as wholes. In Jogjakarta, although ethnic minority status is seemingly almost a sufficient condition for being a reformist, it is certainly not a necessary condition, since the majority of the reformists (including leaders) are of the ethnic Javanese majority. And if ethnicity is controlled by eliminating the very few non-Javanese from the Jogjakarta sample, the relationships between reformism and other variables are not much affected. In sum, ethnicity bears important relations with reformism, but the survey data show that reformism and ethnicity are not the same. Reformism is not simply an ideological expression of ethnic minority status or of an ethnically heterogeneous milieu.

Sex—Sexual status cannot be correlated with reformism on the basis of the household surveys, since all of the respondents identified as reformist or non-reformist on the basis of the household survey were male. The school surveys did differentiate on the basis of sex, however, and these data show no strong sex-linked contrasts. The Jogja madrasah data suggest slightly less Islamic and reformist orientation among females on a few items (e.g., 78% males vs. 61% females believe in *djin*—a contrast that recalls a statement by a Malay Muslim in Singapore that "women should believe in a *polong* [a bottle imp], men in the *djin*"); but overall, the male and female students are equal in their extent of reformist belief. Given the Islamic tradition of favoring males over females, one might accuse the reformists of desiring to spread Islam in order to perpetuate male chauvinism. This interpretation is refuted by the strength of Aisjijah activities, as well as the demonstration by survey and other data that both sexes are similar in their commitment to the basic reformist tenets. Reformism cannot in any direct way be reduced to an expression of maleness or an ideological justification of male dominance.

Occupation—Occupation correlates with reformism. Reformists tend to be merchants and manufacturers, non-reformists to don the white collar. There is even a tendency for merchants and manufacturers to spawn sons who are reformists, and history documents the strong commercial representation in the earliest Indonesian reformist movements. And among the Muslim reformists, as among Weber's Calvinists, there are ideological parallels between a "Protestant Ethic" and a "Spirit of Capitalism." Both orientations favor a type of rationalization.

Reformism does not, however, reduce to occupational status. The correlation between merchant fathers and reformist sons does not prove that it is occupation that gives rise to reformism; correlations have also been shown between reformist fathers and merchant sons. Both correlations must be viewed in the light of history. For 600 years, commerce and Islam have been united in Southeast Asia; for 75 years, commerce and reformism. The merchant fathers were also heirs of a staunch Islam and reformist subculture—and it is this total subculture, rather than merely its occupational component, that has produced the reformist sons. By the same token, the commercial subculture has doubtless played its part, together with reformism, in engendering merchant sons. Commerce and reformism are complexly intertwined—showing, as Weber phrased it, a certain "elective affinity."

Second, while the historical record rarely disentangles the occupational from the reformist elements, there are documented instances where conversion to reformism came first and commercial occupation later. This was true in the West Java village of Pekadjangan, for example, where the entire village first converted to reformist Islam, then went into business as fabric manufacturers, and today is one of the leading Indonesian centers for this enterprise. In Jogjakarta the sequence is more complex, since reformism sprang from a milieu both strongly Islamic and commercial; the founder of Muhammadijah himself, K.H.A. Dahlan, was an Islamic teacher but also a part-time trader.

And third, the relationship between reformism and commercial status does not hold in all times or places, or for all people. Today the national and regional leadership of Muhammadijah are largely bureaucrats rather than businessmen—persons who earn their living as civil servants and government teachers. And even among the rank-and-file reformists, as sampled by the Jogjakarta survey, only a minority work as merchants or manufacturers. In Singapore, reformists tend to be English-educated bureaucrats; and in Kedah, farmers. Reformism would seem unlikely to survive among these groups if it were merely an ideological justification or reflection of the capitalist mode of production or of commercial status, although such activities certainly contribute significantly to the reformist endeavor.

Finally, even though capitalistic occupations are a minority within the reformist group, is it this minority which accounts for what "rationalizing" tendencies the reformists show? Various statistical analyses have failed to show that this is true. The differences between reformists and syncretists in most of the cultural features and some of the psychological ones are too great to be explained by the capitalistic element, and occupation does not correlate strongly with such reformist clusters as those revealed by factor analysis. While capitalistic occupation is extremely important as a source of both resources and values within the reformist culture, that culture is now a force in its own right—showing its own integrity and exercising influence independent of the occupation of its bearers.

In sum, reformism does not appear reducible to such obvious and simple social or demographic variables as ethnicity, sex, or occupation, though it bears important relations to them.

Modernizing Factors—More comprehensive than the demographic variables just considered are such overall trends as modernization and Westernization. Historically and today, Islamic reformism in Southeast Asia shows complex relations to these trends—in some ways influenced by them, in others opposing them. No one aware of the history and ethnography would imagine that reformism is simply modernization or Westernization, that the Islamic element is merely a localized wrinkle on these universal tendencies. At the same time, one would expect relationships; and the surveys do permit some exploration of them.

In the first attempt at exploration, relations were assessed between the reformist orientation and a crude measure of modernized or progressive situation, i.e., being urbanized, educated, and young. The Jogja sample was divided by age ("old" and "young," with 40 as the dividing line); by education ("low" and "high," with high school attendance as the dividing line); and by extent of urbanization ("urban" or "rural" place of residence at present). The cross-tabulations between reformism and the psychological items were then redone, controlling for these three factors which were taken as defining a generally "progressive" (young, urban, well educated) versus "conservative" (old, rural, poorly educated) status. It was asked whether the correlations between reformism and psychological patterns that had been discovered for the sample in general held also *within* each subgroup: the young, the old, the urban, the rural, the highly educated and the poorly educated. Because of the subdivisions, these results were considerably more bulky than those already reported and will not be detailed, but the conclusion is clear: In virtually every case, the general relationship held when these factors were controlled.

A second effort at exploring the question endeavored to define two pure types, a "demographic progressive" and a "sociocultural reformist." The progressives fit on all three demographic counts—they were young, well educated, and urban, as defined above—while the conservatives were opposite on all three counts. Reformists were defined by all three attributes— schooling, membership, and theology—and contrasted with respondents who were syncretist on all three counts. This procedure selected from the Jogjakarta sample 101 demographic purists, either progressive or conservative, and 69 sociocultural purists, either reformist or syncretist. Correlations were then checked between the two groups and the various psychological and cultural items.

In many respects, the resulting configurations were similar. Both progressives and reformists tended more than conservatives and syncretists to reject belief in spirits, *slametans*, and *petungan*, for example; to have hospital births, early release from *kuloni*, early toilet-training, less *momong*, more use of *salaman* and less of *sungkan* at Lebaran, and more market play, and to reject the *tuturi* method; to show concern with planning and with organization of time, to express ambition rather than tranquility, and to choose mobility over security, and independence over conformity. Culturally and psychologically, progressivism and reformism share many patterns.

They differ, however, in areas most closely associated with Islam. Reformists excelled syncretists in seeing life as a calling and mission to follow the command of God, in preferring to die in the desert close to God, and in choosing to satisfy mother rather than father. Progressives did not exceed conservatives in choice of these items, suggesting that it is the Islamic linkage of the items, elucidated earlier, which associated them to reformism but not to progressivism. A similar difference is that reformists exceeded syncretists in reporting a sense of sin, whereas progressives did not exceed conservatives in this attitude (in fact, the reverse was true), again suggesting an Islamic-specific psychology. Early circumcision is found among reformists but not among progressives—and again, this is a specifically Muslim practice.

Finally, reformists differ from progressives in a certain collectivism, which has been suggested earlier as associated with Islam. Reformists exceeded syncretists in desire to associate with famous leaders rather than with friends, whereas progressives were below conservatives on this; perhaps this expresses an Islamic collectivist ethic which differs from a bourgeois, interpersonal one of progressivism or modernity. On HQ I-62, reformists but not progressives excelled in concern with the social contribution of work—a collectivist concern which in other contexts, too, has been interpreted as distinguishing the strongly Islamic from the more progressive, Westernized (e.g. English schooled) respondents.

Reformism and progressivism, then, do not generate identical configurations. The reformists are not simply "progressive," though they share many traits with this group. Rather, the progressives can be distinguished from the reformists in that the latter retain elements derived from Islamic culture: a sense of mission, a sense of sin, early circumcision, and collectivism. Progressives appear to thrust toward a rationalization resembling that of reformists, but stripped of the Islamic cultural baggage and the specific psychologies that derive from this Islamic "Protestant" ethic.

The Malay and Singapore comparisons warn, too, against too simple an identification of reformism with progressivism as reflected in education and urbanity. The Singapore Muslim has a higher level of concern with Western education than the Kedah Muslim (reflected in the much greater frequency of Singapore than of Kedah sons in English schools), and his situation is much more urban than that in Kedah. Yet the Kedah subjects are much stronger than those of Singapore in affirmation of reformism, and they excel the Singaporeans, too, in the measures of psychological rationalization. They also excel the Singapore Malays in precisely those Islamically related motivations by which the Jogjakarta reformist excels the Jogjakarta progressive: sense of sin, feeling of mission, and preferring to die close to God rather than among friends. Here again is a reformist culture and psychology that seems independent of secular progressivism. If it is asked why this psychology should be stronger in Kedah than in Singapore, it can be answered as before: that the Islamic organizations and schools are much stronger in Kedah than in Singapore, and these seemingly encourage the specifically Islamic ideologies and attitudes noted.

A further check was made to see to what extent Westernization (as somewhat distinct from the "modernizing" or "progressive" tendencies) was correlated with reformism. HQ 45 on the Jogjakarta survey asked: "Do you incline to the traditions and identity of Indonesia or to a method of progress rather like that of the West?" Choice of the "Western" alternative did not highly correlate with the various evidences of reformist orientation or with the cultural and psychological tendencies most strongly associated with these. Indeed, reformist respondents tended to reject both the traditional and Western alternatives and to add a third, Islam. Another pattern relevant here is one already noted, the relation between Western as opposed to Islamic schooling and the various psychological and cultural tendencies tapped by the Jogjakarta survey. It will be recalled that in many instances the Western schooled were more allied with the syncretists than with the reformists, and a check showed a low correlation between Western schooling and reformist orientation. This differentiation between Western and reformist Islamic cultural influences is not surprising in the light of Southeast Asian history, where "Western" has often been identified with Christianity, with the elite, and with colonialism—all opponents of Islam. While reformism and Westernization converge in many areas of rationalizing tendency, they remain distinct in others.

Reformist Identity

In sum, the data show significant and important relationships between reformism as a cultural construct and such categories or trends as ethnicity, sexual or occupational status,
modernization, and Westernization.[1] But the evidence also

1. Analysis of the relationship between reformism and external elements or systems could certainly go further (see, for example, Wertheim, 1959, pp. 168-98, and 1965, pp. 133-45, concerning relationships
between reformism and capitalism). Full analysis of these relationships
is beyond the scope of this study for several reasons. First, the focus of
the study is not the relation between reformism and such external
elements as occupation, modernization, or capitalism, but on the reformist *psychology*—that is, the association between reformism as a
cultural complex and a behavioral and attitudinal configuration involv-
ing many elements other than these external ones. Second, the focus is
not on the relation of these external elements to this configuration, but
on the relation to reformism, i.e., on *reformist* psychology. Third, no
claim of causality is made. It is not asserted that reformism causes the
configurations associated with it; rather, the aim is to explore the extent
and character of this configuration and its association with reformism.
Establishing the cause or causes of the reformist complex and associated
psychological configurations is a further step fraught with difficulty.
Tentative exploration suggests, however, that neither reformism nor the
associated configuration can be explained as the result of the more
obvious demographic and social categories or trends—i.e., that reformism is to a degree an independent cultural complex having its own
integrity and a distinctive psychological implication.

The present study has not even begun to analyze relations between
reformism and another type of external system: the wider Islamic
culture of which it is a part. A single quotation from Von Grunebaum
(1955, p. 22) suggests directions such analysis could take:

> So the achievement of Islam in transforming the ancestral Arab
> culture [includes] . . . the delineation of a new "standard" type of
> life, that is, a new human ideal, and a detailed pattern for its
> realization in a model biography extending from conception to
> beyond the day of judgment.

Islam is itself reformist, and the objective of reformism is to restore pure
Islam. Thus, it is not surprising that the psychological implications of
Islam should resemble those of reformism. Modest confirmation of this
similarity is given by the survey, which finds many pan-santri (reformist
or traditionalist) tendencies, set against the non-Islamic or less Islamic

speaks against reduction of reformism to such categories. Islamic reformism is a complex cultural orientation, reflecting myriad forces of history and environment. Despite its involvement in these forces, however, reformism appears to sustain its own integrity and thus to justify designation as a meaningful, independent cultural construct.

The Psychology of Reformism

Complex as the reformist configuration may be, it has integrity; its features interlock. Also, it is explicit. Reformists consciously conceive of the configuration as a whole, discuss it, label it, and formulate various doctrines and manifestos to define it. It is a cultural complex.

Those elements which have been termed "psychological"— modes of child-rearing, patterns of marriage and work, personality dispositions, expressive forms, sequences of life cycle and life history—do not constitute so explicit and integrated a complex in the minds of the Southeast Asian Muslim reformists. The reformists are much aware of certain of these elements, less so of others, and various persons perceive various relationships among various elements, but the group as a whole does not share a conscious, explicit, standardized conception uniting the various elements to each other or to the reformist cultural complex. The lack of such an integrated cultural conception does not, of course, preclude strong functional relationships among the elements, and some of these have been suggested. The surveys, however, reveal, on the whole, much less interrelationship among these "psychological" elements than among those that compose the "cultural" complex. Thus, for example, factor analysis does not reveal the degree of consistency in choice of the psychological elements that is apparent with the cultural ones; a respondent who reports rejecting one slametan

---

syncretist. Yet the reformist santri does differ significantly from the others on many features—thus attesting, again, to the distinctiveness of reformism.

usually rejects all, or all of that type, whereas a respondent who weans early may toilet-train late, for example.

It is also true, on the whole, that the cultural elements correlate more strongly with each other than with the psychological elements. The relation between professing reformist theology and denying the slametan practice is strong, for example, whereas the relation between being a reformist and weaning or toilet-training early or late is slight. Indeed, in some comparisons between reformists and nonreformists, the difference on psychological items is so slight as to warrant remarking on their similarity rather than their differences, as perusal of the footnoted statistics will reveal.

Attenuated relationships may reflect measurement error or inadequate formulation of the questions. They may also reflect a randomness of respondents' opinions with regard to such practices as child-rearing, marriage, or work, such that these do not form a tightly integrated system in their lives or minds. A third possibility is that in many respects the attitudes and actions of the reformists and nonreformists really are similar.

Cultural Roots

Similarity is explicable by two factors: common traditions and common directions of change. Javanese, whether reformists, traditionalists, or syncretists, are Javanese, and Malay reformists and nonreformists are both Malay. Regardless of religious type, all share a strong allegiance to their root culture. The Jogjakarta survey reveals, for example, that both reformists and nonreformists believe strongly that the child should learn *krama* Javanese. This is not surprising, since without knowing krama the Jogjakartan, reformist or not, would be excluded from meaningful and prestigeful association in Jogjakarta. Similarly, the survey revealed a strong commitment by both reformist and nonreformist to such basic Javanese values as *nrima* and *sabar.* Javaneseness has characterized Jogjakarta Muhammadijah since its founding, and indeed, that quality has evoked the criticism of non-Javanese Muhammadijans. K.H.A. Dahlan, the

Jogjakartan founder of Muhammadijah, himself exemplifies the
Javanese ideal. In his final assessment of Dahlan, biographer
Anis characterizes him as a "satriya," the Hinduist warrior who
serves as a model in Javanese culture owing to his ability to
combine action with inner calm; Dahlan is portrayed by Anis
as exemplifying the best of the Javanese character, a patient,
orderly tranquility which nevertheless moves toward its goal.
Thus, as seen by a Javanese Muhammadijan, Dahlan, in the
final analysis, is the good Javanese.[2]

Given common roots, then, can one speak of the reformists
as moving from them toward rationalization, while nonreformists remain traditional? No, for both have moved toward rationalization. Within one to fifteen years of the date of the founding
of Muhammadijah, the syncretists and traditionalists had established their movements too—for example, the Nationalist and
Communist parties for the syncretists, and the NU for the
traditionalist santri. In part, these movements sought to retain
and revitalize old traditions, such as Sufi and Hinduist mysticism. Yet these movements necessarily elaborated notions of
history, of organization and change, of rational relations between means and ends. Doubtless these common experiences of
rationalization explain certain general tendencies toward rationalism and against traditionalism as reflected in the survey in
Jogjakarta. Note, for example, the general preponderence of
"rational" rather than "traditional" choices on the ethos questions (HQ II-26 through 31). The Jogjakarta survey indicates a
general Javanese tendency toward rationalization, and the same
can be said of the Singapore and Kedah surveys in certain areas.

Differences

Reformists and nonreformists do differ in certain respects,
however. These differences are expressed by the Javanese themselves through stereotypes such as *santri modèren* as opposed to
abangan. Having done fieldwork among both the reformists and
the syncretists, I am persuaded that they differ importantly in

2. Anis (1962).

life style, ethos, and demeanor as well as doctrine. I have had the experience of picking strangers in a crowd as Muhammadijan and then checking to confirm that indeed they were, and Muhammadijans assert that they can do the same, although they were not able to define precisely what traits permitted them to do this. In Singapore and Malaya the stereotypes are less prominent, since reformism is more an individual inclination than a group doctrine; but even here, ethnographic observation and life histories do suggest that the reformists are distinctive types of people.

If important differences exist, then, what are they? The findings can be summarized, once again, as follows: The life cycle of reformists becomes rationalized in the sense of being de-ritualized, a pattern which follows logically from the reformist conception that what counts is religious ends, such as salvation, and that the various forms of existence can and should be modified to more efficiently achieve these ends: thus reformists cut Arabic from sermons, streamline the practice of prayer, and eliminate the slametan cycle. Freed from ritualistic linkage to the cosmic cycle at points of entry, transition, and exit, life is more easily conceived as history, as struggle toward objectives.

As a plausible outgrowth of this streamlining of the life cycle, transitions are accelerated: dependency (as in *gendong* and *kuloni, bedong* and *buaian kain*) is terminated earlier, independence (as in circumcision and starting work) begins sooner. Such rationalization is ordered by various disciplines, as in the scheduling of ingestion and excretion, obedience to parents, moral exhortation, and ascetic schooling. Change in practice is reflected in change in conception: the reformist narrator of life history dwells less on nostalgic recollection of a sensuous past and more on forward-looking anticipation of a legalistic and activist future. Reflecting a Muslim as opposed to a bourgeois Protestant outlook, the reformist vision of the future is more collectivist than private, imagining contributions to the wider society, religion, and ethnic group rather than personal and domestic happiness and intimate association with friends.

As God's importance increases, that of human forms declines. Particularism, localism, and hierarchy give way to egalitarianism and transcendentalization, nourished by, and nourishing, mobility and cosmopolitanism. These "rationalizing" social values are to some extent tempered (especially, apparently, in Singapore) by an Islamic patrism, a stress on male dominance; but at least in Jogjakarta and Kedah, the rationalization overrides the patriarchal so that the trend is toward egalitarian cooperation.

Reformists show a kind of Protestant Ethos: an affection for plans and missions, asceticism oriented instrumentally, and individualism of certain types. From Islam and perhaps Malayo-Indonesian culture as well comes a tempering value, *ichlas* (steadfast devotion and obedience). Ichlas parallels the Islamic commitment to at least one form, the scripture, and thus prevents the rampant Protestant rationalization such that all forms are reduced to means. As revealed by psychopathology and literary expression, such rationalization is accompanied by a sense of guilt and sin and an introspective judgment of one's personal actions.

Reformism and Rationalization

Overall, then, it appears that the findings support Weber's hypothesis for Muslim Southeast Asia: Religious reformation is associated with a certain psychological rationalization. Considerable caution, however, is needed concerning the character of this rationalization; Weber used the term in many senses. The sense employed here is the efficient utilization of means toward an end. Do the reformists or the nonreformists better fit this ideal type of rationalization?

The first problem is to define the ends of each group. To simplify, one could hazard that the syncretist's major goals are to maintain harmony of self, society, and the cosmic order. The reformist's goals are salvation of his soul and reform of the nonreformist. From the vantage point of their own goals, the syncretist and the reformist would each seem to have organized their lives and personalities quite efficiently. Both are highly rationalized, and some kind of grotesque cost-effectiveness analysis would be necessary to rate which is more so.

One could get around this problem by arguing that it is erroneous to conceive of the syncretists as having goals in the first place. The ritualization, cyclical patterning, and timelessness of their world-view show that they conceptualize the world in terms other than means and ends. For them the key relationship is perhaps between form and meaning. But while this definition of the difference has merit as an ideal type, the data do not support so stark a contrast. The syncretists' own revolutionary movements demonstrate that for them such apparently nonrational elements as ritual, timelessness, and cycles can become rational at a certain level. Harnessed to ideologies stressing political ceremony, myth, and eschatological conceptions of cyclical history, these traditions become weapons of power: means. More modestly, the survey data reveal considerable inclination to think in terms of rationalization of means, among syncretists as well as reformists.

Given the difficulties of claiming a generally greater degree of rationalization in the psychology of one group as opposed to the other, I am inclined to fall back on a more specific Weberian ideal type, the Protestant Ethic. The Protestant Ethic defines a particular set of rationalizations that serve a special end: salvation. Such rationalizations include the purging of ritual, scheduling of time, and streamlining of work. This complex of means and ends forms a psychological configuration illustrating a certain type of rationalization. Overall, it appears that the reformists do fit this type better than the non-reformists. In terms of the peculiar rationality of the Protestant Ethic, the reformists' psychology is more rationalized. They are Muslim Puritans.

Yet it must be emphasized that their "Puritanism" is "Muslim."[3] If their ethic and ethos bear comparison to the Protestant

3. To link reformism to Puritanism is not to claim that Islam derives from Protestant Christianity; such was the reaction of one Muhammadijan, who then cleverly presented the reverse argument, that Protestantism comes from Islam (via the Crusades). The concept of Protestant

Puritans of Max Weber's concern, the reformists also bear the distinctive stamp of their region and religion, Southeast Asia and Islam. Collectivism and legalism as opposed to individualism and dramatism are among the features that distinguish the Southeast Asian Muslim reformist psychology from that of the Protestant Ethic. The findings affirm the logic of Weber's notion of rationalization, while suggesting both possibilities and limitations for extending that concept into the sphere of psychology and beyond the culture of the West.

Ethic is invoked here because this is the theoretical construct from which this study sprang.

Jogjakarta Household Survey
(English Translation)

Write the name of the respondent's neighborhood _____
(Do not write the person's name)

AIM

A scholar, Professor James L. Peacock, is compiling information and opinions
that are necessary for writing a book. This material concerns the history of
religion in Singapore, Malaysia, and Indonesia. Among the methods chosen in
order to write such a history is the recording of experience and opinions of
people from various groups, including you yourself. The collecting of this
information is not intended for the use of politics or factions, but for
knowledge. Your name will not be linked to your answers. Your name will not
be recorded.

2. What is the ethnic group of your father?

                                      (Encircle the proper number)

3. What is the ethnic group of your mother?

FATHER	MOTHER
1. Javanese	1. Javanese
2. Sundanese	2. Sundanese
3. Minangkabau	3. Minangkabau
4. Atjehnese	4. Atjehnese
5. Arab	5. Arab
6. Other	6. Other
(Record_____)	(Record_____)

4. What is your age?

   1. 20-29 years

   2. 30-39 years

   3. 40-49 years

   4. 50-59 years

   5. 60 and over

5. Do you use a title?

   1. Hadji [one who has made the pilgrimage to Mecca]

   2. Kijai [Muslim teacher]

   3. Sajid [descendent of the Prophet]

   4. Sjech ["sheikh," title given to Muslim scholars in Indonesia]

5. R.M., R.A., KRT, Raden Wedono, and the like [noble status; includes titles theoretically inherited from ancestors who served in the courts]

6. Doctor, Engineer [Dutch name for advanced academic degree], Sardjana [Indonesian name for advanced academic degree], Bachelor's degree

7. Other (Record)_____

6. Exactly what schooling have you had?

1. Indonesian government elementary school [SD] (from class _____ to class _____)

2. Muhammadijah elementary school (from class _____ to class _____)

3. Other Islamic elementary school (from class _____ to class _____)

4. Dutch elementary school (State name _____. From class ____ to class _____)

5. Other elementary school (State name _____. From class ____ to class _____)

6. Indonesian junior high school [SMP] (from class _____ to class ____)

7. Muhammadijah junior high school (from class _____ to class _____)

8. Other Islamic junior high school (state name _____. From class _____ to class _____)

9. Dutch junior high school (State name _____. From class ____ to class _____)

10. Other junior high school (State name _____. From class _____ to class _____)

11. Indonesian government senior high school [SMA] (from class _____ to class _____)

12. Muhammadijah senior high school (from class _____ to class _____)

13. Other Islamic senior high school (state name _____ from class _____ to class _____)

14. Other senior high school (state name _____ from class ____ to class _____)

15. Mualimin [the famous Muhammadijah Islamic boy's school of the Madrasah type in Jogjakarta] (From class _____ to class _____)

16. Other Islamic schools of the <u>Madrasah</u> type (state name _____

from class _____ to class _____)

17. Traditional Qur'anic school (state name _____   From

class _____ to class _____)

18. Other schools (state name _____ from class ___ ___ to

_____)

15.* What is the highest level of education that you have reached? _____

What school have you finished? _____

21. Exactly what schooling did your father have?

[same categories as used in question 6, except that "Dutch high school"

is inserted in place of "other high school" for category 14]

35. Exactly what schooling has your eldest son had?

[same categories as used in question 6]

45. What is the age in years of your eldest son? _____

46. Where were you born?

47. Where was your father born?   (Encircle the proper number)

You yourself	Your father
1. Central Java	1. Central Java
2. East Java	2. East Java
3. West Java	3. West Java
4. West Sumatra	4. West Sumatra
5. North Sumatra	5. North Sumatra
6. South Sumatra	6. South Sumatra
7. Madura	7. Madura
8. South Celebes	8. South Celebes
9. Other (state _____)	9. Other (state _____)

51. Are you still employed? <u>If so</u>, what is your work? <u>If not</u>, what was

your last job?

53. What was your first job? _____

55. What was your father's job? _____

*
In order to accord with the coding convention of the Singapore ques-

tionnaire, these questions are not always numbered consecutively.

57. If your eldest son is still in school or not yet employed, what kind of
     work do you plan for him or does he aspire to? If he already works, what
     is his work?

     Work that is planned after he finishes his schooling _____

     Work that is planned but not yet begun even though he has finished
     school _____

     Work that he has already begun _____

60. What method do you most frequently use in order to increase your profit?

     1. Luckily a profitable situation emerges

     2. With planned endeavors

     3. Social connections

     4. Ask blessings from ancestral spirits or from the spirit children at
         sacred graves

     5. Lotteries

     6. Work hard

     7. Other (state _____)

                         MOST OFTEN _____

                         RATHER OFTEN _____

62. Please look at this list. In your opinion, which job condition is most
     important? Which is also important? Which is somewhat important?

     1. adequate income

     2. high salary

     3. no danger of being fired

     4. short working hours, long leisure hours

     5. good opportunity for promotion to higher rank [pangkat]

     6. the work is important and its results satisfy the heart [hati]

     7. interpersonal relations at the place of work are good

     8. the work contributes to society

     9. the work provides status and prestige

     MOST IMPORTANT _____

     ALSO IMPORTANT _____

     RATHER IMPORTANT _____

65. Do you believe that in the next life persons will be punished by God?

    1. believe (yes)

    2. no

    3. don't know/not certain

66. In your opinion, which sacred action listed below is most important?
    and also important? and rather important?

    1. the five daily prayers

    2. struggling to build a society that is good, prosperous, and secure

    3. struggling to build a family that is secure, prosperous, and happy

    4. an inner/spiritual [batin] relationship with God (meditation)

    5. do good to all mankind

    MOST IMPORTANT _____

    ALSO IMPORTANT _____

    RATHER IMPORTANT _____

69. Do you believe that God more favors those who struggle to get ahead or
    those who are already content with their situation?

    1. struggle

    2. satisfied

    3. not certain

70. Approximately how often do you do the prayers?

    1. five times per day

    2. less than five times per day but more than once per day

    3. less than once per day but more than once per week

    4. seldom

    5. never

71. Was your father a hadji [pilgrim to Mecca], imam [leader of prayers at
    the mosque and/or leader of the Muslim community], kijai [Muslim
    teacher], ustad [Muslim teacher], modin [Muslim official], or other
    holy personage?

    1. Hadji

    2. Imam

    3. Ustad

    4. Kijai

    5. <u>Modin</u>

    6. Other (state _____)

    7. No

<u>II</u>

1. Which of the following sentences most fit your own belief?

    1. religion and daily work are two matters that have no relationship at all

    2. religion and work form a unity that is fixed by God (for example, if you lend money you may not charge interest [due to limitations imposed by religion]).

    3. Certainly religion should influence each individual personality in his work (for example, goad each person to work hard).

2. Which of the following sentences most fits your own belief?

    1. The carrying out of the law of Islam must be cleansed from the folk custom [<u>adat istiadat</u>] that does not fit the teachings of Islam.

    2. Folk customs that have long been followed by Muslims should not be changed.

    3. Not certain.

3. Which of the following sentences most fits your own belief?

    1. Better that an individual draw his own conclusions about the law of Islam from the sacred Qur'an and the codified traditions [<u>sunnah</u>].

    2. Most people are better off depending upon the religious authority [<u>ulama</u>] to inform them about the law of Islam.

    3. Better if each person relies on the inner voice [<u>suara hati nuraninja</u>] of his own heart.

    4. Better if each person relies on the great teachings of the ancestral spirits at the shrines [<u>Keramat</u>] together with his own inner voice.

4. Which of the following sentences most fit your own belief?

    1. Better to pray [<u>sembahjang</u>] every day at a set time.

    2. Better to pray [<u>memohon</u>] to God at whatever time I desire to relate to God.

    3. Not certain.

5. In your opinion, is it fitting that the women [literally the "mother's faction" or <u>kaum ibu</u>] take a larger role than they presently have in the mosque activities?

   1. yes

   2. no

   3. not certain

6. In your opinion, is it fitting that father and mother should work together in educating their child, or that the mother should directly educate and discipline the child while the father, who actually has the authority, seldom exercises it directly?

   1. work together

   2. the mother should do the educating

   3. other answer (record: _____)

8. Can you give an example of an event in the life story [<u>riwajat hidup</u>] of the Prophet Muhammad that made a deep impression on you when you were young? _____

10. At what age were you circumcised?

   1. before 1 year

   2. 1-6 years

   3. 7-9 years

   4. 10-15 years

   5. above 15 years

11. On Lebaran day [the ending of the Muslim fast--Idul Fitri], did you as a child customarily ask forgiveness of your parents?

   1. yes

   2. no

12. What was your age when you first began to work? _____ years

13. What was your age when you first began to live separately from your parents? _____ years

14. What was your age when you first married? _____ years

15. Was your marriage based on love [<u>suka sama suka</u>] or arranged by your parents?

   1. love

    2. arranged

16. Where did you live during the first year after the marriage?

    1. With your wife's parents (in-laws)

    2. With your own parents

    3. In a house separate from either set of parents

    4. Other answer (record _____)

17. Who most influenced matters in your household? Your mother or your

father?

    1. Father

    2. Mother

20. When you educate(d) your eldest son, which of the following traits did

you feel were most important to equip that child for life?

    1. obedience [ta'at]

    2. sociability [pergaulan baik]

    3. ability to think for himself (think out each matter itself, not only

       depend on the opinion of others)

    4. adapt [menjesuaikan diri] and fit into situations

    5. work hard

    6. help others

    7. lead an orderly life

    8. other (state _____)

    MOST IMPORTANT_____

    ALSO IMPORTANT_____

    RATHER IMPORTANT_____

23. Which of the following methods do you most often employ in educating

your eldest son?

    1. punish the child when he fails in a certain endeavor (for example,

       if he fails in an examination), but reward him when he succeeds.

    2. continuously give the child advice [dituturi, probably accompanied

       by prodding and guiding of the child's body].

    3. encourage the child to do things on his own.

    4. try to keep him happy all the time.

    5. other answers (state _____)

MOST FREQUENT_____

ALSO FREQUENT_____

RATHER FREQUENT OR SELDOM_____

26. Below are several statements. Please read them, pair by pair, and then please choose one from each pair that most fits your own personality. Don't hesitate and think a long time before choosing. Just give your first reaction.

    26a) EXAMPLE

        1. I am more attracted to work than to socializing.

        2. I am more attracted to socializing than to work.

        (Choose the statement that most fits with your personality.)

    26b) 1. I more often defend my own opinion even though many persons oppose it.

        2. I more often make sure that I keep good relations with others even though they are not in keeping with my own opinion.

    26c) 1. I always endeavor to seek the highest reward or prestige [prestasi] even though the endeavor disturbs my peace of heart (Ketenteraman hati).

        2. Better to have peace of heart even though the reward or prestige is small.

    27a) 1. I try to satisfy the heart of my mother more than that of my father.

        2. I try to satisfy the heart of my father more than that of my mother.

        3. Satisfy both.

    27b) 1. I more often feel confused [bimbang] when I don't plan the path of my life and my program of work with perfection and efficiency.

        2. I more often simply fantasize about the pleasures of life.

    27c) 1. I dare to sin [dosa] a little if the ultimate results are fairly good.

        2. I believe that drinking liquor, even a little, is always sinful.

28a) 1. More often I feel as though I've sinned.

      2. More often I feel pressed because I must choose between
          demands of work and pleasures of socialization.

28b) 1. More often I believe that there are people who are trying to
          hurt me.

      2. More often I feel homesick [merindukan rumah] for my home,
          family, or mother and father.

28c) 1. I want to work, even though far from the home and my parents,
          and among people who are very different from me, as long as
          the work has results in the end.

      2. Although my work has inadequate results, it doesn't matter so
          long as I stay in my home and community [Kampung].

29a) 1. I desire to plan all of my actions.

      2. I feel sad because neighbors, kinfolk, or friends look down
          on me.

29b) 1. I feel that it is difficult to divide the time of work from
          the time of pleasant socializing [Kesenangan bergaul].

      2. I like to go to parties and ceremonies that are joyful, and
          not to think about difficulties of dividing time.

29c) 1. I often crave to associate with a friend without counting the
          time that is consumed.

      2. I more often crave acquaintance with famous people.

30a) 1. I don't like it when people interrupt me when I am doing some-
          thing important.

      2. When I was still young, I often felt pity/sympathy [kasihan]
          toward my wife, but not a feeling of romantic love [tjinta],
          and I felt that I had sacrificed myself [mengorbankan diri]
          to my parents in marrying according to their wishes and not
          my own desires.

30b) 1. I would rather die alone in the desert while praying to God
          than die at home surrounded by friends but far from God.

      2. On occasion, I have joined two ideologically conflicting
          organizations in order not to insult either.

30c) 1. I feel that I must plan all aspects of life in order that I
          can carry out the command [perintah] of God.

      2. I remember my father as a person whom I venerated [hormati]
          with a manner that was so polite [sopan] that I felt shame
          [segan] when I was in his presence.

31a) 1. If my things are stolen, I let it go with a heart that is
          stoic [ichlas].

      2. I am a person who finds it extremely difficult to acknowledge
          defeat or loss.

31b) 1. I prefer watching the shadow play or movie that is comic
          rather than sad.

      2. I am not able to leave a play or stop reading a novel before
          the story is complete.

      3. Both.

31c) 1. I would rather go hungry than beg.

      2. I often quit a project that I want to carry out if another
          person doesn't like it.

32. Imagine that you are watching the following stories at the movie,
     theatre or ludruk show, which would most sadden you?

     1. A man divorces his wife and marries a woman who is bitchy and mean.
         The child suffers because of this stepmother.

     2. An innocent man is accused of committing a crime. He is attacked
         [dikerojok] by a gang of angry neighbors. At the time he is
         attacked, he defends himself and fights with great courage, and will
         apparently win and escape, but finally he becomes exhausted, loses,
         and is killed.

33. Do you customarily behave as follows:

     1. humbling oneself according to proper
         etiquette when in the presence of a
         superior [Andap-asor]   customarily customarily no

     2. dissimulation [Étok-Étok]   customarily customarily no

     3. steadfast stoicism [Ichlas]   customarily customarily no

     4. patience [sabar]   customarily customarily no

5. acceptance of whatever comes [nrima]   customarily   customarily no

6. enduring and struggling through

   suffering [prihatin]   customarily   customarily no

34. If you feel sad and desire to talk with someone, who do you most often

    seek?

    1. friend

    2. parent

    3. wife

    4. other (record_____)

35. Could you say, or not, that your father was a strict or harsh [keras]

    person?

    1. could say so

    2. no

36. Exactly which of the following ceremonies do you still endeavor to per-

    form?

    1. Slametan tingkeban [feast when the mother is seven months pregnant]

    2. Slametan brokohan (lahir) [feast when the mother gives birth]

    3. Slametan selapanan [feast when the child is one month old]

    4. Slametan weton [birthday feast]

    5. Slametan tedak siten [feast to celebrate the child's setting foot

       on the ground]

    6. Slametan djuma'at Kliwon [feast to celebrate the sacred Javanese

       Friday]

    7. Slametan Kematian [funeral meal three days after death]

    8. funeral meal seven days after death

    9. funeral meal 100 days after death

    10. funeral meal one year after death

    11. funeral meal 1000 days after death

    12. muludan [ceremony to celebrate the birth and death day of the

        Prophet]

    13. maleman [ceremony in the evening toward the end of the fast]

    14. Petungan hari baik [system of calculating proprietous days]

    15. praying at holy shrines

    16. Tarekat Sufi [Islamic mystical order]

38. Do you believe in:

    1. Ratu Adil [messianic figure, the "just prince"]

    2. Pusaka jang punja zat Kesaktian [sacred object ancestral object]

    3. Tujul [genie-like spirit that does its master's or mistress's bidding]

    4. Memedi [frightening, spook-like spirit]

    5. Wé wé [spirit]

    6. Lelembut [possessing spirit]

    7. Djin [Muslim spirit]

    8. Peri [spirit]

    9. Gendruwo [type of possessing spirit]

    10. Wedon [ghost]   (Encircle all that are believed)

39. Have you ever been a member of any of the following organizations? Which ones?

    1. NU [Nahdatul Ulama--conservative Muslim party]

    2. Muhammadijah [reformist Muslim missionary organization]

    3. PSI [Partai Sosialis Indonesia--Indonesian socialist party]

    4. PNI [Partai Nasional Indonesia--Indonesian nationalist party]

    5. PSII [Partai Sarekat Islam Indonesia--Indonesian Islamic Association Party, name for SI adopted in 1929]

    6. HMI [Himpunan Mahasiswa Indonesia--Muslim Student Association]

    7. SI [Sarekat Islam--Islamic Association, original name of PSII]

    8. GMNI [Gerakan Mahasiswa Nasional Indonesia--Indonesian National Student Movement]

    9. Ansor [youth wing of NU]

    10. Gerakan Pemuda Marhaen [youth wing of PNI]

    11. Perti [Persatuan Tarbijah Indonesia--Indonesian Education Association]

    12. Persis [Persatuan Islam--Islamic Union]

    13. Al-Irsjad [reformist Muslim organization]

    14. Partai Muslimin [Muslim Party--reformist Muslim political party]

    15. Masjumi [Madjelis Sjuro Muslimin Indonesia--Council of Indonesian

Muslim Associations]

16. PMII

17. IPNU

18. PII [Peladjar Islam Indonesia--Indonesian Islamic Student's Party]

19. GPI

20. GPII [Gabungan Pemuda Islam Indonesia--Union of Islamic Indonesian
     Youth]

21. PERSAMI

22. GEMSOS

23. GPS

24. SOKSI

25. KOSGORO [a cooperative]

26. GASBIINDO [Gabungan Sarekat Buruh Islam Indonesia--Union of Islamic
     Indonesian Workers]

27. SARBUMUSI [Sarekat Buruh Muslimin Indonesia--Union of Islamic
     Indonesian Workers]

28. BO [Budi Utomo--Noble Endeavor, party founded in 1908 to promote
     Javanese cultural revival]

29. Aliran[2] Kebatinan [meditation groups]

42. Are there other movements or organizations that you have been in to
     improve society? (Record_____)

44. If you were forced to choose, can you say that you more agree with the
     orientation "Islam mazhap" [based on the traditionalist scholastic
     traditions], "Islam tidak mazhap" [not based on these but, by implica-
     tion, on idjtihad] or "Javanese Islam" [syncretism].

     1. Islam mazhap

     2. Islam tidak mazhap

     3. Islam kedjawèn

45. Do you more incline to the traditions and identity of Indonesia or to a
     method of progress rather like that of the West?

     1. tradition

     2. West

     3. other (state_____)

<u>III</u>

THE FOLLOWING QUESTIONS ARE DIRECTED TO THE RESPONDENT'S WIFE, WHO IS TO
GIVE EXPLANATIONS ABOUT THE ELDEST SON (IF THERE IS NO SON, END THE INTER-
VIEW).

46. Where was your eldest son born?

    1. his mother's parents' house

    2. his father's parents' house

    3. his own house

    4. a house of collateral kin or friends

    5. hospital

    6. other (state_____)

47. Was the child cuddled [<u>dikuloni</u>]?

    1. yes

    2. no

48. <u>If yes</u>, from what age to what age? From _____ to _____ (months)

50. Was the child ever carried on the hip in the shawl [<u>digendong</u>]?

    1. yes

    2. no

51. <u>If yes</u>, from what age to what age? From _____ to _____(months)

53. At what age was the child first taught to urinate and defecate in a

    certain place (such as the toilet)?

    1. before one year

    2. 1-1 1/2 year...[remainder of items goes by 1/2 year intervals to "4

       years and over"]

54. At what age was the child weaned [<u>disapih</u>]?

    1. before six months

    2. six months to one year...[remainder of items goes by 1/2 year

       intervals to "six years or more"]

55. At what age was the child circumcised [<u>disunat</u>]?

    1. before 1 year

    2. 1-6 years

    3. 7-9 years

    4. 10-15 years

    5. 15 years or above

56. At what age did the child begin to feel shame [merasa isin]?

    1. before 4 years

    2. 5 years

    3. 6-8 years

    4. more than 8 years

    5. not yet

57. At what age did the child begin to speak refined Javanese [krama] to

    his father? [same intervals as in 56]

58. Did the child frequently play at erecting buildings or houses from

    blocks or stones?

    1. often

    2. seldom

    3. never

59. Did the child ever play market?

    1. often

    2. seldom

    3. never

60. Was the child frequently given snacks [djadjanan] or only occasionally?

    1. frequently

    2. occasionally

61. Was the child often taken care of [dimomong] by an older sibling or

    other relative other than its mother?

    1. frequently

    2. seldom

62. Can you give a brief summary of one story that you often tell the child?

64. Were any of your sons ever adopted [diangkat] by a relative?

    1. yes

    2. never

65. If yes, by relatives of the mother or by relatives of the father?

    1. mother's relatives

    2. father's relatives

66. If by mother's relatives, her male or female relatives?

68. On Lebaran does the eldest son customarily ask forgiveness of his

mother and father?

1. yes

2. no

69. If yes, with the method of bowing, kneeling, or shaking hands?

    1. bowing [<u>sungkem</u>]

    2. kneeling [<u>sembah</u>]

    3. shaking hands [<u>salaman kasih tangan</u>]

Jogjakarta School Survey
(English Translation)

NO NEED TO WRITE YOUR NAME   Name of school_____

                                          Class_____

                                          Sex (male or female)_____

1. What is your age?_____

2. What is your ethnic group [bangsa]_____

3-4. Have you ever attended a religious school (madrasah or pondok-pesan-tren)?

         Name of school_____from class (year) what_____to what_____

         Name of school_____from class (year) what_____to what_____

         Name of school_____from class (year) what_____to what_____

5. Where were you born?_____

6. Where was your father born?_____

7. What is your father's work today?_____

8. Has your father ever attended a Dutch school?

         If so, from about which class_____to which_____?

9-11. Has your father ever attended a Muhmmadijah school?

         Name or type of school_____approximately how many years?_____

         Name or type of school_____approximately how many years?_____

         Name or type of school_____approximately how many years?_____

13-14. Has your father ever attended a pondok-pesantren or madrasah other than Muhammadijah?

         Name or type of school_____approximately how many years?_____

         Name or type of school_____approximately how many years?_____

         Name or type of school_____approximately how many years?_____

15-17. identical with question II-62 on Jogjakarta household survey.

18. identical with question II-4, household survey, except no provision for "not certain."

19.   identical with question II-2, household survey.

20.   identical with question II-1, household survey.

21.   identical with question II-3, household survey.

22.   identical with question II-33, household survey.

23.   identical with question II-38, household survey.

24.   Below are several pairs of sentences. Please read each pair, then
      please choose one statement from the pair that is most in keeping with
      your own personality. No need to doubt and think a long time before
      choosing. Just give your first reaction.

24a. Example:

      1. I am more attracted to study than to socializing.

      2. I am more attracted to socializing than to study.

      (Choose the statement that most fits with your personality.)

24b-27b. equals household II-26c, 27a, 27c, 29b, 29c, 30c, 31b, 31c.

28.   Imagine how your life will be in the future [dimasa depan] and write a
      fantasy-story that depicts yourself while working, at home, and in the
      society twenty-five years from now.

APPENDIX C
Singapore Household Survey
(English Translation)

INFORMANT'S NAME: _____

ADDRESS: _____

_____

DATE OF INTERVIEW: _____

DAY OF INTERVIEW: _____

I certify that this questionnaire is a true record of a face
to face interview with the person named in the left hand col-
umn. All instructions were com-
plied with and any difficulties
have been noted on my report
form.

INTERVIEWER: _____

A scholar, Professor James L. Peacock, is gathering materials for a book.
These materials have to do with the social history of Muslims in Singapore,
Malaysia and Indonesia. One method of writing this history is to record life
histories, past events, and personal experiences of certain individuals, including you, yourself. We are approaching a lot of different people. We
want to get an idea of the experience of a cross-section of people. Your
name will not be mentioned in connection with your particular answers.

I.

1. Title: Environment:

   Haji   1.1   Rural neighborhood [Kampong] 2.1

   [a person who has been   Urban Kampong   .2

   to Mecca]   Other Urban   .3

   Syed   .2   Other (specify)

   [locally taken to mean   _____

   a person who is a de-

   scendant of a prophet]

   Inche   .3

   [Malay term of respect

   equivalent to "mister"]

3. What is the ethnic group [bangsa] of your father?

4. What is the ethnic group of your mother?

	Father	Mother
Arab	3.1	4.1
Indian	.2	.2
Malay	.3	.3
Javanese	.4	.4

226

Buginese	.5	.5
Boyanese	.6	.6
Acheh	.7	.7
Minangkabau	.8	.8
Other (specify)		

5. How old are you?		
	20 - 29	5.1
	30 - 39	.2
	40 - 49	.3
	50 - 59	.4
	60 and over	.5

6. What is the highest standard of school you have completed?

8. Have you ever attended a Malay school? If so, from what standard to what standard?

12. Have you ever attended an English school? If so, from what standard to what standard?

	Highest	MALAY SCHOOL		ENGLISH SCHOOL	
		Started	Completed	Started	Completed
Primary I	6.1	8.1	10.1	12.1	14.1
II	.2	.2	.2	.2	.2
III	.3	.3	.3	.3	.3
IV	.4	.4	.4	.4	.4
V	.5	.5	.5	.5	.5
VI	.6	.6	.6	.6	.6
Secondary 1	.7	.7	.7	.7	.7
2	.8	.8	.8	.8	.8
3	.9	.9	.9	.9	.9
4	.0	.0	.0	.0	.0
Form 5	.X	.X	.X	.X	.X
Post-Sec/Pre U I ...	7.1	9.1	11.1	13.1	15.1
II ..	.2	.2	.2	.2	.2
Higher education	.3	.3	.3	.3	.3
None/not attended ...	.4	.4	.4	.4	.4

16. Have you ever attended a religious school [bersekolah ugama]? If so, from what standard to what standard?

From _____ to _____

16. _____

17. _____

18. Have you ever attended any other type of school? If so, what type?
From what standard to what standard?

    Type of school _____

    From _____ to _____

18. _____

19. _____

20. _____

21. Has your father ever attended a Malay school? If so, from what standard
to what standard?

25. Has your father ever attended an English school? If so, from what standard to what standard?

	MALAY SCHOOL		ENGLISH SCHOOL	
	Started	Completed	Started	Completed
Primary I	21.1	23.1	25.1	27.1
II	.2	.2	.2	.2
III	.3	.3	.3	.3
IV	.4	.4	.4	.4
V	.5	.5	.5	.5
VI	.6	.6	.6	.6
Secondary 1	.7	.7	.7	.7
2	.8	.8	.8	.8
3	.9	.9	.9	.9
4	.0	.0	.0	.0
Form 5	.X	.X	.X	.X
Post-Sec/Pre-U I	22.1	24.1	26.1	28.1
II	.2	.2	.2	.2
Higher education	.3	.3	.3	.3
None/not attended	.4	.4	.4	.4

29. Has your father ever attended a religious school? If so, what type?
From what standard to what standard?

Type of school _____

From _____ to _____

29. _____

30. _____

31. _____

32. Has your father ever attended any other type of school?

If so, what type? From what standard to what standard?

Type of school _____

From _____ to _____

32. _____

33. _____

34. _____

35. Has your eldest son ever attended a Malay school? If so, from what standard to what standard?

39. Has your eldest son ever attended an English school? If so, from what standard to what standard?

	MALAY SCHOOL		ENGLISH SCHOOL	
	Started	Completed	Started	Completed
Primary I	35.1	37.1	39.1	41.1
II	.2	.2	.2	.2
III	.3	.3	.3	.3
IV	.4	.4	.4	.4
V	.5	.5	.5	.5
VI	.6	.6	.6	.6
Secondary 1	.7	.7	.7	.7
2	.8	.8	.8	.8
3	.9	.9	.9	.9
4	.0	.0	.0	.0
Form 5	.X	.X	.X	.X
Post-Sec/Pre-U I	36.1	38.1	40.1	42.1
II	.2	.2	.2	.2
Higher education	.3	.3	.3	.3
None/not attended	.4	.4	.4	.4

43. Has your eldest son ever attended a religious school? If so, from what standard to what standard?

     From _____ to _____

                                                 43. _____

                                                 44. _____

45. Has your eldest son ever attended any other type of school? If so, what type? From what standard to what standard?

     Type of school _____

     From _____ to _____

                                                 45. _____

                                             46. _____

47. Where were you born?

49. Where was your father born?

	Respondent	Respondent's father
Perlis	47.1	49.1
Kedah	.2	.2
Penang or Province Wellesley	.3	.3
Perak	.4	.4
Selangor	.5	.5
Negri Sembilan	.6	.6
Malacca	.7	.7
Kelantan	.8	.8
Trengganu	.9	.9
Pahang	.0	.0
Johore	.X	.X
Singapore	.Y	.Y
Java	48.1	50.1
Sumatra	.2	.2
Bawean	.3	.3
Other Indonesia	.4	.4
Pakistan	.5	.5
India	.6	.6

Saudi Arabia   .7   .7

Others (specify)   _____

---

51. Are you working at present? If yes, what job do you do? If not, what

was your last job? (Probe for full details)

_____

_____

51. _____

52. _____

---

53. What was your first job? (Probe for details)

_____

_____

53. _____

54. _____

---

55. What is your father's work?

_____

55. _____

56. _____

---

57. If eldest son is in school or has not yet started work, what work have

you prepared him to go into? If already employed, what is his work?

In school   57.1

Left school, not working   .2

Working   .3

58. _____

59. _____

---

60. What method do you ordinarily use to try to increase your income? Can

you choose one from this list? (Read out list below) Can you choose

one more?

	First Chosen	Second Chosen
Readiness to make use of lucky opportunity	60.1	61.1
Careful planning	.2	.2
Social connections	.3	.3
Sheer struggle [se-mata^2 perjuangan]	.4	.4
Other (write in)		

_____

62. Please look at this list and choose <u>one trait</u> that you feel is the most
     important concerning a job. (Show Card A) And second most important
     And third most important?

	1st	2nd	3rd
High salary	62.1	63.1	64.1
No danger of being fired	.2	.2	.2
Short working hours, lots of free time	.3	.3	.3
Good chance for promotion [<u>naik pangkat</u>]	.4	.4	.4
The work is important and gives a feeling			
of accomplishment [<u>perasaan puas hati</u>]	.5	.5	.5
Pleasant social relations at work	.6	.6	.6
The work contributes to society	.7	.7	.7

65. Do you believe that in the next life, some people will be punished and
     others rewarded by God?

                         Yes   65.1
                         No   .2
                         Unsure   .3

66. In your opinion, which of these sins is worst? And second worst, and
     third worst? (Show Card B)

	Worst	2nd Worst	3rd Worst
Not carrying out the responsibility of doing			
the five prayers [<u>salat</u>]	66.1	67.1	68.1
Not having faith [<u>beriman</u>] in God	.2	.2	.2
Not striving to build a good Muslim			
community [<u>ummat</u>]	.3	.3	.3
Not working diligently at your job	.4	.4	.4
Not spiritually communicating [<u>berhubong</u>			
<u>batin</u>] with God	.5	.5	.5

69. Do you believe God is more pleased when individuals struggle to push
     ahead or when they are satisfied with what they have?

     Struggle [<u>bergerak maju</u>] to push ahead   69.1
     Satisfied [<u>berpuas hati</u>] with what they have   .2
     Unsure   .3

70. Approximately how often do you pray?

      More than 5 times per day   70.1

      Less than 5 times but more

          than once a day   .2

      Less than once per day but

          more than once per week   .3

      Rarely   .4

      Never   .5

71. Was your father a haji, imam, ustaz or otherwise an unusually pious man?

      Haji [pilgrim]   71.1

      Imam [mosque prayer leader]   .2

      Ustaz [religious teacher]   .3

      Other special qualifications

          (specify)   ____

      No   .Y

II.

1. Which of the following statements best fits your own belief? (Read out)

      Every act in life should be an act of devotion

          [Ibadat] including work.   1.1

      Religion [ugama] and work [pekerjaan] are

          separate.   .2

2. Which of the following statements best fits your own belief? (Read out)

      Islam must purify itself of custom and ritual

          [adat istiadat] that are not true religion

          [ugama]   2.1

      Hallowed custom and ritual long observed by

          Muslims should not be changed.   .2

      Unsure.   .3

3. Which of the following statements best fits your own belief? (Read out)

      Each individual should draw his own conclusions

          regarding Muslim law by examining the teach-

          ings [ajaran] of the Holy Qur'an   3.1

      Most people should depend on the religious

authorities [pehak$_2$ berkuasa ugama] to inform

them about the law of Islam.   .2

---

4. Which of the following statements best fits your own belief? (Read out)

    Prayer should be each day at a set time.   4.1

    One should pray to God whenever one yearns

        to communicate [berhubong] with him.   .2

    Unsure.   .3

---

5. Are you most attracted to takdir or to jihad?

    Takdir [a divine decree setting the course of a

        person's life]   5.1

    Jihad [holy crusade or holy war]   .2

    Understand terms but unsure.   .3

    Does not understand terms [Arabic terms

        possibly not understood by Malays if little

        religious schooling].   .4

---

6. In your opinion, should women play a stronger role than they now play in

    activities of the mosque [pergerakan mesjid]?

        Yes   6.1

        No   .2

        Unsure   .3

---

7. In your opinion, should father and mother co-operate in raising the

    child, or should it be the mother who most directly disciplines the

    child, while the father, though having authority, rarely deals so

    directly with it?

        Co-operate   7.1

        Mother should discipline .2

        Other answer (write in)   _____

        Unsure   .4

---

8. Can you give one example of an event in the life history of Nabi

    Mohammed s.a.w. [s.a.w. stands for Sallalla-hu-'ala-hi-was, salam, or

    'God Bless his name'] which made a strong impression on you when you

    were young?

    _____

_____ 8. _____

_____ 9. _____

10. At what age were you circumcised?

Under 1	10.1
1 - 6	.2
7 - 9	.3
10 - 15	.4
Over 15	.5

11. On Hari Raya Puasa [the holiday celebrating breaking of the fast] did
     you as a child ordinarily ask forgiveness from your parents?

Yes	11.1
No	.2

12. How old were you when you first started work?

13. How old were you when you first left home?

14. How old were you when you first married?

	Started Work	First Left Home	First Married
Up to 15 years	12.1	13.1	14.1
16 years	.2	.2	.2
17 years	.3	.3	.3
18 years	.4	.4	.4
19 years	.5	.5	.5
20 years	.6	.6	.6
21 years	.7	.7	.7
22 years	.8	.8	.8
23 years	.9	.9	.9
24 years	.0	.0	.0
25 years or over	.X	.X	.X
Other answer (specify)			
_____	.Y	.Y	.Y

15. Was this marriage by "love" [suka sama suka] or arranged by parents and
     relatives?

Love	15.1
Arranged	.2

16. Where did you live after this marriage?

     With the bride's parents   16.1

     With your parents   .2

     In a house separate from that

       of either parent, an

       independent household   .3

     Other answer (write in)   _____

17. (If lived at man's parents' home): Did your father or your mother most

    influence [berchampor-tangan] your household affairs?

     Father   17.1

     Mother   .2

18. If lived at separate house. How far was your house from that of your

    mother and father?

     Under 1/2 mile   18.1

     1/2 mile but under 1 mile   .2

     1 mile but under 2 miles   .3

     2 miles but under 5 miles   .4

     5 miles or more   .5

19. If lived at separate house. Who came most frequently to visit you –

    your mother or father?

     Mother   19.1

     Father   .2

20. When you were trying to raise your eldest son, which of the following

    qualities did you consider most important for him to acquire in prepara-

    tion for life? (Show Card C) Which is second most important? And

    which is third?

	1st	2nd	3rd
Obedience [ta'at]	20.1	21.1	22.1
Getting along well with people [pergaulan baik]	.2	.2	.2
Thinking for himself	.3	.3	.3
Adapting [menyesuaikan diri] to every situation	.4	.4	.4
Working diligently	.5	.5	.5
Helping others	.6	.6	.6

	1st	2nd	3rd
Disciplined habits	.7	.7	.7

Other (write in) _____

---

23. Which of the following methods did you (or do you) most often use in rearing your eldest son? (Show Card D) Which would you choose second? Which third?

	1st	2nd	3rd
Punish the child when he fails in some endeavor (for instance, if he fails to pass an exam), but reward him when he succeeds	23.1	24.1	25.1
Constantly tell the child what to do so that he rarely has a chance to fail or do wrong	.2	.2	.2
Encourage the child to attempt tasks on his own, then reward him when he succeeds	.3	.3	.3
Try to keep him happy at all times	.4	.4	.4

Other answers (write in) _____

I am going to read out some pairs of statements. As I read them out, please choose the sentence, first or second that most nearly applies to you. Don't hesitate long in answering. Just give your first reaction.

26(a) I always try to keep strictly on schedule.   26.1

   Sometimes I put off until tomorrow what I ought to do today.   .2

 (b) I frequently find it necessary to stand up for what I think is right.   .5

   I always strive to have pleasant relations with others.   .6

 (c) I work hard at everything I undertake until I am satisfied with the results.   .9

   No matter what, I try to keep a calm heart and tranquil spirit [bertenang].   .0

27(a) I try to satisfy my mother more than my father.   27.1

   I try to satisfy my father more than my mother.   .2

 (b) I feel anxious when I do not plan my career [jalan hidup] well and am inefficient.   .5

   I often think how I would like to wear expensive clothes.   .6

(c). I prefer to risk a little to gain [beruntong] a lot.   .9

I believe that moderate drinking is always sinful.   .0

28(a) Often I feel as if I have done many wrongs and am sinful
[berdosa].   28.1

I feel tense about having to separate my work from my
social life.   .2

(b) I believe people are plotting against me.   .5

Sometimes I feel homesick [merindukan rumah].   .6

(c) I like working with a project that will produce results,
even though it is far from my home and parents, and
among people very different from me.   .9

I like to stay in my home or kampong.   .0

29(a) I feel a desire to schedule all my activities in order
that nothing is left disorganized.   29.1

I worry about neighbors or kinfolks looking down on me
[memandangkan].   .2

(b) I feel tense [payah] about trying to decide between the
demands of work and the demands of life.   .5

I like to go to parties and other gatherings that are
noisy and jolly.   .6

(c) I often yearn for a friend with whom I can associate
without worrying about wasting time.   .9

I like to know important people.   .0

30(a) I don't like people to ask advice or otherwise interrupt
me when I am working on something important.   30.1

When I was young, I often felt sympathy [kasehan] but not
love [chintaan] and desire toward my wife, and I felt
that I had sacrificed myself to my parents by marrying
according to their wish rather than mine.   .2

(b) I would rather die alone in the desert while praying to
God than at home in bed surrounded by friends but
without God.   .5

I have sometimes joined two groups that possess conflicting

       views so as to avoid offending either group.   .6

(c) I feel that I must plan my entire life in order to perform

       the mission that God has set for me.   .9

       I remember my father as a man whom I respected and venerated

       with a manner most polite, until I felt very shy and

       embarrassed in his presence.   .0

31(a) If my goods are stolen, I just let them go with a heart

       that is _ichlas_.   31.1

       Frequently I am the last to give up.   .2

(b) I prefer comedy to tragedy at the cinema.   .5

       I cannot leave a cinema film or stop reading a novel until

       it is finished.   .6

(c) I would rather go hungry than ask a favor.   .9

       I am apt to forego something I want to do when others feel

       that it isn't worth doing.   .0

---

32. Imagine that you see the following stories at a cinema.

      Which would most sadden you?

(a) A man divorces his wife and marries another who is mean and

       cruel. His child suffers because of this step-mother.   32.1

(b) A man is wrongly accused of a crime. In the end he is

       trapped by angry neighbors whom he was actually trying

       to help. When the crowd attacks him, he fights coura-

       geously, and apparently will win and get away, but

       finally becomes exhausted, is overwhelmed and killed.   .2

---

33. Have you ever been active in any of the following organizations?

      PAP [People's Action Party - the party of Prime Minister

      Lee Kuan Yew in power] DAP [Democratic Action Party]   33.1

      PMIP [Pan Malayan Islamic Party]   .2

      UMNO [United Malay National Organization, the main Malay

      party of Malaya]

      PKM [Partai Kebangsaan Melayu - the main Malay party of

      Singapore]   .3

      4 PM [Persatuan Persunatan Pemuda Pemudi Melayu - Malay

                youth literary association]   .4

            All Malayan Muslim   .5

            Missionary Society

            Ahmaddiyya [radical sect believed by many to reject

                    orthodox Islamic worship]   .6

            Muhammadiyah   .7

            Tarekat (sufi) Club   .8

            Pentjak [fighting] Club   .9

            Other (specify)   _____

34. Are there any other activities which you have engaged in to reform

     society?

                        _____

                        _____

                                                    34. _____

                                                    35. _____

36. If you were forced to choose, would you say you are more inclined

     toward the "Kaum muda" [modernist] or the "Kaum tua" [conservatist]

     position within Islam?

            Kaum muda   36.1

            Kaum tua   .2

            Understand terms but unsure   .3

            Do not understand terms   .4

III. Ask subsequent questions of respondent's wife about her eldest son. If

     no son in house, close interview.

37. Was your eldest son born in the house of your mother?

                        Yes   37.1

                        No   .2

38. If no, where was he born

                        Husband's father's house 38.1

                        Own house   .2

                        House of other relatives   .3

                        Hospital   .4

                        Other (specify)   _____

39. Was he wrapped in a <u>bedong</u> [swaddling]?

                    Yes   39.1

                    No   .2

40. If yes, from what age to what age?

                    From:_____ to _____ (months)

                                          40. _____

                                        41. _____

42. Was your eldest son suspended in a <u>buaian kain</u> [hammock]?

                    Yes   42.1

                    No   .2

43. If yes, from what age to what age?

                    From:_____ to _____ (months)

                                          43. _____

                                        44. _____

45. At what age did your oldest son learn to urinate and defecate in a suitable place (hole or toilet)?

                    Under 1 1/2 years   45.1

                    1 1/2 years but under 2 years   .2

                    2 years but under 2 1/2 years   .3

                    2 1/2 years but under 3 years   .4

                    3 years but under 3 1/2 years   .5

                    3 1/2 years but under 4 years   .6

                    4 years or over   .7

46. At what age was the child weaned?

                    Under 6 months   46.1

                    6 months but under 1 year   .2

                    1 year but under 1 1/2 years   .3

                    2 years but under 2 1/2 years   .4

                    2 1/2 years but under 3 years   .5

                    3 years or more   .6

47. At what age was the child circumcised?

                    Under 6 months   47.1

                    6 months but under 1 year   .2

```
                1 year but under 1 1/2 years          .3

                2 years but under 2 1/2 years          .4

                2 1/2 years but under 3 years          .5

                3 years or more                        .6
```

48. Do you feel that caring for your eldest son (feeding, nursing, changing
     it) was burdensome or pleasant?

                Burdensome   48.1

                Pleasant   .2

49. If the child, <u>for example</u>, crawled close to the fire or played with a
     knife, would you teach him to be careful by (read out).

                Letting him feel the heat or cut

                    himself a little, then remark,

                    "Hot, eh?" or "Sharp, eh?" and

                    making a disapproving face.   49.1

                Spanking him.   .2

                Constantly telling him that he

                    should not do these things,

                    and what he should do.   .3

                Other answer (write in)   _____

                                               _____

50. When the child asked for money to buy sweets and other things, was he
     given as much as he requested?

                Yes   50.1

                No   .2

51. Did the child's older relatives often care for the child?

                Yes   51.1

                No   .2

52. Can you briefly summarize a story that you have often told the child?

                _____

                _____

                _____

                                              52. _____

                                              53. _____

54. Did your eldest son eat the evening meal with the father before the age
     of sixteen?

                         Yes   54.1

                         No   .2

55. If yes, at what age did he start doing so?

                         Up to 6 years   55.1

                         7 - 8   .2

                         9 - 10 years   .3

                         11 years   .4

                         12 years   .5

                         13 years   .6

                         14 years   .7

                         15 years   .8

56. Have any of your sons been adopted by relatives?

                         Yes   56.1

                         No   .2

57. If yes to 56. Which relatives? His father's or his mother's?

                         Father's   57.1

                         Mother's   .2

58. On Hari Raya Puasa does the child ordinarily ask forgiveness from his
     parents?

                         Yes   58.1

                         No   .2

APPENDIX D
Singapore School Questionnaire
(English Translation)

NO NEED TO WRITE YOUR NAME

1. What is your age?_____

2. What is your ethnic [bangsa] group?_____

3. Have you ever attended a Malay school? If so, from what class_____
    to what_____?

4. Have you ever attended an English school? If so, from what class_____
    to what_____?

5. Have you ever studied in a Madrasah? If so, from what class_____
    to what_____? Name of the school?_____

6. Where were you born?_____

7. Where was your father born?_____

8. What is your father's work?_____

9. Has your father ever attended Malay school? From class_____to
    what_____?

10. Has your father ever attended an English school? From class_____
    to what_____?

11. Has your father ever studied at a Madrasah [religious school]?
    Class_____to what_____?

12. Has your father ever studied at a pondok [religious boarding school]?
    How many years_____? Name of the pondok_____?

13. Please look at this list and choose one trait that you consider most
    important with respect to a job:

    a. high salary

    b. no danger of getting fired

    c. short working hours, much time off

    d. good opportunity to be promoted to higher rank

    e. the work is important and gives a feeling that satifies the heart.

    f. good social relations at the working place

    g. the work contributes to society.

    h. other_____

14. Which is second (most important)?_____

15. Which is third (most important)?_____

16. Which of the following is truly suitable to you yourself?

    a. pray every day at a fixed time

    b. pray to God at a time when you want to relate to Him

17. Which of the following truly fits your own belief?

    a. Islam must be cleansed from custom that is not truly religion.

    b. Custom that has long been followed by Muslims should not be changed.

18. Which of the following truly fits your own belief?

    a. Every action is worship, including work.

    b. Religion and work are separate.

19. Imagine how your life will be in the future, and write a fantasy-story depicting you yourself at work, at home, and in the society twenty years from now.

Glossary

ABANGAN—Syncretic Javanese Muslim culture; its beliefs and practices combine Hindu-Buddhist, animistic-Javanese, and Muslim elements.

ACHLAK—Morality.

ADAT—Custom, tradition.

AGAMA—Religion

AHMADIYYA—A Muslim reformist organization originating in Pakistan which proclaims Mirza Ghulam Ahmat the new Prophet.

'AISJIJAH—The women's branch of Muhammadijah.

AKAL—Rationality.

ALUS—Refined, civilized, polished, cultural. (Cf. *kasar.*)

BANGSA—Ethnicity, race.

BEDONG—Swaddling of a child.

BUAIAN KAIN—Soft, constraining hammock for a child.

DA'WAH—Evangelism.

DJIN—Genies, supernatural creatures recognized by Islam.

DOSA—Sin.

GENDONG—The practice of carrying a child in a soft, constraining sling.

GOTONG-ROJONG—Mutual cooperation.

HADJ—The pilgrimage to Mecca.

HADJI—A Muslim who has made the pilgrimage to Mecca.

HAWA NAFSU—Greed, lust, instinct.

HIJRAH—Muhammad's journey from Mecca to Medina in 622 A.D.

247

HMI (Himpunan Mahasiswa Islam)—Islamic college student association, a reformist Muslim youth movement in Indonesia.

Ichlas—Stoic commitment.

Idjtihad—Rational personal interpretation of Muslim scripture and tradition. (cf. *taklid buta.*)

IMM (Ikatan Mahasiswa Muhammadijah)—Muhammadijah college student association.

IPM (Ikatan Peladjar Muhammadijah)—Muhammadijah secondary school student association.

Isin—Embarrassment, as in the presence of superiors.

Isra Mir'adj—The miracle of Muhammad's ascension to heaven and his experience of revelation in heaven.

Jawi peranakan—Children of marriage between Indian father and Malay mother.

Kaget—Shock which disturbs equilibrium, causes confusion.

Kampung—A rural Indonesian or Malay village, or an urban neighborhood with many features of such a village.

Kasar—Crude, uncouth, natural. (Cf. *alus*)

Kathi—Muslim religious official especially concerned with marriage.

Kaum Muda—Reformist Islam, reformists.

Kaum Tua—Traditionalist Islam, traditionalists.

Kebatinan—Syncretic mysticism or theosophy; the search for inner *(batin)* meaning.

Kijai—Indonesian Muslim religious teacher of a traditionalist type; title indicates sacred Islamic status.

Krama—A level of Javanese language considered high, refined, formal. (Cf. *ngoko.*)

Kuloni—To cuddle a child.

Latah—A personality disorder characterized by obsessive imitation of the speech and action of others.

Lebaran—The day celebrating the end of the month of fasting, and the customary day in Malayo-Muslim culture for asking forgiveness from one's parents.

Ludruk—Popular *abangan* drama.

Madrasah—Reformist religious school.

Madzhap—Schools of Islamic law derived from medieval scholars.

Maleman—Ceremony celebrating the end of a fast period.

MASJUMI—An Indonesian political party, largely of reformist Muslim persuasion.

MAULUD—Feast celebrating the birth and death of Muhammad.

MIR'ADJ—Feast celebrating Muhammad's ascension.

MOMONG—Brief care of a child by persons other than its mother.

MUFTI—Religious official authorized to interpret Muslim law.

MUHAMMADIJAH—Islamic reform movement, founded in 1912.

MULUDAN—Feast celebrating birth and death day of Muhammad.

MUSJARAWAH—A method of reaching a decision by consensus rather than by vote.

NGOKO—A level of Javanese language considered low, unrefined, informal. (Cf. *krama.*)

NRIMA—Passive acceptance.

NU (NAHDATUL ULAMA)—A traditionalist Muslim party of Indonesia.

PENGADJIAN—Study sessions.

PESANTREN—Traditional Javanese Islamic school.

PETUNGAN—Counting, divining; a mode of coordinating ritual or other events with the cosmos.

PKM (PARTAI KESATUAN MELAYU)—Malayo-Muslim political party emphasizing interests of this ethnic-religious group.

PMI (PARTAI MUSLIM INDONESIA)—Javanese Muslim reformist political party.

PMIP (PAN-MALAYA ISLAMIC PARTY OR PERSATUAN ISLAM SA-MELAYU)—Malayo-Muslim political party emphasizing interests of this ethnic-religious group.

PNI (PARTAI NASIONAL INDONESIA)—Javanese nationalist political party of rather *abangan* sentiment.

PONDOK—Traditionalist Malay Islamic school.

PRIJAJI—Aristocratic Javanese.

QUR'AN—The Koran, Muslim sacred scripture.

RUKUN—Cooperation and harmony, emphasizing solidarity.

SABAR—Patience.

SALAMAN—Greeting by shaking hands.

SALAT—Islamic prayers.

SANTRI—Purist, pious Muslims; also, students.

SANTRI KOLOT—Traditionalist Muslims.

SANTRI MODÈREN—Reformist Muslims.

SAYED—Title or term for descendants of the Prophet.

SD—(See SR.)

SEMBAH—A kneeling posture of veneration.

SJARIAH—The Islamic law.

SLAMETAN—Communal feast, supposed to create social and spiritual harmony among the celebrants and thus make their souls calm and *slamet* (safe).

SMA (SEKOLAH MENENGAH ATAS)—Senior high school.

SMP (SEKOLAH MENENGAH PERTAMA)—Junior high school.

SR (SEKOLAH RAKJAT)—Elementary school, also known as Sekolah Dasar (SD).

SUNGKAN—Neutralization of *isin* by proper manners.

SUNGKEM—Bowing one's head and kneeling to show respect.

TAAT—Obedience to rules.

TAKLID BUTA—Reliance on authorities. (Cf. *idjtihad.*)

TAMAN SISWA—A Javanese *abangan* educational movement and type of school.

TATA-KRAMA—Etiquette.

TAUHID—The unity or oneness of God.

TUTURI—Continuous kinesic molding and verbal instruction of children.

UGAMA—Religion.

ULAMA—Muslim official and scholar.

UMMAT—The Muslim community.

UMNO (UNITED MALAYS NATIONAL ORGANIZATION)—Moderate Malay party with a strong Islamic element.

URMAT—Respect, emphasizing hierarchy.

VERSTEHEN—Understanding, specifically (as defined by Max Weber) through interpretation of the actor's viewpoint. (German.)

WAHJU—Charisma, spiritual power, as of the Javanese god-king.

WAJANG KULIT—Puppet shadow-play.

References

Aaron, Raymond
  1964 German Sociology. Mary and Thomas Bottomore, trans. New York: Free Press.
Abdullah, Taufik
  1966 Adat and Islam: An Examination of Conflict in Minangkabau. Indonesia 2:1-24.
  1971 Schools and Politics: The Kaum Muda Movement in West Sumatra (1927–1933). Ithaca, N.Y.: Cornell University Modern Indonesia Project.
Aberle, David F.
  1952 Arctic Hysteria and Latah in Mongolia. New York Academy of Science Transactions, Series II, 14:291-297.
Adikusumo, Arman
  1969 Homoseksualitas dan Psikosis (Homosexuality and Psychosis). Dijwa 2 (April):64-71.
Ahmat, Sharom
  1969 Transition and Change in a Malay State: A Study of Economic and Political Development of Kedah. Ph.D. dissertation, University of London.
Al-Attas, Syed Hussein
  1963a On the Need for an Historical Study of Malaysian Islamization. Journal of Southeast Asian History 4: 62-74.
  1963b The Weber Thesis in Southeast Asia. Archives de Sociologie des Religions 8(15):21-34.

1968a Islam in Social Change in Malaya. The Malaysian So-
      ciety of Orientalists Seminar on Religion in Social
      Change with Reference to Malaysia. University of Ma-
      laya, Kuala Lumpur.
1968b The Grading of Occupational Prestige Among the Ma-
      lays in Malaysia. Journal of the Malaysian Branch of the
      Royal Asian Society 41:146-156.

Al-Attas, Syed Muhammed Naguib
  1963 Some Aspects of Sufism as Understood and Practiced
       Among the Malays. Singapore: Malaysian Sociological
       Research Institute, Ltd.
  1967 New Light on the Life of Hamzah Fansuri. Journal of the
       Malaysian Branch of the Royal Asiatic Society of Great
       Britain and Ireland 40:42-51.

Alfian
  1970 Modernism in Indonesian Politics: The Muhammadijan
       Movement During the Dutch Colonial Period, 1912–
       1942. Ph.D. dissertation, University of Wisconsin.
  1971 Agama dan Masalah Perkembangan Ekonomi (Religion
       and the Problem of Economic Development in Indo-
       nesia). Indonesia Magazine 9:16-26.

Ali, A. Mukti
  1957 The Muhammadijah Movement: A Bibliographical In-
       troduction. M.A. thesis, McGill University, Montreal.

Ames, Michael
  1964 Religion, Politics, and Economic Development in Cey-
       lon: An Interpretation of the Weber Thesis. In Sympo-
       sium on New Approaches to the Study of Religion. June
       Helm, ed. Seattle: University of Washington Press.

Amir, M.
  1934 De Transvestieten van Batavia (The Transvestites of
       Batavia). Geneeskundig Tijdschrift van Nederlandsch
       Indie 74:1081-1083.

Anderson, Benedict R. O'G.
  1965 Mythology and the Tolerance of the Javanese. Ithaca,
       N.Y.: Cornell University Modern Indonesia Project.
  1972a The Idea of Power in Javanese Culture. In Culture and
        Politics in Indonesia. Claire Holt, ed. Ithaca, N.Y.:
        Cornell University Press.

1972b Java in a Time of Revolution: Occupation and Resistance 1944–1946. Ithaca, N.Y.: Cornell University Press.

Anis, H. M. Junus
1962 Riwajat Hidup K.H.A. Dahlan, Dan Perdjoangannja (Life Story of K.H.A. Dahlan, and His Struggle). Jogjakarta: Pimpinan Pusat Muhammadijah.

Annual Report on the Social and Economic Progress of the
1936 People of the State of Kedah (Unfederated Malay States), 1935–1936. London: His Majesty's Stationery Office.

Arasaratnam, S.
1970 Indians in Malaysia and Singapore. London: Oxford University Press.

Archer, Raymond
1937 Muhammadan Mysticism in Sumatra. Journal of the Malayan Branch of the Royal Asiatic Society 15(2): 1-126.

Aulia
1960 Kepentingan Agama Untuk Ilmu Kedokteran (Importance of Religion for Medical Science). Madjallah Kedokteran Indonesia 10(12):507-514.

Bador, Abdul Kahar bin
1964 Reformisme Islamique et Politique en Malaisie, Un Cas Historique. Archives de Sociologie des Religions 9(17): 68-84.

Baginda, Abdullah bin
1959 Boyanese of Singapore. Social Studies Department paper, University of Malaysia.

Banks, David J.
n.d. Islam and the Spirits of Kinship in Northwestern Malaysia. Unpublished paper.

Bateson, Gregory
1936 Naven. Cambridge: Cambridge University Press.

Bateson, Gregory, and Margaret Mead
1942 Balinese Character: A Photographic Analysis. New York: New York Academy of Science.

Becker, Alton L.
1974 Plot as Symbolic Action: Two Essays. Paper presented at the Conference on Symbolic Systems in Indonesia,

Malaysia, and the Philippines. Ann Arbor: University of Michigan Center for South and Southeast Asian Studies.

Becker, Judith
  1974 Time and Tune in Java. Paper presented at the Conference on Symbolic Systems in Indonesia, Malaysia, and the Philippines. Ann Arbor: University of Michigan Center for South and Southeast Asian Studies.

Bellah, R. N.
  1957 Tokugawa Religion: The Values of Pre-Industrial Japan. Glencoe, Ill.: Free Press.
  1963 Reflections on the Protestant Ethic Analogy in Asia. Journal of Social Issues 19:52-60.
  1965 Religion and Progress in Modern Asia. New York: Doubleday.

Benda, Harry J.
  1958 The Crescent and the Rising Sun: Indonesian Islam Under the Japanese Occupation, 1942-1945. The Hague: van Hoeve.
  1970 South-East Asian Islam in the Twentieth Century. In The Cambridge History of Islam. P.M. Holt, Ann K. S. Lambton, and Bernard Lewis, eds. Cambridge: Cambridge University Press.

Bendix, Reinhard
  1962 Max Weber: An Intellectual Portrait. New York: Doubleday.

Benjamin, Geoffrey
  1974 Indigenous Religious Systems of the Malay Peninsula. Paper presented at the Conference on Symbolic Systems in Indonesia, Malaysia, and the Philippines. Ann Arbor: University of Michigan Center for South and Southeast Asian Studies.

Berg, C. C.
  1932 Indonesia. In Whither Islam? A Survey of Modern Movements in the Moslem World. H.S.R. Gibb, ed. London: Victor Gollancz.

Boland, B. J.
  1971 The Struggle of Islam in Modern Indonesia. The Hague: Martinus Nijhoff.

Boon, James A.
  1975 Bali Hindu Versus Islam: Circumcision Rituals and Reli-
       gious Change. Paper presented at the Conference on
       Mysticism and Rationalism in Islam. Durham, N.C.:
       Duke University South Asia Committee.

Brandon, James
  1967 Theater in Southeast Asia. Cambridge, Mass.: Harvard
       University Press.

Castles, Lance
  1966 Notes on the Islamic School at Gontor. Indonesia
       1:30-45.
  1967 Religion, Politics, and Economic Behavior in Java: The
       Kudus Cigarette Industry. New Haven: Yale University
       Southeast Asia Studies.

Chabot, Hendrik Theodorus
  1950 Verwantschap, Stand en Sexe in Zuid Celebes (Kinship,
       Status, and Sex in South Sulawesi). Groningen and
       Djakarta: J. B. Wolters.

Chander, R.
  1972 Gulongan Masharakat: Community Groups (1970
       Population and Housing Census of Malaysia). Kuala
       Lumpur: Jabatan Perangkan Malaysia.

Chua, S. C.
  1964 Report on the Census of Population, 1957. State of
       Singapore.

Cremin, Lawrence A.
  1970 American Education: The Colonial Experience, 1697–
       1783. New York: Harper and Row.

Cunningham, Clark
  1965 Order and Change in an Atoni Diarchy. Southwestern
       Journal of Anthropology 21:359-382.

Dahm, Bernard
  1969 Sukarno and the Struggle for Indonesian Independence.
       Mary F. Sommers Heidhues, trans. Ithaca, N.Y.: Cor-
       nell University Press.

Danziger, K.
  1960 Independence Training and Social Class in Java, Indo-
       nesia. Journal of Social Psychology 51:65-74.

de Josselin de Jong, P. E.
  1960 Minangkabau and Negeri Sembilan: Socio-Political
       Structure in Indonesia. Djakarta: Bhratara.
Demos, John
  1971 A Little Commonwealth. New York: Oxford University
       Press.
Dewey, Alice D. G.
  1962 Peasant Marketing in Java. New York: Free Press.
Dipojono, Bonokamsi
  1972 Javanese Mystical Groups. In Transcultural Research in
       Mental Health. William P. Lebra, ed. Honolulu: East-
       West Center.
Djajadiningrat, Pangeran Aria Achmad
  1936 Herinneringen (Remembrances). Amsterdam-Batavia:
       G. Kolff.
Djamour, Judith
  1965 Malay Kinship and Marriage in Singapore. London:
       Athlone.
  1966 The Muslim Matrimonial Court in Singapore. London:
       Athlone.
Drewes, G. W. J.
  1955 Indonesia: Mysticism and Activism. In Unity and Vari-
       ety in Muslim Civilization. G. E. von Grunebaum, ed.
       Chicago: University of Chicago Press.
Drewes, G. W. J., ed. and trans.
  1969 The Admonitions of Seh Bari: A Sixteenth-Century
       Javanese Muslim Text Attributed to the Saint of Bonan.
       The Hague: Martinus Nijhoff.
Eisenstadt, S. N.
  1968 The Protestant Ethic and Modernization: A Compara-
       tive View. New York: Basic Books.
Ellis, Gilmore W.
  1896 Notes and News: Medico-Psychological Association
       General Meeting. Journal of Medical Science 42:209-212.
  1897 A Mental Malady of the Malays. Journal of Mental
       Science 43:32-40.
Emmerson, Donald
  Forth- The Ramayana Complex. Honolulu: University of Ha-
  coming waii Press.
Endicott, Kirk Michael
  1970 An Analysis of Malay Magic. Oxford: Clarendon Press.

Fagg, Donald R.
   1958 Authority and Social Structure: A Study of Javanese
          Bureaucracy. Ph.D. dissertation, Harvard University.
Federspiel, Howard M.
   1970 The Muhammadijah: A Study of an Orthodox Islamic
          Movement in Indonesia. Indonesia 10:57-80.
Geertz, Clifford
   1959 Ritual and Social Change: A Javanese Case. American
          Anthropologist 59:32-54.
   1960a The Javanese Kijaji: The Changing Role of a Cultural
          Broker. Comparative Studies in Society and History
          2:228-249.
   1960b The Religion of Java. Glencoe, Ill.: Free Press.
   1963 Peddlers and Princes: Social Change and Economic
          Modernization in Two Indonesian Towns. Chicago:
          University of Chicago Press.
   1966 Person, Time and Conduct in Bali: An Essay in Cultural
          Analysis. Cultural Report No. 14. New Haven: Yale
          University Southeast Asia Studies.
   1968 Islam Observed: Religious Development in Morocco
          and Indonesia. New Haven: Yale University Press.
   1973 The Interpretation of Culture. New York: Basic Books.
Geertz, Hildred
   1959 The Vocabulary of Emotion. Psychiatry 22:225-237.
   1961 The Javanese Family. New York: Free Press.
   1968 Latah in Java: A Theoretical Paradox. Indonesia 5:
          93-104.
Gerth, H. H., and C. W. Mills, eds. and trans.
   1958 From Max Weber: Essays in Sociology. New York:
          Oxford University Press.
Gluckman, Max
   1962 Les Rites de Passage. In Essays on the Ritual of Social
          Relations. Max Gluckman, ed. Manchester, Eng.: Uni-
          versity of Manchester Press.
Goethals, Peter R.
   1961 Aspects of Local Government in a Sumbawan Village.
          Ithaca, N.Y.: Cornell University Modern Indonesia Pro-
          ject.
Green, Robert, ed.
   1959 Protestantism and Capitalism: The Weber Thesis and Its
          Critics. Boston: Heath.

Hadiwijono
  1967 Man in the Present Javanese Mysticism. Baarn, Netherlands: Bosch and Kenning.
Hagen, Everett
  1962 On the Theory of Social Change: How Economic
       Growth Begins. Homewood, Ill.: Dorsey Press.
Hamka
  1957 Ajahku: Riwajat Hidup Dr. H. Abd. Karim Amrullah
       dan Perdjuangan Kaum Agama di Sumatera (My Father: Life Story of Dr. H. Abd. Karim Amrullah and the
       Religous Struggle in Sumatra), 3rd ed. Djakarta:
       Djajamurni.
  1966 Kenang-kenangan Hidup (Memoirs). Kuala Lumpur:
       Pustaka Antara.
Hawkins, Everett D.
  1957 Entrepreneurship in the Batik Industry of Indonesia.
       Indonesia Project Publications, Vol. 3. Boston: Massachussetts Institute of Technology Center for International Studies.
  1961 The Batik Industry: The Role of the Javanese Entrepreneur. In Entrepreneurship and Labor Skills in Indonesian Economic Development. Benjamin Higgins, ed.
       Monograph Series No. 1. New Haven: Yale University
       Southeast Asia Studies.
Hoek, Jan
  1949 Dajakpriesters: Een Bijdrage Tot de Analyse Van de
       Religie de Dajaks (Dyak Priests: Analysis of Dyak Religion). Ph.D. dissertation, University of Amsterdam.
Holt, Claire
  1939 Dance Quest in Celebes. Paris: Les Archives Internationales de la Danse.
  1967 Art in Indonesia: Continuities and Change. Ithaca,
       N.Y.: Cornell University Press.
Honigmann, John J.
  1967 Personality in Culture. New York: Harper and Row.
Hudson, Alfred B.
  1972 Padju Epat: The Ma'anyan of Indonesian Borneo. New
       York: Holt, Rinehart and Winston.
Hussain, Zahar Ahmad bin Haji Fazal
  1965- Growth of Islamic Education in Malaysia. Education
  1966 Journal 3:54-66.

1969 Politics and Policies in Malay Education in Singapore, 1951–65, With Special Reference to the Development of the Secondary School System. M.A. thesis, University of Singapore.

Indonesia, Biro Pusat Statistik (Central Office of Statistics)

1961 Statistical Pocketbook of Indonesia. Djakarta: Biro Pusat Statistik.

1971 Indonesia: Sensus Penduduk 1971 (1971 Population Census). Djakarta: Biro Pusat Statistik.

Iskandar

n.d. Kamus Dewan (Malay language dictionary). Kuala Lumpur: Dewan Bahasa dan Pustaka (Council of Language and Literature).

Jay, Robert

1963 Religion and Politics in Rural Central Java. Cultural Report No. 12. New Haven: Yale University Southeast Asia Studies.

1969 Javanese Villagers: Social Relations in Rural Modjokuto. Cambridge, Mass.: Massachusetts Institute of Technology Press.

Johar, Azis B.

1961 The Javanese People of Singapore, 1960/61. Social Science Department paper, University of Singapore.

Johns, A. H.

1965 The Gift Addressed to the Spirit of the Prophet. Oriental Monograph Series No. 1. Canberra: Australian National University Center for Oriental Studies.

1966 From Buddhism to Islam: An Interpretation of the Javanese Literature of the Transition. Comparative Studies in Society and History 9 (October): 40-50.

Kartini, R. A.

1921 Letters of a Javanese Princess. Agnes Louis Couperus, trans. London: Duckworth and Co.

Kats, J.

1923 Het Javaansche Toneel, Deel I, Wajang Poerwa (The Javanese Theater, Part I, Puppet Plays). Weltevreden, Netherlands: Volkslectuur.

Kechik, Abbas B.

1961 Mosque: A Comparative Study of a Suburban and a City Mosque. Social Science Department paper, University of Singapore.

Kern, R.
    1925 Mailrapport No. 644x/2A. Verslag van March 1925
          Jogjakarta Congress Muhammadijah (Report on the
          1925 Jogjakarta Muhammadijah Congress). The Hague:
          Department of Colonial Affairs, Ministry of Interior.
Kessler, Clive S.
    1974 Muslim Identity and Political Behavior in Kelantan. In
          Kelantan. William Roff, ed. Kuala Lumpur: Oxford
          University Press.
Kirsch, A. T.
    1967 Thai Buddhist Syncretism. Ph.D. dissertation, Harvard
          University.
Koentjaraningrat, R. M.
    1961 Some Social Anthropological Observations on Gotong
          Rojong Practices in Two Villages of Central Java.
          Ithaca, N.Y.: Cornell University Modern Indonesia Pro-
          ject.
    1969 Rintangan Mental Dalam Pembangunan Ekonomi di
          Indonesia (Mental Obstacles to Economic Development
          in Indonesia). Djakarta: Bharata.
    n.d. Angket Nilai-Nilai Budaja: Faktor-Faktor Mental Da-
          lam Pembangunan Ekonomi di Indonesia: Program
          Pelita Tahap II (Inquiry into Cultural Values: Mental
          Factors in Indonesian Economic Development, Illumi-
          nation Program, Phase II). Djakarta: Lembaga Ilmu
          Pengetahuan Indonesia (Indonesia Science Council).
Kraemer, H. (supplemented by C.A.O. van Nieuwenhuijze)
    1952 Agama Islam (Islamic Religion). Djakarta: Badan Pen-
          erbit Kristen.
Kuchiba, Masuo, and Yoshihiro Tsubouchi
    1968 Cooperative Patterns in a Malay Village. Asian Survey,
          8 (October):836-839.
Kumton, Rozhan B.
    1957 Muslim Religious Schools in Malaya. Social Studies
          Department paper, University of Singapore.
Kuntowidjojo
    1971 Economic and Religious Attitudes of Entrepreneurs in a
          Village Industry: Notes on the Community of Batur.
          Mitusuo Nakamura, trans. Indonesia 12:47-56.
Leighton, Alexander
    1959 My Name Is Legion. New York: Basic Books.

Lenski, Gerhard
  1963 The Religious Factor. New York: Doubleday.
LeVine, Robert
  1973 Culture, Behavior, and Personality. Chicago: Aldine.
Levy, Marion J., Jr.
  1966 Modernization and the Structure of Societies: A Setting
    for the Study of International Affairs, Vols. 1 and 2.
    Princeton, N.J.: Princeton University Press.
Ling, Tan Tjiauw
  1968 Beberapa Segi Daripada Laporan Preliminer Projek Re-
    search "Bantji." (Several Facets of the Preliminary
    Report on the Research Project on Transvestites). Djiwa
    2(April):45-54.
Loh, C. H.
  1963 The Arab Population of Singapore, 1819-1959. Geog-
    raphy Department paper, University of Singapore.
Mangkunegara II of Surakarta, K.G.P.A.A.
  1957 On the Wajang Kulit (Purwa) and Its Symbolic and
    Mystical Elements. Claire Holt, trans. Ithaca, N.Y.:
    Cornell University Modern Indonesia Project.
Masdani, J.
  1968 Pemeriksaan Psikologik Pada Bantji (Psychological
    Analysis of Transvestites). Djiwa 2 (April):55-60.
Matthes, B. F.
  1872 Over de Bissoe's of Heidensche Priesters en Priesteres-
    sen der Boeginezen (On the Holy Priests and Priestesses
    of the Buginese). Verhandelingen der Koniklijke Aca-
    demie van Wetenschapen 7:1-50.
McClelland, David C.
  1967 The Achieving Society. New York: Free Press.
McDougall, John Arthur
  1968 Shared Burdens: A Study of Communal Discrimination
    by the Political Parties of Malaysia and Singapore.
    Ph.D. dissertation, Harvard University.
McVey, Ruth T.
  1963 Indonesia. New Haven: Human Relations Area Files.
  1970 Introduction. In Nationalism, Islam and Marxism, by
    Sukarno. Ithaca, N.Y.: Cornell University Modern
    Indonesia Project.
Mulder, J. A. Niels
  1970 Aliran Kebatinan as an Expression of the Javanese

Worldview. Journal of Southeast Asian Studies 1:105–114.

1975 Mysticism and Daily Life in Contemporary Java: A Cultural Analysis of Javanese Worldview and Ethic as Embodied in Kebatinan and Everyday Experience. Ph.D. dissertation, University of Amsterdam.

Murphy, H. B. M.
1959 Culture and Mental Disorder in Singapore. *In* Culture and Mental Health. Marvin K. Opler, ed. New York: Macmillan.

Muskens, M. P. M.
1970 Indonesie: Een Strijd om National Identiteit, Nationalisten, Islamiet, Katholieken (Indonesia: A Struggle Toward National Identity, Nationalist, Islamic, and Catholic). Bussum, Netherlands: Paul Brand.

Nash, Manning
1974 Ethnicity, Centrality, and Education in Pasir Mas. *In* Kelantan. William Roff, ed. Kuala Lumpur: Oxford University Press.

Needham, Rodney
1960 The Left Hand of the Mugwe: An Analytical Note on the Structure of Meru Symbolism. Africa 30:20-33.

Nieuwenhuijze, C. A. O. van
1945 Samsu 'L-Din Van Pasai: Bijdrage tot de Kennis der Sumatraansche Mystiek (Inquiry Into the Knowledge of a Sumatran Mystic). Leiden: E. J. Brill.

Nitsastro, Widjojo
1970 Population Trends in Indonesia. Ithaca, N. Y.: Cornell University Press.

Noer, Deliar
1960 Masjumi: Its Organization, Ideology, and Political Role in Indonesia. M.A. thesis, Cornell University.

1973 The Modernist Muslim Movement in Indonesia, 1900–1942. London: Oxford University Press.

Noteboom, D.
1948 Aantekeningen over de Cultuur der Boeginezen en Makassaren (Notes on the Culture of the Buginese and Makassarese). Indonesia 3 (November):244-255.

Opler, Marvin K.
1956 Culture, Psychiatry, and Human Values. Springfield, Ill.: Charles C. Thomas.

Palmier, L. H.
1954 Modern Islam in Indonesia: The Muhammadijah After Independence. Pacific Affairs 27:255-263.
Parsons, Talcott
1968 The Structure of Social Action. New York: Free Press.
Peacock, James L.
1967 Anti-Dutch, Anti-Muslim Drama Among Surabaja Proletariana. Indonesia 4(October):44-73.
1968 Rites of Modernization: Symbolic and Social Aspects of Indonesian Proletarian Drama. Chicago: University of Chicago Press.
1973a Indonesia: An Anthropological Perspective. Los Angeles: Goodyear.
1973b Religion, Communications, and Modernization: A Weberian Critique of Some Recent Views. Human Organization 28:35-41.
1975a Consciousness and Change: Symbolic Anthropology in Evolutionary Perspective. Oxford: Blackwells.
1975b Weberian, Southern Baptist, and Indonesian Muslim Conceptions of Belief and Action. Proceedings of the Southern Anthropological Society. Athens: University of Georgia Press.
In Symbolic Classification and Social History: Clown and
Press Transvestite in Java. In Reversible World. Roger Abrahams and Susan Babcock-Abrahams, eds. Ithaca, N.Y.: Cornell University Press.
Forth- Muhammadijah: A Muslim Reformist Movement in
coming Southeast Asia. Palo Alto, Calif.: Cummings.
Penerangan Ugama Negeri Kedah (Kedah Division of Religious Information)
1968 Laporan Kemadjuan Islam Kedah (The Progress of Islam in Kedah). Alor Setar: Penerangan Ugama Negeri Kedah.
Pfeiffer, Wolfgang M.
1967 Psychiatrische Besonderheiten in Indonesien. Beitraege zur Vergleichenden Psychiatrie, Vol. I. N. Petrilowitsch, ed. Basel: Karger.
1971 Transkulturelle Psychiatrie: Ergebnisse und Problems. Stuttgart: Georg Thieme Verlag.
Pigeaud, T.
1938 Javanese Volksvertoningen: Bijdrage Tot de Beschrij-

ving van Land en Volk (Javanese Folk Plays: Inquiries Into Folklore). Batavia: Volkslectuur.

1967 Literature of Java, Vol. 1. The Hague: Martinus Nijhoff.

n.d. The Romance of Amir Hamza in Java. Bingkisan Budi. Leiden: Sijthoff.

Pijper, G. F.
1934 Fragmenta Islamica: Studien Over het Islamisme in Nederlandsche-Indië. (Islamic Pieces: Studies of Islam in Indonesia). Leiden: E. J. Brill.

Piker, Steven
1973 Some Comments on Religion and Economic Development in Southeast Asia. Paper presented at the Symposium on Religion in Southeast Asia, Association for Asian Studies Annual Meeting, Chicago.

n.d. The Weber Thesis and Southeast Asia: Alternative Considerations. Unpublished paper.

Poerbatjakara, R. M. N.
1940 Beschrijving der Handschriften Menak (Study of the Menak Manuscript). Bandoeng: A. C. Nix.

Polak, J. B. A. F.
1973 De Herleving Van Het Hindoeisme Op Oost Java (Revival of Hinduism in East Java). Amsterdam: South and Southeast Asia Anthropological-Sociological Center, University of Amsterdam.

Provencher, Ronald
1974 Eating Symbols and Having Them, Too: Orality as a Pattern of Symbolism in Malay Psychiatry. Paper presented at the Conference on Symbolic Systems in Indonesia, Malaysia, and the Philippines. Ann Arbor: University of Michigan Center for South and Southeast Asian Studies.

Radjab, Muhammad
1950 Semasa Ketjil DiKampung (1913–1928): Autobiografi Seorang Anak Minangkabau (Childhood in the Village: Autobiography of a Minangkabau). Djakarta: Baali Pustaka.

Ras, J.
1973 The Panji Romance and W. H. Rassers' Analysis of Its Theme. Bijdragen Tot de Taal-, Land- en Volkenkunde 129:411-456.

Rassers, W. H.
   1959 Panji, the Culture Hero: A Structural Study of Religion
         in Java. The Hague: Martinus Nijhoff.
Ratnam, K. J.
   1965 Communalism and the Political Process in Malaya.
         London: Oxford University Press.
Reid, A. J. S.
   1967 Nineteenth-Century Pan-Islam in Indonesia and Malay-
         sia. Journal of Asian Studies 26:267-283.
Roff, William R.
   1967 The Origins of Malay Nationalism. Kuala Lumpur and
         New Haven: University of Malaya Press and Yale Uni-
         versity Press.
   1970 South-East Asian Islam in the Nineteenth Century. In
         Cambridge History of Islam. Cambridge: Cambridge
         University Press.
   1974 Kelantan. Kuala Lumpur: Oxford University Press.
Salam, Solichin
   1965 Muhammadijah dan Kebangunan Islam di Indonesia
         (Muhammadijah and the Emergence of Islam in Indo-
         nesia). Djakarta: N. V. Mega.
Samson, Allan A.
   1968 Islam in Indonesian Politics. Asian Survey 8:1001-1017.
Samuelsson, Kurt
   1961 Religion and Economic Action: A Critique of Max
         Weber. Stockholm: Scandinavian University Books.
Sardjono, Koes
   1947 De Botjah-Angon (Herdersjongen) in de Javaanse Cul-
         tuur (The Shepherd Boy in Javanese Culture). Ph.D.
         dissertation, University of Leiden.
Shärer, Hans
   1963 Ngaju Religion. Rodney Needham, trans. The Hague:
         Martinus Nijhoff.
Schrieke, E.
   1921- Allerlei Over de Besnijdnis in den Indischen Archipel
   1922 (On Circumcision in Indonesia). Tijdschrift Voor In-
         dische Taal-, Land- en Volkenkunde 60:373-578; 61:
         1-94.
Selosoemardjan
   1962 Social Changes in Jogjakarta. Ithaca, N.Y.: Cornell
         University Press.

Setyonegoro, Kusmanto
  1970 Mengenai Fenomena Latah Aspek Kultural Dalam Ilmu
       Kedokteran Djiwa (On the Phenomenon of Latah as a
       Cultural Aspect in Psychiatry). Djiwa 1 (January):
       36-58.
Shadily, Hasan
  1955 A Preliminary Study of the Impact of Islam on a Com-
       munity and Its Culture in Indonesia. M.A. thesis, Cor-
       nell University.
Shamsudin, A. S.
  1957 Patterns of Child-Rearing in Malay Families. Social
       Science Department paper, University of Singapore.
Siegel, J. T.
  1969 The Rope of God. Berkeley and Los Angeles: University
       of California Press.
Singapore Department of Statistics
  1967 Yearbook of Statistics, Singapore 1967. Singapore: De-
       partment of Statistics.
Singarimban, Masri, and Chris Manning
  1974 Marriage and Divorce in Mojolama. Indonesia 17
       (April):67-82.
Skeat, Walter W.
  1967 Malay Magic. New York: Dover.
Snouck-Hurgronje, C.
  1927a Brieven van een Wedono Pension (Letters from a Dis-
        trict Officer's Guest House). Verspreide Geshriften, Vol.
        4, Part I (Geschriften Betreffende den Islam in Neder-
        lansch Indie). Leiden: E. J. Brill.
  1927b Over een Bamboe-Gamelan (About a Bamboo Instru-
        ment). Verspreide Geschriften, Vol. 6. Leiden: E. J.
        Brill.
Soebardi
  1971 Santri Religious Elements as Reflected in the Book of
       Tjentini. Bijdragen Tot de Taal-, Land- en Volkenkunde
       127(3):331-349.
Spiro, Melford
  1970 Buddhism and Society. New York: Harper and Row.
Swettenham, Frank A.
  1895 Malay Sketches. New York: Macmillan.

Tamney, Joseph B.
  n.d. Muslim and Christian Attitudes Toward Fasting in Southeast Asia. Unpublished paper.
Tan, P. C. K.
  1967 Report on the Registration of Births and Deaths and Marriages. Singapore: Government Printing Office.
Toer, Pramudya Ananta
  1952 Tjerita dari Blora (Tales of Blora). Djakarta: Balai Pustaka.
Uhlenbeck, E. M.
  1955 A Critical Survey of Studies on the Languages of Java and Madura. Koninklijk Instituut vor Taal-, Land- en Volkenkunde, Bibliographic Series 7. The Hague: Martinus Nijhoff.
van Loon, F. H. G.
  1927 Amok and Latah. Journal of Abnormal and Social Psychology 21:434.
van Nieuwenhuijze, C. A. O.
  1958 Aspects of Islam in Post-Colonial Indonesia. The Hague: van Hoeve.
Von Grunebaum, Gustave E.
  1955 Unity and Variety in Muslim Civilization. Chicago: University of Chicago Press.
Wahie, Nursan b. Mohammad
  1959 The Arabs in Singapore. Research paper, Department of Social Studies, University of Singapore.
Wallace, A. F. C.
  1956 Revitalization Movements. American Anthropologist 58:264-281.
Weber, Max
  1947 The Theory of Social and Economic Organization. Talcott Parsons and A. M. Henderson, trans. New York: Oxford University Press.
  1951 The Religion of China: Confucianism and Taoism. H. Gerth, trans. Glencoe, Ill.: Free Press.
  1958 The Protestant Ethic and the Spirit of Capitalism. Talcott Parsons, trans. New York: Scribner.
  1964 The Sociology of Religion. E. Fischer, trans. Boston: Beacon Press.

1966 Soziologische Grundbegriffe. Tubingen: J. C. B. Mohr.

1967a The Religion of India. H. Gerth and D. Martindale, trans. New York: Free Press.

1967b Ancient Judaism. H. Gerth and D. Martindale, trans. New York: Free Press.

Wertheim, W. F.

1959 Indonesian Society in Transition: A Study of Social Change, 2nd rev. ed. The Hague: Van Hoeve.

1965 East-West Parallels: Sociological Approaches to Modern Asia. Chicago: Quadrangle.

Whiting, John W. M., and Irvin L. Child

1953 Child Training and Personality: A Cross-Cultural Study. New Haven: Yale University Press.

Wilder, William

1968 Islam, Other Factors, and Malay Backwardness: Comments on an Argument. Modern Asian Studies 2:155-164.

1970 Socialization and Social Structure in a Malay Village. In Socialization. Philip Mayer, ed. A. S. A. Monographs. London: Tavistock.

Wilken, G. A.

1912 De Verspreide Geschriften (Collected Works). Semarang, Surabaja, 'S-Gravenhage: G. C. T. van Dorp.

Winckelmann, Johannes

1972 Max Weber: Die Protestantische Ethik. II: Kritiken und Antikritiken. Hamburg: Siebenstern Taschenbuch Verlag.

1973 Max Weber: Die Protestantische Ethik. I: Eine Aufsammlung. Hamburg: Siebenstern Taschenbuch Verlag.

Winzeler, Robert

1970 Malay Religion, Society, and Politics in Kelantan. Ph.D. dissertation, University of Chicago.

1974 The Social Organization of Islam in Kelantan. In Kelantan. William Roff, ed. Kuala Lumpur: Oxford University Press.

Wood, Larry

1975 A Quantitative Analysis of Southeast Asian Reformism. M.A. thesis, University of North Carolina.

Yap, P. M.

1951 Mental Diseases Peculiar to Certain Cultures: A Survey of Comparative Psychiatry. Journal of Mental Science 97:313.

1952 The Latah Reaction: Its Pathodynamics and Neurological Position. Journal of Mental Science 98:516-564.

1962 Words and Things in Comparative Psychiatry: With Special Reference to the Exotic Psychosis. Acta Psychiatrica Scandinavica 38:163.

1967 Classification of the Culture-Bound Reactive Syndromes. Australian and New Zealand Journal of Psychiatry 1:172-179.

1969 The Culture-Bound Reactive Syndromes. *In* Mental Health Research in Asia and the Pacific. William Caudill and Tsung-y Lin, eds. Honolulu: East-West Center.

Zaki, Mohamed Abdulkhin

1965 Modern Muslim Thought in Egypt and Its Impact on Islam in Malaya. Ph.D. dissertation, University of London.

Index

271

Hierarchy, 204
  in Java, 101–11, 142
  in language. *See* Ngoko
  in Singapore, 153–4
Hijrah, 90, 152
Himpunan Mahasiswa Islam. *See* HMI
Hindu mysticism, 202
Hindu myth, Javanized, 118
Hinduism, 17, 18, 112, 136
HMI (Himpunan Mahasiswa Islam), 34, 38, 39*n*, 48*n*, 70–2

Ichlas (ikhlas), 95, 136, 137*n*, 139–41, 142, 178, 183, 184, 204. *See also* Asceticism
Idjtihad, 6, 18, 34, 39, 50, 152, 171, 173, 180, 184, 188–90
Idul Adha, 150
Idul Fitre, 150
Ikhlas. *See* Ichlas
IMM, 72*n*
Indians
  in Malaya, 16, 17
  in Singapore, 144, 145, 148, 150
Indonesia, 15–9, 21–2, 23
Indonesian language, 108
Isin, 57, 101, 106
Islamic ethic, 47, 48*n*, 50, 52, 70, 85, 100, 138, 142, 183
Isra Mir'adj, 90, 92, 153

Java, 10, 16, 19, 63, 114, 124, 132, 144
Javanese language, 102, 108. *See also* Ngoko
Jawi Peranakan, 145, 155
Jibril. *See* Gabriel
Johore, 155

Ka'bah, 91
Kaget, 134
Kalidjaga, Sunan, 109
Kalimantan, Borneo, 124
Kampung, 23, 24, 154
Kantjil, 119–20, 182
Karang Kadjen, Jogjakarta, 25, 28, 189

Kasar, 125, 134, 135
Kathi, 145, 146
Kaum muda, 18–20, 146–7, 178, 180, 190
Kaum tua, 146, 172, 178, 180
Kauman, Jogjakarta, 23, 25, 28, 106, 108, 189
Kawin, 183
Kedah, Malaya, 22, 176–7
Kijai, 82*n*, 104
Kinship systems
  in Java, 79–83, 102, 111
  in Malaya, 182–3
  in Singapore, 163–4, 173, 174
Kitab Berzanji, 150
Kota Baru, 29
Krama, 57, 101, 106, 132, 201
Kramat, 150
Kraton, 29, 106
Kresna, 124
Kuloni, 55, 98, 99, 157, 196, 203

Latah, 129–32, 141, 142, 166. *See also* Psychopathology
Lebaran, 41, 106, 180
Lepas hari, 156
Life history, 86–100, 169–72, 190
Literature
  and psychopathology, 134–5, 204
  children's, 119–21
  Javanese, 117–28, 142
  popular, 121–3, 142
  syncretist vs. santri, 87–8
  see also Drama; Folktale; Life history; Myth; Parable; Poetry; Wajang kulit
Ludruk, 118*n*, 121–7. *See also* Drama

Madrasah, 26, 31, 33, 39, 66–7, 71, 77, 89, 139*n*, 144–6, 149, 161, 167–8, 178, 179, 189, 193. *See also* Schools and education
Madzhab, 35*n*, 107
Mahabharata, 126
Mahdi, 119